DISEQUILIBRIA

A Journal of Nonfiction Narrative

RIVER TEETH LITERARY NONFICTION PRIZE

Daniel Lehman and Joe Mackall, Series Editors

The River Teeth Literary Nonfiction Prize is awarded to the best work of literary nonfiction submitted to the annual contest sponsored by *River Teeth: A Journal of Nonfiction Narrative*.

Also available in the River Teeth Literary Nonfiction Prize series:

What Cannot Be Undone Walter M. Robinson
The Rock Cycle by Kevin Honold
Try to Get Lost by Joan Frank
I Am a Stranger Here Myself by Debra Gwartney
MINE: Essays by Sarah Viren
Rough Crossing: An Alaskan Fisherwoman's Memoir by Rosemary McGuire
The Girls in My Town: Essays by Angela Morales

DISEQUILIBRIA

MEDITATIONS ON MISSINGNESS
Robert Lunday

UNIVERSITY OF NEW MEXICO PRESS | ALBUQUERQUE

Library of Congress Cataloging-in-Publication Data

Names: Lunday, Robert, author.

Title: Disequilibria: meditations on missingness / Robert Lunday.

Other titles: River teeth literary nonfiction prize (Series)

Description: Albuquerque: University of New Mexico Press, 2023. | Series: River teeth
literary nonfiction prize

Identifiers: LCCN 2022037833 (print) | LCCN 2022037834 (e-book) |
ISBN 9780826364678 (paperback) | ISBN 9780826364685 (e-pub)

Subjects: LCSH: Lewis, Jim (Veteran) | Lunday, Robert. | Missing persons—Biography. |
Missing persons—North Carolina—Fayetteville. | LCGFT: Biographies.

Classification: LCC HV6762.A3 L76 2023 (print) | LCC HV6762.A3 (e-book) | DDC
363.2/336092 [B]—dc23/eng/20220902

LC record available at https://lccn.loc.gov/2022037833

LC e-book record available at https://lccn.loc.gov/2022037834

Founded in 1889, the University of New Mexico sits on the traditional homelands of
the Pueblo of Sandia. The original peoples of New Mexico —Pueblo, Navajo, and
Apache— since time immemorial have deep connections to the land and have made
significant contributions to the broader community statewide. We honor the land
itself and those who remain stewards of this land throughout the generations and
also acknowledge our committed relationship to Indigenous peoples. We gratefully
recognize our history.

Cover photographs courtesy of Robert Lunday

Cover design by Felicia Cedillos

Interior text design by Isaac Morris

Composed in Myriad and Jenson 11 | 14

We began to dig. After a little while, I heard an old farmer called Barz shout that there was something there. I went to look. Yes, there was something. "Do I keep digging?" asked Barz. "Don't be stupid," I answered, "cover it up again, leave it as it was."

—ROBERTO BOLAÑO

CONTENTS

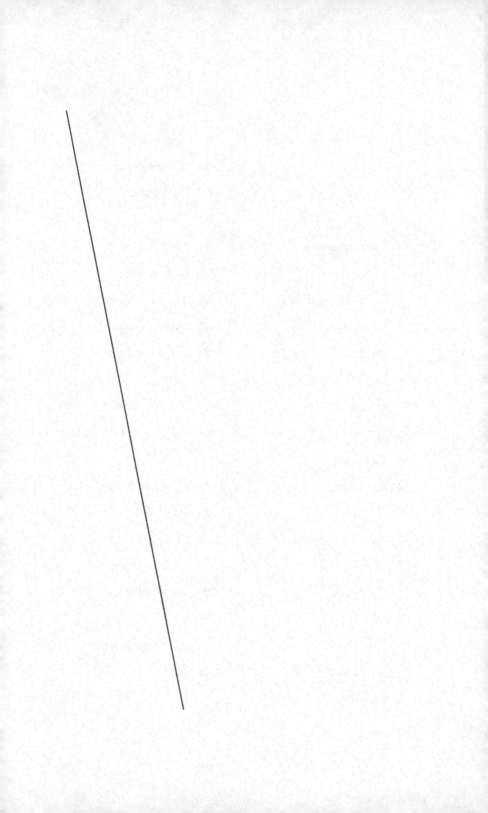

FINDING; UNDERSTANDING

IT'S HARD TO say when my stepfather, James Edward Lewis, disappeared. We know when he left our home in Fayetteville, North Carolina: Sunday morning, October 3, 1982. He drove his white Ford Fiesta and was headed, he told us, to Vero Beach, Florida. Can we say he went missing that day?

Or should it be the day we filed the missing-persons report? The photocopy in my hand is dated October 9. It was I who went down to the Cumberland County Sheriff's Department. Closing my eyes, I see metal desks and windows with dingy blinds. The slouching, uniformed men at the desks are uninterested.

A few months later my mother received a call from long-term parking at the Fayetteville Municipal Airport. "We got a car here," the voice said, "registered to y'all. Been parked since October 6. It's collecting some fees." Should that be the day of my stepfather's disappearance? Was it he who left the car there? Under what circumstances? What happened in the three days between his leaving our home and the parking of the car?

Sometimes life veers into something other than death. That third state might resemble a car driving down the road, turning and vanishing from sight. Say one more goodbye to the vacancy itself. I see my mother waving, waiting for time's loop to close.

There was fidelity in our waiting, and maybe we're waiting still, but each in different ways. I believe my mother found acceptance many years ago. My baby brother, Kevin, doesn't simply wait, but searches. His searching has become a mission, a way of life. As time goes by, the more urgent grows his search.

Kevin's father, my stepfather, had just retired from twenty-five years in the army. So Kevin tracks down old army veterans, talks to them, writes them letters or emails, scours websites, collects names, fills in the life of the man before the disappearance: the career, the friendships, the achievements, every document or scrap of information that helps fill in a gap in the timeline, a blank spot on the map of his father's journey to the point of vanishing.

The long arc or the vector of his leaving was familiar: James Lewis drove away, flew away many times in his life, and always returned. We look back on moments of departure, on the last-time-seens, to see prophetic signs of disappearance. It's vertiginous: something of which the gravity, the speed of light, the angularity are changed in memory.

Lewis's death by now might seem a near-certainty, but the *near* is hard as diamond. One might think of such a sentiment—a ratio, maybe, between mere survival and the striving it takes—as an early formulation of the profit-above-all ethos of late-stage capitalism. It is, for me, more locally, the ratio defining someone like Lewis: to what extent he'd go away from us to find his pulse in the horizon line.

The little white car Lewis was driving, the Ford Fiesta, backed out of the garage and drove down the street. We waved goodbye from the porch, or my mother did, alone. The car turned right at the stop sign. He waved one last time, turned left onto the larger road that led out of the housing area and out of sight. If that's what happened, it wasn't worth remembering. It was what Lewis did routinely, though this time for a few days' absence.

Once we knew a few months later that the car was parked at the airport, the image and spare narrative of the man getting on a plane was clear, though fantailing somewhat: what airline, what plane, what destination? There's an interface between the man and his location as we imagine him. That he or someone else driving the car flew away was a narrative we could connect to something. The car found next to a bridge or a cliff would be a different narrative.

We project back on the scene our later feelings: that he had a deeper seriousness, taciturnity, rigidity of body; that his tone of voice was slightly altered: something coded, involuntarily expressive of a more-permanent goodbye. Or was he just too good at the game? Coldly abandoning his family, out the door and driving away, releasing all our futures blithely with the backward wave of a hand momentarily released from the wheel.

The stories vary because none possess much fact. We've thought them, talked about them, dreamed them, and then undone the different narratives in our doubts and self-recriminations. After so long a time, it's hard to sort the varied stories: as if that one man, so clearly an individual, a "Jim," a "Lewis," of distinctive voice and face, were several blurring, blending, and ultimately dispersing presences. Death, too, a certain death, can cause the personality to collapse: posthumous evidence can reveal the flaws, weaknesses, indiscretions; or a survivor's memory and imagination outstrip the static, fragmented images of the dead, the ones we valorize, make monuments to—for the dead, who inhabit some corner in our psyches, slowly fading.

In "The Need for an Ending," an essay about missingness in war, journalist and veteran Andy Owen[1] shares the thinking of Jikisai Minami, a Buddhist priest, reflecting on the 2011 Fukushima disaster. Minami defines the virtual as what can be turned off and on. The virtual can be put out of mind. The real, on the other hand, is unavoidable. A missing person is real, Minami argues, whether alive or dead. You can't simply put them out of mind. So, more than constructing or receiving the virtual, he argues, we should engage the real—both present and absent.

I use Minami's terms oppositely, because it's not raw reality we concern ourselves with, but illusion. The real was never there when the missing were present. The real is exactly what we turn on or off. That's what the brain is for. But the takeaway is that when we can't find the missing, or bring back the dead, we can still, as Owen says, "follow through on known wishes, ask for advice, and say goodbyes that were never said."

Idra Novey's narrator in her novel *Ways to Disappear*[2] observes of the protagonist, a translator for a recently vanished novelist in Brazil: "For so long, she'd willingly sought the in-between. She'd thought of herself as fated to live suspended, floating between two countries, in the vapor between languages." We're comfortable in our illusions, operating the virtual lives we think we've shaped for ourselves. But sometimes we end up near the event horizon of the real. What's the difference? Often, no more than a change in perspective, a slight movement or lean this way or that. But it can be all the difference between life and death, or life and another life. In Tim O'Brien's novel *The Lake in the Woods*,[3] the narrator says of a war veteran's missing wife: "She belongs to the angle. Not quite present, not quite gone, she swims in the blending twilight of in between."

Tim Krabbé's twice-filmed novella *The Vanishing*[4] switches between its killer and a man searching for his missing girlfriend. As the couple drive through France on vacation, the woman, Saskia, is kidnapped at a rest stop. For eight years the boyfriend searches, until the killer stands before him, offering a choice. If Rex, the boyfriend, accompanies Lemorne, the killer, he will finally learn Saskia's fate. To know, Rex has to die himself, in the same way Saskia died. The finding and the understanding, according to this rule, can exist at all only if he achieves them instantaneously.

It's microcosmic of our general agreement with life itself. We know we're going to die, and we keep moving toward that death, through the choices that every day draw it closer.

"You're insane," Lex says to Lemorne as they drive again south, to which the killer replies, "That is irrelevant." Sanity matters only in the virtual world. Sanity is the expectation of patterns. In the real world, where Rex is already buried alive, every choice annihilates the last.

"Knowing would coincide with the destruction of the one who knew," Rex thinks as he decides to go with Lemorne. Then what's knowing? I imagine finding the missing person, dead or alive. I imagine knowing, though perhaps without solid proof—no habeas corpus. Then I try to think of understanding. The latter requires no more proof than what we already possess of self-knowledge, which is to say, of what we know about the boundaries between ourselves and the world.

In Kazuo Ishiguro's *When We Were Orphans*,[5] a detective, Christopher Banks, who had lived as a small boy in prewar Shanghai, returns there as the Japanese are invading. He's looking for his parents, who both went missing before he was packed off to private school in England. His father, he learns, had run off with a lover, abandoning wife and child, dying soon after. The mother, an antiopium crusader, offended a criminal boss and became his slave. In exchange, her son would be provided with financial support.

Such is Banks's life, there in all its weight, when he learns these truths near the end of the tale. In the final act, years after the war, he finds his mother in Hong Kong in an asylum. She doesn't recognize him. His lifelong effort to find her has been inextricably woven into a grander effort to save the world.

Which is likelier? After the war, in the Hong Kong asylum, in the midst of the world's refusal to be saved, his mother refuses to acknowledge him or leave with him. Is it her madness or the world's? Finding her is the impossibility of saving her.

The mother, sitting at a table on a shady lawn, is neither lost nor found. "I had assumed she was playing solitaire," says Banks, "but as I watched, she was following some odd system of her own. At one point the breeze lifted a few cards off the table, but she appeared not to care." He collects the cards from the lawn, but she tells him, smiling, "There's no need to do that, you know." She lets them fly away, and sooner or later she gathers them back.

This is the lightness of the world. This is how Christopher Banks finds himself, letting the cards flutter away without chasing each one every time. "After all," his mother tells him, "they can't fly away off the hill altogether, can they?"

DOUBLES

BELOW IS THE first letter my stepfather, then–First Lieutenant Lewis, wrote home to my mother, Patsy Lewis, in 1969 at the start of his third combat tour in Southeast Asia. The first was in Laos in 1962, the second in Pleiku, South Vietnam, in 1966, and the last in Long Binh.

> 3 Feb 69
> Dearest Patsy,
>   I have to write this in a hurry, so it will be short. I leave for the field at 0600 tomorrow. I will be acting CO because the CO was killed yesterday.
>   I sent a check for $700.00 which should arrive a couple of days after you receive this; also, for the next three months, you will receive $320 per month starting this month. When I make CPT you will get another $100.00. Try to stay within your budget and save some money if possible.
>   I love and miss all of my family. I love you more than anything.
> Love
> Jim[1]

The experience, tersely related, is a specimen of clean, clear rhetoric: tomorrow/yesterday, acting/killed, CO/CO. This is to be Lewis's first leadership assignment as an officer in a combat environment. He will be precise. He will be bracing and direct, sometimes to the point of cruelty. He will be passionate, cool, and sharp. All of it, in the end, is love. Is that obscene to you? It is war, and it is love.

That's the word he uses most in the 145 letters he wrote to my mother, and in the few cassette-tape letters that remain. Love mostly to his wife, but sometimes to the children, and sometimes love by itself, with his sharp and angled exclamation points: bayonets of love, love the only postage one might need for love. I can see it beyond the pen, the paper: love, just love.

From 13,000 miles away he manages the squad back home, relays commands to his wife/staff sergeant, devising financial maneuvers down to the dollar and cent—all while commanding a ranger platoon half a world away. It was as if there were two of him, one at home and the other across the world.

In *The Invention of Solitude*, Paul Auster[2] writes: "Each thing leads a double life, at once in the world and in our minds, and to deny either one of those lives is to kill the thing in both its lives at once." We say "double," but maybe it's more a series of echoes or reflections—from some locus—and I'm not sure the person writing this now isn't one of the echoes.

The Missing One might seem a singular vanishing presence, but it's a minimum of two: of the present, embodied person, and of the reputation. Are we this corporeal substance, or are we the last choice we made in a long line of choices? We can't know someone's experience, wrote R. D. Laing,[3] but only their behaviors. If we inventory a person's behaviors, do we have their reputation? And is that their personality—that which comprises "the series of successful gestures" as Nick Carraway calls it in *The Great Gatsby*? As such, people have the reality of constellations, ceasing to exist when one's perspective has somewhat changed.

One might have other experiences beyond the ordinary: flow-states, peak experiences, trauma, ecstasies. Some of us might never have them, or will turn away, happily or not. We study the air, the water, the strata of rock, learning systems, taxonomies, labels, extreme states that reframe the normative states, charging them suddenly with new meaning. Our more complex ways of looking, being, choosing, or enduring can be simple, momentary acts multiplied across the span of years. What if we could refocus, shift the distance and angle, at just the right time, in just the right place, to see what's really there? Might it be something or someone we've sought for so long? Right there, on the sidewalk, in front of us, as the crowds flow by.

If a map of the missing included time, time as a meta-topographical loop, we might find the traces of the Missing Ones. We might find, at least, the places where they vanish. "Temporal bandwidth," we learn in Thomas Pynchon's *Gravity's Rainbow*,[4] "is the width of your present, your *now*. It is the familiar 'Δt' considered as a dependent variable. The more you dwell in the past and in the future, the thicker your bandwidth, the more solid your persona. But the narrower your sense of Now, the more tenuous you are." *Attenuation*: a reduction down to the dollars and cents, scrounging, surviving, or not; trying to pick up the playing cards blowing across the lawn, as if we really needed all fifty-two.

In his February 4 letter, Lewis tells his wife the new company was hit pretty hard. "But they've bounced back," he assures her, under his command. This is Lewis's element. It's what he was made for, or what he made himself for. "I'm staying very busy and that is the way I like it. I can feel the weight falling off a drop of sweat at a time." Attenuation—then another reminder about finances. Throughout the letters, across the many months, his two front lines will be the jungle and the bank account. He micromanages both.

In a photograph from the night my mother met Lewis in early 1964, they're sitting together at someone's house. It's a party and she's in heavy makeup, big white earrings, styled hair, looking at Jim Lewis with interest and admiration. He looks back, lips slightly open, charming her with small talk. Each has a drink in one hand, a cigarette dangling from the other. His head is shaved and he has no neck: broad shoulders, then the flat-topped head directly attached, or so it looks. My mother's single again, a mere thirty-one, but Lewis, at twenty-three, seems older. His earlier photos show a hard-edged man-boy, someone always older than his years. In that party photo, his debonair, seductive smile draws the line of our future. Our mother, coyly, steps across.

ORACLES

I'VE NEVER BEEN to Vero Beach, Florida, the destination Lewis announced before his trip on October 3, 1982. We noted references through the 1980s to Vero Beach as a hub for cocaine smuggling, but that's because we were looking for such news. In our minds, it was a vortex of missingness.

Except for occasional flying gigs, Lewis was essentially unemployed after retiring from the army. Most of his days were spent at a friend's airfield, where he flew for skydivers. I don't know if he was paid much for it, though he was a skilled and experienced pilot. When he went missing, he was traveling to interview for a job ferrying small airplanes from dealer to buyer. So he said. When we tracked down businesses that sold airplanes in South Florida, we found no one who'd heard of Lewis or invited him for an interview.

All we could prove was that he'd existed. We couldn't prove he still existed. We couldn't prove he was living; we couldn't prove he was dead. We couldn't prove he wanted to be found or that he didn't want to be found. To believe anything was an act of imagination starting over every day.

By now, decades later, we've looked for Lewis in old drawers and closets, down the street, on the map of the world, through the mails, and, in this era, online. We've looked for him inside ourselves. My youngest brother Kevin moved to Florida, hoping for magical coincidence: that if he were going to cross paths with his father someday, it would be there. "I look for him in every man I see of that age," he told me some years back.

"But Kevin," said I, "you know that's unlikely—"

"Nothing about this business is likely!—I know, I know. It's just a way to make myself believe I'm doing something."

"You might as well play the Megamillions or whatever."

"Hey—I buy lottery tickets every week, big brother; with the same hope. Why the hell not?"

My baby brother had a heart attack a few years ago. It woke him up. He quit alcohol, started exercising and eating organic food. All of that makes more sense than buying lottery tickets, but down at a raw, visceral level, maybe they're on the same scale of what we can control: winning at lotto, believing in food labels. It's the System of Systems that wins the long game.

A week or so after that October 9 when I filed the missing-persons report, I visited the local FBI office. The lone agent, an ex-soldier himself, was kind enough to speak with me. Already I'd begun to expect blankness and refusal, resisting the same impulses in myself. He took notes, or maybe he pretended to take notes. "I don't think we can do anything, really"—like a surgeon delivering a death sentence to a cancer patient, as if the truth in such circumstances was the one saving grace, and his kindness was in laying it out firmly but gently in one sentence. He guided me to the door with a smile. I could tell Jim Lewis was already erased from his mental notepad.

Maybe we were out of line: A man had gone away. So what? Sometimes, searching for a missing person seems to violate an unspoken code. Aren't we all free to go away? Didn't we have our own lives to carry on with? There was no clearance between past and present. The problem wasn't localized—except in that empty La-Z-Boy and the fading smell of cigarette smoke in my mother's living room.

I gave a photograph to a private investigator and never got it back. That was too bad, because we have few photos of Lewis from that time. The investigator was reasonably polite, took notes more studiously than the FBI agent, and even made a file before I left. "I'll let you know," he told me, "if I think of anything I can do." He never got back to us and never charged a fee. This one, he must have thought, wasn't going to be a guy shacking up with a broad or shaking off debtors.

We asked around, but an eerie silence quarantined us. My mother called some of his army buddies. I could hear the embarrassed phone-silence across the room. My mother's voice is like onion skin, soft and wavy. When she spoke on the phone about her husband's absence, her voice grew even thinner. She'd end the call on a vaguely apologetic note, as if she'd been begging somebody for a loan.

People knew nothing and offered nothing: no help, no information, no hand-holding. It was as if retired-Major Jim Lewis had been wiped from their memories. Maybe they also believed a man could leave as he saw fit, no matter how cruel an act it was. Maybe they envied him, or were cheering him on, as the speaker seems to do in Philip Larkin's "Poetry of Departures":[1]

> Sometimes you hear, fifth-hand,
> As epitaph:
> He chucked up everything
> And just cleared off,
> And always the voice will sound
> Certain you approve
> This audacious, purifying,
> Elemental move.

Why "elemental"? As a romantic gesture, escape is being true to oneself. But it would be like envying someone their virginity. Larkin undoes the sentiment:

> Surely I can, if he did?
> And that helps me to stay
> Sober and industrious.
> But I'd go today—

Does knowing you can leave *prevent* you from going? Apollo 11 astronaut Michael Collins said "a man loses something if he has the option to go and he does not take it."[2] But the poet stays inside his poem, and we know where to find him. In fact, soon after those lines Larkin doesn't *end* the poem so much as turn around and walk back into it, closing the door.

After retirement, most of those soldiers settled down in places like Fayetteville and stayed to the end. The end, often, was emphysema, lung cancer, liver failure, heart disease. We prefer what we know even when we know it's going to kill us. Maybe the uncanniness of Lewis's departure precluded what help or consolation such men could give. A funeral offers release, but vanishing has a life of its own.

We tried to interest the local newspaper, but they passed. Years later they printed something, though. We sent a letter to the DEA. No response. I wrote to the Social Security Administration after a few months to see if they could forward a letter. Then I wrote the credit-card companies to ask if they could check for activity. I called the FAA to see if they had any flight records, and the State Department to see if they could query embassies about arrested or hospitalized foreigners. My mother approached the Judge Advocate General's office at Fort Bragg, then some former superiors, but all begged off. We called the VA to see if they had any recently admitted, amnesiac patients. I wrote our congressman, who replied with a letter of sympathy and a few suggestions: all of the above, already tried.

We never made fliers to distribute at airports, skydiving clubs, bars where retired soldiers hung out. We didn't raise money to pay for a coordinated search effort. Other than calling the local paper, we didn't work the media. We didn't track down everyone who ever knew him, didn't write every US embassy and consulate in countries with conflicts, didn't offer a reward for information. We didn't petition law enforcement very hard but took their nonchalance passively, with frustration but no rage.

We ransacked our memories, and as years went by, we talked to each other on the phone about it. My sister and I rarely made it back to Fayetteville, but when we did, whoever was there—two, three, or all of us—stayed up late talking about Lewis. We studied every scrap of paper, notebook, flying journal, and financial record he'd left behind.

We compared notes with Lewis's mother and sister in Texas while they were alive. Both had died by the mid-nineties. My Aunt Pam, Lewis's baby sister, was keen on conspiracy theories. "Bubba told me a few years ago," she claimed, "he was part of that Delta Force business to free the hostages in Iran!" It was her singular jewel: that her big brother, who had taken care of her and her mother for so many years, was at the center of things—and so, how could he be *missing*? In the mid-eighties I made enquiries, just to remove that stray thread of possibility. Over the phone, I spoke briefly with an associate of Colonel Beckwith, former Delta Force commander. "Never heard of him," the man said when I asked about James Lewis, and he hung up on me.

No sightings. Jim Lewis, as far as we know, was never seen in a crowd. No one but us seemed to be looking for him, and what does that mean, "looking" for him? We could have stood outside the front door, walked down the driveway, peered down the road out of the subdivision. Nothing was there. Once you go down the road, there are further roads in all directions, and he might have taken any of them. In imagination, he took all of them.

Hester Parr and her colleagues,[3] British geographers, define the distinction between *searching* and *looking*. Looking is living your life with an ear open to news. You live alongside the absence. Searching is the intense, panicked, scouring, no-stone-unturned effort at the start of the missingness. It's also the habitual, methodical, never-say-die detective work necessary in the long-term cases, at least when someone has reason or passion to keep looking. Such searching can consume the searcher's life: they quit their jobs, sell their businesses, start missing-persons groups. This is not so rare among parents of the missing. Some wind up finding other people's missing persons, if not their own.

Parr is one of several geographers in the UK who've attempted to bring the massive data of missingness into more intelligible, comprehensible form. She and her colleague Lucy Holmes worked with health professionals on a system meant to help returnees and families cope, but also to reduce reoccurrences. After interviewing returnees, they defined several recommendations for social services. Returned missing people told their interviewers they felt a need for more effective and empathetic police response. Beyond law enforcement involvement, returnees believed there should be opportunities to talk with nonpolice professionals, support to overcome the social legacies of having been reported missing, support to reestablish family and community relations and trust, support to address the drivers of the missing episode to prevent future incidents.

Penny Woolnough[4] worked with police to develop "spatial profiles" based on past cases—thousands of them—allowing the study of patterns according to many variables that would have a quantifiable or definable value in all cases: age, sex, previous disappearances, family situations, psychological/mental health profiles, and so forth. Comparing cases in the past allowed greater insight and predictive ability regarding "outcome characteristics": where someone might have gone, by what route, their survival choices, and more. So, to some extent, the missing persons of the past help the missing persons of today and tomorrow.

For me, to find Lewis would have been satisfying and unsettling at the same time. It was an extension of the love-hate-fear I'd always felt toward my stepfather, wishing deep down that Lewis would not return from war, that he would go away and no longer be married to my mother.

That was when I was a child. In the first weeks of his disappearance, when I was grown, still it felt like a game. Part of me wanted the game to continue. But after a few months, his absence was more frightening than his presence had ever been, and I realized the man who'd left was not the stern stepfather of my childhood. He was instead the graying, overweight, somewhat-tired-looking man who cared for my mother and loved me as his son.

It seems wrong these days for a person, living or dead, not to have a digital life. I write to that almost as much as to my other purposes: encomium or accusation, search for self, search for the missing man. How and why does it matter? As I look through the hard-copy and scanned military forms, photos, letters, newspaper clippings, certificates, and various other documents, I realize how important the recordkeeping is to military life, showing achievement, fellowship, validation. This effort now, these words: it's making an effigy. I want a conjuration that could be questioned, tell a story, reveal an ending.

Then 1982 became 1983. A few months after the disappearance, after we'd run out of ideas and people to contact, we got that call from the long-term parking lot. I drove down to the airport and looked through the car window. We didn't have a spare key, so I called the sheriff's office again, hoping they'd take action. One deputy drove to the parking lot and talked to me for a few minutes, shrugged at the car, then left. "I hope you find your dad," he called out as he drove off, as if the search itself was no work other than hope.

Before I could look further, the finance company drove the vehicle away. My mother had stopped writing the monthly checks for a car that was lost somewhere in the world. I'd noted a few flight maps on the passenger seat, all for the Southeastern US, no marks; not much else, but now even those traces were lost.

In the airport terminal, I inquired at various counters and windows. Had a man by this name flown anywhere on or near that date? Had a man by this name chartered a small plane or filed a flight plan? Did you see a man who looked like this, a few months back?

In February 1983, my mother went into the army hospital for a hysterectomy. It was the same industrial-looking tower where she'd given birth to two of her four children. That evening she lay recuperating in her darkened room, dazed and dry-mouthed, as the nurses in their camouflage fatigues rushed by in the brightly lit hall. I held her hand, then looked out the window at the winter parking lot, near empty, one car circling for some reason, as if deciding which of the many empty spots to choose. I imagined Lewis driving into the lot, getting out, coming up to the room with flowers. He had to be circling somewhere. In my mind's eye I tried to picture it. My mother's state was a dazed, drugged semiconsciousness at that moment, framed by the cold and the dark outside, the thin fluorescence inside, and my own fecklessness as I sat beside her. Now it seems like the general state of her life in those early days—more alone, more vulnerable than I allowed myself to see.

Through those first several years, my mother's emotions, at least as I sensed them in brief visits home and infrequent phone conversations, covered a spectrum: guilt, worry, anger, fear, sadness, loneliness, embarrassment, blame, and self-blame. She didn't speak of the experience analytically to me. She didn't complain but rather stated the facts—focusing sometimes on one segment or another, the prologue of Lewis's retirement or the days before his trip, the days and weeks of absence, the steps we'd followed, the frustrating conversations with friends, the suspicions of covert or illegal acts. I heard the litany dozens of times. Eventually she seemed to move on.

Not long after, I went back to New York. My dreams were feverish and repetitive. I called my mother often from New York and listened. Within my own compact life, I felt a certain aura from the whole affair, as if something had happened to *me*. It became a story to tell strangers at a party.

Searching for a place to live, I made my way out to a boardinghouse in Park Slope, in Brooklyn. The landlady was a self-professed clairvoyant. Lewis's disappearance came out while I was talking to her in the room she was renting, and I let the story work along the line of acquaintance between us just to see where it would go. She brought me to someone's Manhattan apartment where another, more-psychic psychic listened to my story and did his magic.

We performed a small ritual that included listening to a tape—a blank tape—through which the voice of St. Germain spoke oracular messages. Then the psychic asked some questions and gave his interpretation of the voice on the blank cassette. It must have seemed right to offer a little hope, or what they took for hope, and tell me the man I sought (*was* I seeking him?) still lived. Lewis, they told me, was in a hospital bed somewhere in South America.

We bade farewell to the high priest of St. Germain. The boardinghouse lady took me aside near the elevators where she placed a magic stone under my shirt. She pressed her hand against me firmly for several minutes. Her many rings lay ice-cold against my skin as she sang "The Battle Hymn of the Republic" with closed eyes.

RELICS

IN THE EARLY nineties, my mother saw news of remains found in a Carolina swamp: a swatch of denim and a wristwatch along with bones. She contacted the detective in charge of the case and forwarded Lewis's dental records. "There's no record of your husband's disappearance," the detective told my mother, "in the NCIC database."[1] He entered the data, though a decade late. He had the dental records compared, but the remains turned out to be someone else's.

Around the same time, she hired a lawyer to make Lewis dead. The whole thing took about a year, like a lingering illness. Something was said in court, some documents were stamped and mailed, copies put in a drawer somewhere, and a death filed away to bookend the birth. No explanation as to the death itself; no funeral and no grave.

After the disappearance, my mother kept Lewis's clothes for several years. They were hung in the closet and neatly folded in the dresser drawers: short-sleeved shirts, jackets, dress blues, fatigues starched thick as boards. Sometimes I imagined him in those early years of the disappearance wasting away in a cell or disintegrating on a forest floor. The clothes reminded of his size, his stance, his purposes: on duty, off duty, out to the barracks, or, come the weekend, off to the airfield or drop zone.

After the death declaration, my mother called Purple Heart to take the clothes away. The decision was one step in a narrative: that her husband would have worn them out, that menswear had changed. But it also seemed to me she was freeing herself: not from loving him, but from believing in his return.

We'd moved so many times over so many years. Some belongings traveled with us, some got jettisoned, some got lost along the way. In 1984 my mother settled into the home she still occupies. At first, she resisted clutter. After several years, she allowed herself to inhabit the space as her own: put watercolors on the walls, photographs of her children and grandchildren; let the closets fill with her own old clothes, awkward Christmas presents of years past, her children's castoffs, and things that just seemed to appear in corners or drawers. She kept calendars, magazines, wrapping, junk mail, receipts. The clutter became thick and many-layered. It seemed a way of anchoring her ambiguous present in some abstract but solid past. She keeps the curtains closed, never uses the front door to the house. She rented the house for many years, then took the bold step of asking her land-lady—another ex-army wife—to sell it outright. She wanted to sever even that slight cord to anyone who knew about the abandonment—and to have that little box of a house, if that's all there was, in her own name.

The dresser in her bedroom holds the symbolically charged ob-jects: each a relic, neat, stacked, evidentiary. Remnants of the man are preserved: military and other records, medals, photographs. There's also a decades-old, half-full can of Brasso under the bathroom sink, the tin of bootblack, even the soiled cloths and shoe brush. It had been my task to tend to the careful polishing of bars, crests, wings, and buttons; to shine and buff the jump boots and dress shoes. Why keep such things with the more-permanent objects? To stand, per-haps, for the patterns of attention.

That the Missing One wore clothes, that he kept old wallets in the back of a dresser drawer, that he owned cufflinks rarely worn—from one angle these are signs of his singularity. From another, they indicate the general form of manhood. The first, says Lama Anagarika Govinda,[2] is part of what allows us to become conscious of our uni-versality. "But it is a continual process of molting," the sage concludes. The dead pare down to a point, the missing to a line, or a ray, starting here, pointing beyond.

It's not as if death itself has such clarity. Reports of death, proto-cols, the red tape—they vary from one locality to the next, but also, from one agency to the next. "One report [goes] to the funeral di-rector, another to the public health department," Bowker and Leigh[3] report in *Sorting Things Out*. We see, in framing life and death through paper forms, the failure of Form. It is, though, a contradiction with a certain elegance: "the substitution of precision for validity," reminding me of the messy metaphors nonphysicists make of Heisenberg's Uncertainty Principle—that we can know the spin or the location of a particle, but never both. Or to make another such mess of scientific models: Is the edge between death and life a fractal space? The closer one looks, the more complicated the transition, until there's none.

THE ASYMPTOTE

BEFORE LEWIS, MY mother was married to my biological father, Robert Gailey Lunday, also a soldier. Lunday and Lewis met in Laos, when both were part of Operation White Star in 1962, a Special Forces mission to train and assist the Laotian Kingdom against the communist Pathet Lao. Lunday was Special Forces, and Lewis was on TDY, temporary duty, as an aerial-delivery specialist with the 549th QM (Air Supply) based in Camp Zama, Japan.

The advisors worked in the field with Hmong soldiers. I've got a series of grainy, faded, black-and-white photographs of the two men among others, Americans and Laotians, in the field. In one image, saddled horses wait behind soldiers sitting on a log. The men are in civilian clothes. In other shots they're wearing jumpsuits. The scattered records I've found show they trained parachutists at one point. In other images, they wear the usual olive drab fatigues. They pal around with the Hmong and government troops, some smiling, some dead-serious. The American men are there for the same reason, different reasons, no good reason at all—but from the photographs, I get the sense they're astride the globe.

Men like those hovered over my youth. I was born at Fort Jackson, Richland County, South Carolina: summer, whitewalls spinning down the road, the maternity clinic a converted WWII barracks just like the kindergarten I attended later at Fort Bragg in North Carolina. There's a color photograph of my mother, large with me in the passenger seat of a Buick. She tells the future POW Raymond C. Schrump that this is his most important mission. He's another crew-cut, short-sleeved, boar-necked fellow. He laughs and tells my mother, "Hold on tight, Mrs. Lunday! Make that kid wait a little longer."

At the clinic, my father rushes toward them just as Schrump's car pulls up to the wooden steps. So, Lunday was there: in one of her retellings my mother must have mentioned it, giving him some credit. In fatigues and field cap fresh from grenade practice, where his aim was true: he had the dust of his profession on him. They kept him from the ward, but he waited outside.

My parents divorced when I was six. Lewis came on the scene soon after. Lunday retired a few years before Lewis, in 1976, and floundered. Both men had done little in adult life besides soldiering. In 1977 Lunday died, his own father beside him, in a glider that cut loose too low from its tow plane—maybe, investigators said, to avoid pulling the plane down with it, in a wind shear. I went to both funerals, one in Florida and the other in Tennessee, both closed-coffined.

At my father's funeral my Uncle Don, another veteran, gave me Lunday's Montagnard bracelet. Such bracelets were given to many Special Forces soldiers during the war, marking a bond of fellowship. For me, it was a talisman of my first father, and I wore it for thirty years. I had the habit of squeezing it nervously with my opposite hand, and the brass very gradually became thinner, until one day I noticed it had become very attenuated and frail-looking. The stretched, tired-looking wire was a part of me, but I took it off and placed it in a small box with other keepsakes. It was a second burial of sorts.

Many years after, in the digital age, an old veteran contacted me, perhaps finding the ghostly name I shared with my father online: two Robert Lundays, but the elder one doesn't Google much, so I came up in the search—same name, face like my father's. Finding that it was son rather than father, the man claimed he'd seen Lunday in the 1980s, in Maine, at a flea market. Maine, to my knowledge, was never part of Lunday's personal geography. I assumed the old man was confused, grasping for some strand of the past, or, in some perverse way, trying to give me a thread of possibility.

Generally agnostic, I deny certainty about anything. It seems likely my father's dead, and that his cadaver lay in the coffin I saw with my own eyes, though the lid was shut. Five years after the funeral, I stumbled drunk down the Avenue of the Americas. Reaching my sublet on West 25th Street, I dug in my pocket for a dime to call my roommate so she could let me up. I'd lost my key along with some of my clothes and my shoes. I fumbled and dropped the dime. A man in a green beret walked toward me from the west side of the street, plucked the dime from the sidewalk, and dialed for me. He was a vision of my father. His spirit had urged me to drink a fifth of mescal that night, strip off my coat and shirt, my shoes, everything but my jeans, and search the freezing January night for home. Then it appeared, that spirit, and helped me. I haven't seen it since, nor any of its type, except in true, sleeping dreams. It's never my first father I see in those dreams, but Lewis. He's always just returned, to my dream-self's dismay, bringing with him the unease of my childhood.

A curve pulls closer and closer to a line but never reaches it: That's the asymptote. Mathematically the curve and line are both of zero width. People such as my brother Kevin and I, family of the missing, obsessively gather and process every scrap of information. We can refine what we compile toward a knowledge of Lewis's fate, but my default position within all the details is that we'll never know what happened.

We can't calculate such knowledge. The asymptote is a distraction from despair, though it might define the outer limits of the search. We're always at the head of the line, getting closer and closer.

However, even when I consider the point of knowledge regarding my first father—whose funeral I attended, whose death was recorded in newspapers—my coexistence in time with his death is asymptotic. The death is virtual or real. The news clippings are real enough, but they state the matter virtually, for such is the capacity of details in a newspaper or of the name and dates on a gravestone.

There's another photograph, much larger, that I kept on my chest of drawers while growing up: The two men together, close-up in a studio portrait, both in clean plaid shirts of different colors—looking almost pretty, the two of them, in the hand-tinted image. Lewis is unusually thin-faced and young. Lunday is wedge-faced, crew-cut, smiling broadly. Lewis's smile is a bit subtler, or he isn't smiling at all. He's looking clear about things, without any need to speak. Bob

Lunday looks like he needs to broadcast something: his face is made for it, even his jutting ears are made for it, and his good white teeth.

That photograph, more than anything else, made real the strangeness of having two fathers. There they were in hand-painted color, smiling at me from the same abstract space. The two men were comrades, briefly enemies, then family. I don't know exactly when the portrait was taken: maybe when they met in Laos, or later in Vietnam.

Lunday spent close to seven years in both countries. After White Star, he was part of a Special Forces effort known as Project Delta. Then he took over as the assistant commandant of the Recondo School in Nha Trang. A bit later, as the war was winding down, he helped lead POW recovery efforts. Various published accounts describe Lunday as "five foot nothing," though in fact he was five-four; and dedicated, sometimes even obsessed, with his mission, whatever it was at the moment. George Veith,[1] in his history of POW rescue efforts during the Vietnam war, briefly describes Lunday's focus not only on American POWs, but on ARVN (South Vietnamese) prisoners as well. After the war, he devoted part of his life to advocating for many of his former comrades in the South Vietnamese military, writing letter after letter to help them and their families immigrate to the US.

Lunday was a phantom most of my early life. Now he's faded near to vanishing. Lewis has made a dogged spirit of himself in disappearance. He invades my dreams serially, insistently. Though he might stay silent for a few years, he comes back, then fades again. Since he isn't dead for sure, I think he's talking to us from somewhere far: tropical, maybe, marked on the map of empire.

PARALLAX

MY MOTHER'S FAVORITE stress-release was bowling. I see her in capri pants, nicely coiffed, biting her lip, aiming the round missile toward the pins that might be the men in her life or maybe us kids. Most of the time, the black ball sat in its bag on the floor of the hall closet, cartoon bomb without the fuse, ballast that kept us from floating away. Eventually it disappeared—lost in a move, given to a neighbor—but for a while, my mother was intent on the sport, and sometimes one of us could tag along.

The emblematic memory for me is from 1963 or thereabouts. Lunday was at Bragg and the marriage was falling apart. While bowling one afternoon, she told me decades later, my mother overheard two women gossiping about her husband: "That Bob Lunday! The men say he's a great soldier; but he's a lousy husband."

It was the Space Age, Atomic Age, the time of spies. Women had flared eyeglasses; men wore horn rims. Our Melmac had starbursts, and comets flew so close you could clean with them. The cosmos was our home. On the back wall of the Post Exchange bowling alley was a mural of the universe, glittery and deep-dark. It was overpopulated, a celestial Times Square with asteroids, comets, satellites, rockets, and more than one Saturn in cockeyed rings. It spread out to the left of plate-glass windows facing the parking lot.

I'm plopped down on a swooped, molded seat at a chrome and Formica table, soda and French fries, while my mother bowls. I stare into space—that crammed cosmos on the wall—and the defeated pins make a sound midway between thwacking wood and breaking glass. The strikes spark out of my mother's hands, the ball orbits back from the aphelion of the pin deck, and the cycle repeats: my mother's at war and she's winning. It's the law of physics. The universe is on the wall and I'm waiting for the game to finish, waxy Coke cup in my palms, somewhere on Earth.

Two men gone was a parallax of fathers crossed from two to one to twice-none. Distance is a father, absence a father. Sometimes the army itself was our father. Not Uncle Sam, not the Pentagon, but in my mind's eye a presence figured by a standard army image: an old tank parked on a platform near one of the invasion beaches in France, its treads frozen, gun barrel raised toward the Evening Star. The sky's just going from baby blue to cerulean, but the star is a white beauty mark on each side of the turret. It's a flat, homely, symmetrical star, unspiritual, unambiguous. This is the army, this is us.

The true and proven reality of my fathers was brought home in parachute silk, starched fatigues, K-rations, P-38 can openers, Zippo lighters, entrenchment tools, and canvas with grommets. Grommets could make anything more durable and real. Everything that mattered was dyed army green, stenciled with a stock number and that peculiar military grammar: Truck, comma, Utility; Potatoes, comma, Mashed.

That helter-skelter year of 1969, the strange, vibrant-green jungles of Southeast Asia curled and shadowed the back of my brain and were pinned to the kitchen wall in the form of a newsprint red-and-green map courtesy of the *Fayetteville Observer*, on which we marked Lewis's and Lunday's X's near place-names we couldn't pronounce.

We lived in Fayetteville but would go to Bragg for the PX, commissary, or clinic by driving down Bragg Boulevard, which was the used-car, Korean-food, pawn-shop, massage-parlor artery between post and downtown. Everything on Bragg Boulevard looked ready to pack up and move at a moment's notice.

But my view into the world that year was mainly Fayetteville, off-post, where we lived while waiting for Lewis: staring down the curved street of yet another home-for-a-year, peering into the arc as if I might see past it into the maps and the evening news, as if Vietnam were just around the corner. You could almost hear it, and in a way, you did: artillery thunder you felt in your bones, miles from the firing ranges, all the windows rattling.

Street names on Bragg travel through victories and retreats: Yorktown, Ardennes, Bastogne, Luzon, Normandy; then Son Tay, Kuwait, Just Cause, Desert Storm: Drives and Boulevards and Avenues, and not a few circles and cul-de-sacs: thoroughfares modeling foreign policy.

NOMADS AND EXILES

WHERE ARE YOU *from?* is the classic challenge for military brats. They have no answer or too many. "We grew up strangers to ourselves," Pat Conroy[1] says. "We were transients, we came and went like rented furniture, serviceable when you needed it, but unremarked upon after it was gone."

"I was always leaving behind what I was just about ready to become," Conroy adds later in his remembrance. "I could never catch up to the boy I might have been if I'd grown up in one place." In my mind, those places, those boys slide by like exits on a turnpike, each one a life I didn't live, or lived for no more than a moment.

A passage in Ammianus Marcellinus's *Roman History*[2] hyperbolically captures the nomadism of the military family. "None of them plough, or even touch the plough-handle," writes Ammianus, "for they have no settled abode, but are homeless and lawless perpetually wandering in their wagons; in fact they seem to be a people always in flight." The barbarian, he says, can't tell you where he was born, because "he was conceived in one place, born in another at a great distance, and brought up in another still more remote." The expansion of the clauses is what I find familiar. It resembles the declension that brought me here: so near to myself, yet so far from what matters to me.

One measure of the seasons of a move was the changing presence of cardboard boxes. After arrival, we'd wait for them, then live among the stacks for days. With the furniture in place, we'd still have islands of boxes waiting weeks for a decision. Some would be stored out of sight, but before long we'd be filling up new ones for another move.

The discovery of friends was a discovery of doubles and complements. Most faces fit over those I'd left behind. It was the association of friends with certain places, but also, a collection of faces framed within feeling: This child's drooping eyes and small mouth suggested the same sorrow I'd seen in the face of another child, on another playground. The face itself recalled me to the earlier feeling, becoming the emblem of pity in my tarot-deck of faces.

What a curse it is to feel the present moment as impoverished, unless it bears the corona of all past moments. It's a small, jeweled curse the Portuguese call *saudade*. Some moment long past should have consumed me in its fire, but again and again I slipped through. What mission moves me forward?

Our constant moving led me to believe in what Georg Simmel[3] called "the possibility of a second world alongside the obvious world," a world of secrets that affects this seeming-real world: the world where delusions are the ratio of secrecy, as Simmel calls it, by which any two groups or individuals negotiate a shared virtuality.

The renegade, beyond ratio, strips down to a shadow, sometimes catching a glimpse of his own scarred flesh in puddles or plate-glass windows in inhospitable towns. He has been, Richard Hofstadter[4] says, "in the cave of the arcana, returning with proof of suspicions which might otherwise have been doubted by a skeptical world." This knowledge is the new sense of self: the rightness, and the eclipse of what's right, the thin edge of one's own life as the shadow moves across the image of the true world. Across a boundary between worlds, "the unbelievable is the only thing that can be believed."

There's a softer possibility. I turn to Yoshida Kenkō:[5] "I agree with Akimoto no Chunagon's remark, 'It is as if one were gazing at the moon in some far distant place of exile, to which, however, no crime had banished one.'" Or it might be as in Alfred de Musset:[6] "Some said, 'The emperor has fallen because the people wished no more of him'; others added, 'The people wished the king—no, liberty!—no, reason!—no, religion, the English constitution, absolutism!' and the last one said: 'No, none of these things; give us, instead, repose.'"

Such a passage leads us to the middle distance of ourselves, where sky and waves are inside as much as out.

Missingness sometimes makes the Missing One a god. But it might also make them into miniatures: almost nothing, but still something. We can look for the missing Jesus, for whom apotheosis was the answer to the vacant tomb. The burly angels were his proxies, and as the synoptic view of things is an excellent specimen of the virtual, we turn easily in John's account to one more quick appearance. "Hands off, Dear," says Jesus to Mary, "for I am neither here nor there."

IN THE CLOUD

DURING THE COVID-19 pandemic, I've been locked down only a little more firmly than I had been living my sequestered, solitary life before. Nearly two years ago, my wife and I sold our home in the country and moved to Houston, renting an apartment. Then, Yukiko went to Japan—rural Southern Kyushu—planning to travel back and forth, setting up a horsemanship/parenting program there, and returning here between sessions. The pandemic forced her to stay, and we've had a Zoom marriage, still ongoing.

During that time, I taught remotely. I also exercised, read, and listened to music chosen deliberately to expand and deepen my melancholy: modal jazz, Romantic classical (Ravel and such), dream pop, ambient—whatever drew out memory and loss, whatever shrank the present within the broad, deep field of the past and the unknown future.

I also embarked on several hobbies, following through on obsessive practices already established: cataloging my books, scanning family photos and reading notes from years back, repacking keepsakes so that the boxes, all modular, work like wonder-cabinets that correspond to the abstract files in my mind.

The obsession compounded on itself. I got better and better at scanning and organizing, reducing, and digitizing. I photographed the objects, getting rid of the things themselves, except for the most-precious items. I fit everything into schemes: the digital files are tagged for date, place, and symbolic meaning.

The books have become an emotional burden. Having them but knowing I won't read most of them ever again—won't get around to reading the hundreds of books I bought, fondled, skimmed, but never finished, saving for some future moment—hurts. Those future moments seem transferred, of late, to an alternate life.

Lately I've been scanning the books themselves. I want the physical library to be packable and moveable within a day, able to be loaded into a rental trailer so I can do it myself, if necessary. The benchmark is my move to New York in 1976, dragging two duffel bags crammed with all my possessions down Avenue of the Americas from the Port Authority Bus Terminal. Perhaps before actual death, I won't ever again achieve such compactness; but aiming for the extreme, part of me believes I'll arrive at a clean, renewed version of myself, capable of flight.

I've loaded the family photographs into a digital frame, and as the sad, modal music plays, random images prick me with feeling. My son is still alive and well, but the many versions of him as a child are gone forever. My young selves, my young wife's selves, the several friends and family who are dead—the irrevocable loss becomes the greater part of me.

It's sadness or melancholy. It's the part of happiness that hurts, exposing a mind too tight around itself in a vast and mysterious world. The immobile sense of self that sometimes threatens to adhere, to stall the heart, is an illusion. The self is a flow, a wind or stream. Let yourself vanish sometimes, like a dead leaf that finally drifts into the mass of organic, undifferentiated matter. If your heart beats still, you'll reappear in some discrete, modest form soon enough. If no one is near enough to call your name, some homunculus within—an older or imminent you, the spirit of a loved one—will call you from inside.

I studied myself as I scanned, cataloged, consolidated, and digitized. I found the smallest hard drive to hold it all: every book, note, and photograph in the palm of my hand.

This scanning, digitizing, organizing, and reducing comes from the nomadic part of myself, the child who always seemed to be packing and moving and unpacking, who saw the next town, neighborhood, school, or pack of friends as a new beginning. I was always hopeful before a move. Starting over, getting things right with the new set of circumstances: avoiding social awkwardness this time, becoming cool, becoming admired—it was possible, it stayed possible. That was not only the sense of youth, but the sense of life. To live was to move, or to be just-moved and filled with potential, whatever mistakes might accrue.

The pandemic pushed me closer to the logico-spiritual conclusion of that nomadic frame of life: that death, whether it will take me tomorrow or in thirty years, was the singular sense of self that provides the backing for everything else, ephemeral and dear. Mortality *is* the self, always here, the music behind the music. Thus, this obsessive compacting of the ephemera of my life, the dear things—books, notes, photographs, tiny idols, and gems—means, I think, that I'm preparing for the Last Big Move. Moving has been my life. Moving is also the illusion that death, the sum total of one's choices and fortunes, can be delayed forever.

The Last Big Move is one more try at cheating death. You can't take it with you—or can you? If I reduce it all down to a tiny rectangle or disc that I can hide in my hand, maybe I can. Besides that, I've recently started uploading everything. In that magical part of my brain, it makes sense that the dead have access to the cloud.

THE MIDDLE DISTANCE

I WAS SIX when Lewis came into our lives. That was also the year my wandering extended past my mother's sight, though I didn't know yet how "road" and "route" were different. Which was it I traveled at various ages? When did I understand the various lies and truths of maps? "For an infant," wrote Havelock Ellis in *The Dance of Life*,[1] "the moon is no farther away than his mother's breast." Rebecca Solnit[2] gives more context: "There is no distance in childhood: for a baby, a mother in the other room is gone forever, for a child the time until a birthday is endless. Whatever is absent is impossible, irretrievable, unreachable. Their mental landscape is like that of medieval paintings: a foreground full of vivid things and then a wall."

It's loss, yearning, melancholy that bring distance into our hearts. What goes out the door never comes back exactly so. Space-time is a rumpled fabric. "Some children," writes Kenneth Hill,[3] "may not even understand that locations have a fixed, linear direction with respect to each other." Emotionally, what's "fixed, linear direction"? Even according to the fundamental forces of adult life—finances, employment, regulations—don't we all take rambling paths? Most of us get lost, and often.

My family's moving was a perpetual getting-lost because there was never a way back, no matter how clear and firm the army's orders were. As we neared the end of our stay in one place, its spirit seemed to pool about near the end of the time-tunnel we inhabited: intensifying placeness, making the furniture of place denser, brighter.

Moving, we would enter a new grid: neighborhoods and landscapes that stood behind them, a map to be drawn mainly through streets and vistas from bicycle or the back seat of the car. The initial grid of the first few weeks was scant and abstract: the lay of the land peculiar to that place, to my child's-eye view into it, had to be filled in and become canny enough to forget.

The place would become no- or every-place. Utopia. It would become here as opposed to elsewhere by virtue of its shortcuts. Shortcuts—down alleys, across lots or fields, in woods, under bridges, past menacing buildings, through forbidding neighborhoods—were the intelligence shared between space and self.

In first grade, kids paid a dime to the bus driver to go home. One day I took the dime from the pocket of my corduroy pants and placed it in the desk, under the lid in that tan-metallic space filled with dried gum, pencil shavings, and eraser waste. I forgot the dime, and assuming the bus driver would forbid my passage without it, I walked. Perhaps it was two miles. I have no memory of how I knew the way. A guardian spirit led me. It was partly through woods that I walked, so it was not the bus route. There was a wooden fence, a pasture, and a farmer with a shotgun—did I make that up?—and I remember the sense that he looked at me as a threat, though I was a cowlicked six-year-old kid. Encountering monsters is the risk of seeking the measure of the world. Which of us was the monster?

It was late when I got home. My mother had been worried, and Jim Lewis, recently installed as our father, whipped me. Not a slap or punch like later, but simply a spanking. Still, it seemed unfair. Had I not returned?

FACE OF SHADOWS

IN THE MID-1950S, in France where they were stationed, Lunday had a portrait painted of my mother. I have a copy of the photograph the artist worked from. That young woman still exists, more than if we had the photograph and not her. Painted portraits are effigies in a way I don't feel from photographs. But that person in the photograph is slowly fading: some layer of the younger woman I knew, and who happens to be my mother.

That quality is not fully in my memory, nor fully in the image, but somewhere between, like a fairy-tale version of the woman before she was my mother: her innocence, her simplicity, which she still possesses. That innocence sustains me, balances me, from several states away.

The painting of my mother stays in a cedar chest her stepmother gave her as a wedding gift. The chest is very old, has followed her through every move, and was recently refinished. Slowly, she's been giving each child its contents, but it's still nearly full.

The painting, wrapped in a Sears shopping bag, is about the size of a bathroom mirror. The face is a simple, full-front portrait from the bust. She wears a black dress with a black-and-white polka-dotted scarf, and her hair is as black as the dress, with sheens of red the portraitist might have thought would look dramatic. It's an accurate likeness, neat and balanced, if slightly mechanical.

In the same bag is a crayon-on-cardboard replica I drew when I was eight: a bit squarish in the head, the eyes too wide, but with enough effort at detail and countenance that it must have mattered to me. It shows no effort at chiaroscuro or perspective.

The portrait I'd copied had a frame for a while and hung in two or three homes we lived in after I was born. I remember it in the hallway across from a room where I slept. With the door cracked open and the hall light shining on it, the face in the portrait was terrifying. I knew it was my mother's face, but the shadows turned the eyes down demonically at night. In daylight, they were wide open and expectant as my mother's eyes truly were. She was beautiful, I knew, but at night it was something terrible that watched over me, a forties noir dame à la Dr. Moreau.

Simone de Beauvoir *in The Second Sex*[1] says: "the Woman-Mother has a face of shadows: she is the chaos whence all have come and whither all must one-day return; she is Nothingness." The image, or my reaction to it, my childish perceptions of it, was the intimacy of birth with death.

This frightening and lovely face was the same as the mother who held me before sleep and read to me, the same who put on makeup for special occasions, haloed herself with hairspray, armored her ears, neck, wrists, and fingers with jewelry from the lacquer box Lewis had sent back from Vietnam on an earlier tour. Her face, when I stood beside her at the dresser mirror, had a droopy eye that fascinated me, because it was droopy only in the mirror. This woman who wore makeup and set her hair was the same who did dishes and laundry, but they looked different. I noted the difference as a curiosity I couldn't yet identify in other women, since it was she alone whom I saw in glamour as well as grind.

They went out sometimes, mother in her glamour and Lewis in his dress whites or blues. Since I went to sleep before our parents came back, she was her morning-self, loose hair and pale lips, the next I'd see her. The party face went out but never returned.

The matter of scale seems particularly complex in childhood, with confusions not only in youth, but far beyond—if one is fortunate. "A landmark is not necessarily a large object," observed the spatial theorist Kevin Lynch;[2] "it may be a doorknob as well as a dome." What counts for large, and what counts for intense, deep, magnetic, repulsive, self-defining, self-denying? Try to remember the sense of scale and boundary that defines the child's world: that the edges of things were always near, and, at the same time, that we were always at the center. How could the *I* not be both the center and precipice of existence? When we're older, and we are worked into the systems we serve, though they ultimately devour us, sometimes in the din of it we will feel that childish absolute still there, like the eye of a hurricane of time.

Call it madness, revelation, or simply the gong hour of most Sunday evenings, as we prepare again to lock into the machine. But sometimes, a body does more than stare at the hole, and close eyes, and close them more, and fall in. The world is fractal but so are we.

Things real and unreal consorted with one another like real and mythical animals in a medieval bestiary. Box tops, piggybanks, kites, fishing poles, magic carpets, yoyos, thresholds, hinges, invisibility rings—all were as solid as they were insubstantial. "The peaks of a child's experiences," write Iona and Peter Opie,[3] "are . . . occasions when he escapes into places that are disused and overgrown and silent." That telescope I had at twelve made me want more than the stars and planets, but to travel by sight the same way I traveled by sound when I turned on the radio. These devices were magic as much as technology. But they worked less by science or magic than by desire.

Through carved scrollwork, acanthus leaves, and other flourishes, designs of things made secret spaces. Henri Focillon[4] wrote of form that "it prolongs and diffuses itself through our dreams and fancies: we regard it, as it were, as a kind of fissure through which crowds of images aspiring to birth may be introduced into some indefinite realm."

The seriousness of toys—of tin soldiers, dolls, Lego blocks, or anything that reduces the world to the child's hand—is in the ways those hours of play, preferably solitary, suggest the existence not of a God but of a giant hand. We make ourselves in wonder, the opposite of trauma.

We moved from place to place, which made it more important to have places I could carry with me: cabinets in the mind, though some were physical boxes, jars, or drawers, or patterns of outdoor space I sought in bowers, tunnels, tree-spaces, vistas.

In 1966, on one of his rare visits, Lunday gave me my own transistor radio. I cherished it: size of a cigarette carton, black sleeve, green-luminous dial. It was by my bedside for years, turned low. I don't know how to recreate the feeling now: the part that wasn't the music, exactly, but the sense of distance and invisibility; the hiss, the waves of sound; radio-life folded into the night air, threading sleep into my head. I'd hear haunting melodies in my drowsiness and try to wait for the announcer's ID of the song. Sometimes I recalled melodies for years without knowing what title, what artist had sung me to sleep.

UROBOROS

NOT LONG AGO a three-year-old boy in eastern North Carolina went missing in the woods near his home for a few days. After he was found, damp and scratched, the boy told his family a bear had kept him company. The fairy-tale logic is hard to separate from the likelihood. It might be that a real and a fantasy bear chaperoned the boy. Which was more real in the child's world?[1]

At five, wandering the woods behind our house, I saw a leprechaun. We looked at each other and went our separate ways. Down the trail I told two older boys building a tree house high above me about the little man. They scoffed and jeered without stopping their work. So high above me in the tree, the boys seemed queerer than the leprechaun.

I found a snapping turtle in a creek under a bridge. He clamped on the chuff of my right hand when I tried to take him home. It was the Earth itself clapping onto me. He was a big rock-shaped thing, but I yanked my hand free without thunder.

Neighborhood kids found the turtle or some other creature and smashed it to bits. I saw pieces of the shell like a broken toy and strands of innards littering the road. The sickness I felt was not from gore. It was the immediacy of witness. I knew what they did wasn't for love of me. Vigilantism loves itself.

A waterwheel turned somewhere in the woods near Acorn Street, the first place we lived after Lewis married my mother. It was in the same stream the turtle had inhabited, up from the reservoir. It became my private waterwheel, the first I'd seen outside a picture book, and I sat watching for a long time as its turning told a story through moss-stained paddles, the muscular creak of the machinery, the angry-looking axle, and the suffering water's rising and falling.

Every walk was a search for the uroboros, world-center or some substation thereof. What made things move? What rounded off every instant before it dropped back into the stream? How could anything in such a world be lost?

I wanted to find Ultima Thule, or what I would have called it then: somewhere my father was, though he was a god, a face in a cloud. Even movie stars were more real than he.

I knew I could trace it belowground if need be. I had seen an advertisement in a comic book or a *Boy's Life* for a miniature submarine—on the same page as the ads for X-Ray Specs and Sea Monkeys. The drawing of the little boy at the helm (facing right, toward Progress) was determined and happy. I was taken with the idea that this was the real thing, that I could order it for six dollars, assemble it, and launch it into the secret ocean. As for Sea Monkeys, they're real: genus Artemia, species salina.

I kept an animal graveyard in the lot across from our house on Acorn Street: last rites for rats, possums, mice, birds, frogs, lizards, whatever littered the woods and sidewalks above the level of insect. Shoeboxes became coffins, popsicle sticks made crosses. My mistake was in thinking it sacred. A kid named Doug from the top of the hill trashed it when I was elsewhere, dug up the graves, strewed the bones and broke the crosses. Strange that I remember his name: possibly the pun of his name and act. Doug was my double, my undoing. It taught inertia: the animal graveyard is meant to be everywhere. It was my not-so-secret garden where I played out brief stewardship of fellow beings.

Years ago, I saw a startling film called *Forbidden Games*, made in 1952. It won a foreign-film Oscar. Set during the early days of the Second World War, the story unfolds the friendship between a five-year-old girl recently orphaned and the slightly older son of the peasant family who take her in. The two children collect dead animals, burying them in their own pet cemetery. The boy steals crosses from human graves, including his own dead brother's. At the end authorities remove the girl from the home, but she escapes from the

Red Cross worker in the final frames, running through a crowded train station, calling alternately for the boy and her dead mother, disappearing into the crowd.

In 1965 we left Fayetteville for Waco, Texas, Lewis's hometown. Looking through the rear window as the little house on Acorn Street receded, then Fayetteville itself, I was full of hate toward my stepfather. The energy of it lasted for miles into the dark, from a punishment for an infraction I can't remember. How large is a six-year-old's hatred? How many watts? It seemed to fill the car and more. I kept it deep inside me, lest he hear my thoughts. We drove all night and the road opened to the world, the car radio emitted starlight and soft music, and our parents talked about complicated things. Lewis drove one-handed and smoked with his window open. The cigarette led the way. I slept and pretended to sleep.

Automobiles are a second home, and our family lived in more houses than we owned cars. The long black Studebaker was my favorite because it was the most alive. It seemed to be thinking under its hood about us. I see it now, shot and buried in a pit. For a vehicle older than a decade or so, you have to provide a name and respect its emotional life. The Studebaker was Bessie, and to bless her journeys you had to pat her lovingly on the dash and call her name.

Amelia Earhart[2] said of her Lockheed Electra, "We said goodnight to it and petted its nose and almost fed it apples." David Kern, John Updike's alter ego in "Packed Dirt, Churchgoing, a Dying Cat, a Traded Car,"[3] bestows life on his new vehicle when he's driven it a fair distance: "Beginning as a mechanical assembly of molecules," Kern says, the car "evolved into something soft and organic and consciously brave." If we didn't animate our things, if we didn't mourn their passing, from where would we seize our own life? We get it from giving it. We live inside the life of everything.

On the way to Waco, through the rust holes in the floorboard, I watched the road rush by. The coarse aggregate scrolled back into view when we slowed or stopped. So many particulars in the world, journeying from the local into the world's ongoingness. All one can do is sleep.

On the road, at a Howard Johnsons, Richard Petty and his entourage came by our table to hand out signed images of the race-car driver. Lewis rebuffed him, and the two almost came to blows. I understood Petty was famous, especially in North Carolina. Lewis's brush-off of the star seemed quite audacious and brave. I admired him for it, even in that moment. It was nothing less than primal, essential irony as apprehensible to a child.

Lewis moved us in with his mother, Mildred, and teen sister, Pam, the better to care for all on his master sergeant's pay. The new home was an old farmhouse, though even by 1965 the neighborhood was near the center of town. It was large and organic, with improvisational spaces: haunted, of course—ghost-catching angles and corners; scrolling, beveling, baffling in the surfaces that filled my head with ancient languages. It was the first house we had that asserted itself vertically, though its main life was still the first-floor rooms, alcoves, and central hallway. We stayed only eighteen months, but it was long enough for those rooms to become the floor plan of my house of houses.

Baby Kevin slept in our mother's room. Lewis was away most of that year, so it wasn't his room exactly. The whole house was his, though, and his dark awareness wrapped around it. This was his first absence since he'd become our father.

From books I knew every old house had an attic, a hearth, a basement, and a storm cellar. This one in Waco had them all. Thanks to my new step-grandmother, it also had a Victrola, which she kept in the living room. She showed me how the instrument worked. It towered in a wooden cabinet like a house of its own, its horn flared into a robot blossom. I wanted to crawl through and down into whatever world was there, but it was kept in an alcove that spooked me: a turn in the asymmetrical house that abhorred children and forced me back when I was alone.

My brother Donny and I shared a room off from the kitchen. My bed was next to a window with a fan. At night, crawling into the sound of the fan, I flew. The drone of all night and eternity came through its blades, the breath of possibilities too quick to catch. It didn't stop until sleep shut the doors and windows in me.

Waco was a new town and a new school. The worst kind of move was from the military post to a civilian community, and on top of that, to start the new school in the middle of the year. I sat outside the principal's office while my mother arranged my enrollment at Provident Heights Elementary. Even then it was a very old building. Gainsborough's "Blue Boy" looked down from a high wall, some window into another world. I had no concept of reproductions, no art-history knowledge, but the scale of it, its authority, its drama, the boy's challenge to my own presence there—which of us was more real?—humbled me. The haughty young man taunted me with his familiarity of the world. It was my world more than his, but the school was his domain. Something glowed behind him in the Rococo trees and clouds.

The wait, like any waiting, was long. The blue, the stare, becoming that boy, my sitting on the hard bench, daylight competing for dominance of the present; midmorning angled sun, a stairway; the timid, seated boy, motley and original and still there; the real air of an oil painting, and its shadows as deep as the trek through a fairy tale. Awareness had fallen back on me from some future moment, accordioned out, a suspension, then the collapse; someone calling my name and the cafeteria smells catching me once again in the dread of time.

In October, the school had a carnival. Lewis was due back and already on my mind. Strange to be in the classrooms after dark, and the teachers costumed; rooms emptied of desks for haunted houses, bean-bag tosses, and bake sales. I tried the cakewalk, then musical chairs, and luck was always to the left or right. I despaired at ever winning anything. The carnival was winding down, and in a corner of a bed-sheeted classroom was a fortune teller, someone's mother in headscarf and hoop earrings. Thinking of my immediate future, I asked, "Will my stepdad ever beat me again?" and the crystal gazer looked at me with equal pity and bother. "Likely, darlin', very likely," she drawled, and took my ticket. I was stunned by her nonchalance. Such was my fortune, but I didn't know what "likely" meant. Where did it fit between "never" and "always"? The oracle left me in the dark, as oracles do.

The great dread in my life was Lewis's wrath. More specifically, it was the seething, tight-lipped menace, a narrowing of the eyes, verbal insults followed by a blow, and I was left with a fat lip, a knot on my skull, or a forehead bruise. On one occasion I was ordered to clean up the blood. But then Lewis would hug me and tell me he loved me.

My mother and sister didn't interfere, but it was their petitions that eventually made him stop. Past a certain point he hardly needed to strike more blows. We all learned to stay keen to his moods.

On the playground at school, another little boy, seven like me, stood near, crying grief-laden tears—for what, I didn't know. I felt it—not as my own, not taking it from him, but touching it, like a textured thing: his grief, perhaps from a ball bouncing off his head, other kids teasing him—but a thing I could touch. It wasn't empathy so much as the Platonic form of sorrow.

"Injustice in this world," writes George Santayana,[4] "is not something comparative; the wrong is deep, clear, and absolute in each private fate. A bruised child wailing in the street, his small world for the moment utterly black and cruel before him, does not fetch his unhappiness from sophisticated comparisons or irrational envy; nor can any compensations and celestial harmonies supervening later ever expunge or justify that moment's bitterness."

"The wrong is deep, clear, and absolute in each private fate": Santayana's absolute seems a transcendent source, the original object of grief, refracted once again in the world of the child. I stood there a few times, with many other moments washed away from memory, or rifted into the few; on streets from which all other beings had been whisked away by the sharp, precise fatefulness of the world. How ridiculous the harm must have been: the loss of a toy, name-calling, rejection, and when older, and even now, the failures and losses and degradations that are equally absurd and petty as those childish things. They all refract, with varying degrees of clarity and force, that transcendent feeling.

Sometimes the father bent more toward the warrior. "The two

personalities could succeed each other," asserts J. Glenn Gray[5] in his classic study of the warrior identity, "with lightning rapidity." Most of the time Lewis's violence was triggered by my forgetting to take out the trash. It was my main chore, and remarkably, I could not keep track of trash day. I feel now almost as if something in me wanted to draw his wrath, which seemed horribly out of balance. Being struck was the most precise sensation of the immediate moment. I don't mean I enjoyed it, but nothing else in my life had seemed so real.

At the end of the Second World War, a sociologist named Willard Waller published a book called *Veteran Comes Back*.[6] I imagine it was meant to ease the transition for civilians at home of those several million servicemen. The soldier "can never excuse himself by saying, 'I forgot,'" says Waller, "because drill sergeants, understanding that a man can remember anything that he really wants to remember, treat every such forgetting as rebellion." That had been my phrase— my shield, which I used every time I saw the violence coming: "I'm sorry—I forgot," which never shielded me.

THE SUN AND I

HOME, AS ALFRED Schuetz[1] defines it, is "a common vivid present"—a space where our commonality overcomes our difference. It's the true inside, respiring and settling. "Home" for me was never a geographic place. It always shifted, in the present and in memory. Home was a foreign feeling. We picked up and moved our household goods, but the household gods were always borrowed: ragged spirits that barely knew our names. We honored them by cleaning exceptionally well before departing.

Before Lewis left for his third Vietnam tour, we were settled back Stateside, off-post in Fayetteville after two years in West Germany, '67–68. Some moves stand out as experiences in memory, but mostly, like other trauma, they pass quickly in a subterranean space: We flew, but it seems we tunneled, home again to the States. Back in Fayetteville, Lewis set us up in the new house and was gone. His absence was palpable and sweet for me. I hardly noticed my mother's grieving.

I kept Lunday by my bed in the form of a wallet-size picture in a drug-store frame, gold-lettered Nha Trang stamped in the bottom corner, salmon-tinted backdrop, the lush-green beret with the 5th Special Forces pin, his eyes sharp and focused on something besides me. I'd take the photo down and try to gaze it to life, draw his fire, but the eyes' aim at the periphery never changed.

After Lewis returned from the '69–70 tour, we moved to Fort Benning for the first of two times. Briefest of our moves: nine months. We lived on Kandle Drive in a neighborhood named for Custer. At the bottom of the hill was a diseased old tree hanging over the street. It had a cavity filled with bees that streamed forth like a shout when harassed.

At twelve I was convinced, for a time, that my birthday had slipped everyone's notice. Consequently, I stayed twelve for two years. In that way my body-mind interpreted the onset of puberty. That was also the year, or years as it were, that I resigned from Halloween. Was I child or a man? Consciousness was itself the uncertainty about it. Play had become awkward. In a Tilt-a-Whirl at the carnival, thrown against the insides of the car, I crossed my arms and frowned.

Lieutenant William Calley, court-martialed for his role in the massacre at My Lai, was at Benning in 1970, confined to post not far from where we lived. We saw him, Lewis and I, while on an errand. Parked behind some woman's Triumph, we observed the lieutenant assist her in giving it a push. "I bet they got her husband in the trunk," Lewis wryly if not too cleverly remarked to me. I knew about My Lai and stared at my second celebrity (after the racer, Richard Petty). To my twelve-year-old eyes Calley looked truly hapless, as if starting that stalled sportscar was another test of character. Calley didn't look like the officers I knew: too pasty and squat. The woman was blonde, bouffant, and bouncy. Maybe for Lewis, sex-farce, "ordinary" crime—spouses in the trunks of sports cars—was a way to distance the taint of My Lai. I don't know what mixture of judgments he held: the atrocity itself, the man's poor soldiering, or how someone so plain and baby-faced had come to represent the Warrior.

Lewis had gone to Officers' Candidate School around the same time as Calley. He was distancing himself in his own crude way, but for whose benefit? I was twelve. For a time, he let his hair get one millimeter longer, bought an eight-track player for his Karmann Ghia, and listened to rock rather than Roger Miller or Johnny Cash. He seemed to express the slightest air of alienation from army life. If I was youth culture there by his side, then the tossed-off joke about the bland lieutenant was as close to counterculture as Lewis would go.

After that first short stay in Benning, we went to Omaha for two years. Lewis stayed active duty while bootstrapping, as they called it, to finish a college degree he'd started in the University of Maryland's correspondence school back when he'd met my mother in 1964.

We arrived in Omaha in the dead of winter at the first house Lewis had ever bought, in a brand-new subdivision with only a few finished streets. It seemed in fact only partially sketched out on the terrain, as if we were moving into something that moments earlier had been a blueprint. In part my memory is so framed because of whiteness. On the day of our arrival, Omaha was dominated by snow drifts to the eaves of every house. Midwestern flatness still stretches across that part of my mind. Snow made things disappear. Nothing lay behind our house except white: white ground, white sky. Lew Welch conveys the sameness in his "Chicago Poem":[2]

> The land's too flat. Ugly sullen and big it
> pounds men down past humbleness. They
> stoop at 35 possibly cringing from the heavy and
> terrible sky.

Wright Morris[3] proposed that silos, along with the high facades of commercial buildings, added the relief of some vertical lines to the overwhelmingly horizontal. He saw it not as a matter of vanity, but a problem of being. It's the idea of emptiness: the flatness is fullness, the sky is plenitude. As for Lewis, he didn't stoop but seemed to bloat and bruise from inaction. Occasional skydiving helped, but even at twelve I could tell he was a man who needed risk, torque, pressure. Criminology lectures at the university weren't enough.

Some years ago, decades after we lived in the just-annexed hamlet of Millard, to the west of Omaha, in that new cul-de-sac that was then open and sparse, I visited my sister, Debi, who'd settled there and never left. The sapling the developers had planted—the one little tree we'd had—marveled with its girth and height. Shade waits for the tree to make it.

In 1970 the Nebraska light, or my emotional state, was grim. Sun seemed always to come in dirty through the windows. What was it out of doors, the flatness, the paltriness of buildings under so much sky, that made any effort seem squalid and pointless? Adolescence was near. Its flag was the condom-windsock a scabrous scout held out to passing cars when our patrol went on a roadside hike to the only tree for miles.

This same boy was in my class at the junior high. He brought to homeroom black-and-white Polaroids of his sister having sex. I remember pointedly not looking at them when they were passed around, then regretting. That boy had dirty blond hair and always wore a T-shirt of some off-white hue.

I'd brought along from the first stay at Fort Benning my Sears telescope, having practiced tuning the device through many backyard sessions. I might have hallucinated spying Saturn in its rings for a quivering instant: touch the tube only slightly and you careen off-target millions of miles. I spent the rest of the night trying to center it again. I remember the wobble of the rings, the haze of interrupted light, a living thing. It was a powerful suck through the tube into the very spot where I might have hovered in space. I traveled forward to the face of the planet, and it shone down into my mind for a half-second. I tried two hours more to catch it again and failed.

After mixed success with Saturn, I turned my Sears telescope on the sun, devising an investigation into its spots. The Sears package came with filter attachments for the sun and the moon: the moon's was a greenish glass, and the sun's was orange. For a few weeks I drew sunspots onto several sheets of notebook paper taped into a panoramic scroll, using colored pencils to draw lines for each one as it moved, or as I thought it moved, across the sun's face. But I suspected randomness. I inked them in like beauty marks, then took a ruler to reach down the makeshift scroll to plot their vanishing. The colored-pencil lines were my cat's cradle of science. Kenning such imagined lands, I had no method beyond the obsessive and aesthetic lines. It was I and the sun, staring at each other.

HITCHHIKE

IN 1972 WE returned to Benning. Fourteen, I discovered obsessive hitchhiking: going nowhere, traveling in big circles around the post and Columbus, Georgia. My walkabout. When I put out my thumb, I wasn't going anywhere but around, finding the verge. Social life was little more than scattered moments of bad behavior. Everything new was a transgression, no way forward but consequence or its avoidance.

My hitchhiking domain was the area around the post and town, downtown, and sometimes out toward the countryside, but only furtively on the post itself, buzzing with MPs who might snag and drop me home with a Delinquent Report, the dreaded DR, for my stepfather. That would have been the death of me, but it was a perverse source of power as well.

That sort of travel, walking-standing-hitchhiking, was an organic measure of time-space, the factoring of chance as a reduction or growth of the world. I returned as the combination of rides allowed. I knew I might not return. It was the habit of staying in motion.

It mattered that I couldn't drive on my own yet. A few times I'd gotten so angry at Lewis I considered running away in his new Karmann Ghia, sneaking into the master bedroom to pocket the keys. Somewhere in my brain I knew it mattered that I had never learned to drive and would not get far. The idea of stealing the car was freedom and suicide, which have a passing acquaintance with each other. There would have been no coming back, so I hitchhiked around the county going nowhere but home.

Often, I went downtown, out the long, wooded road that separated Fort Benning from Columbus, down the boulevard toward the dying center, with its cobbled, half-tarred streets and disused trolley tracks. Or out the other side toward Alabama, where country folks were known to nosh on chunks of white clay. Partway to the state line was a park where kids hung out and hunted magic mushrooms. Near town I bloodied the other thumb when a sliding door on a bread truck slammed shut. The lady and gent who picked me up next offered to buy me Band-Aids at K-Mart. Instead, the lady sat in the middle and massaged my thumb, aiming to draw it down under her outlandish miniskirt—outlandish to me, because she was fortyish to my fourteen.

The gall of it made no matter and I came on contact. The anticlimax was my escape when they hung a slow right near the post office. "I need to buy stamps," I yelled as I leaped from the car. Then, creamed jeans and all, I bought stamps. I was a Boy Scout and aimed to make my lies come true.

A chatty gun salesman had me drag his samples case out of the back seat and hold the merchandise while he recited the specs. A young soldier home from the war but not quite home, eyes straight ahead, drove me where I asked, never uttering a word.

Walking in a freeway city: you and the bums and the whores and the newly arrived without wheels, or the people who don't like to trouble their friends when their car's broken down; or people without friends. The bus feels like a trap, slower even than walking sometimes, and God knows where it's really going. I've gone miles out of my way because I was too stubborn to get off the wrong bus and go back. Why go back when you know the world's round?

They're two different dimensions, fast and slow. Walking through a neighborhood you usually drive, you get pulled into windows and the houses talk to you. If you stop walking, the world keeps traveling and you feel it. You sink a little, then you know that the universe and its choices are infinite if bounded.

The last I recall was a ride out to the park. I'd scored my first hit of LSD. It was a concert day at the park and kids were everywhere. I swallowed the tab and waited. Nothing happened until after I'd forgotten something was supposed to happen. I'd expected it to be like stepping into a Peter Max painting or a Fillmore poster. It was a hot day. The music stuck to the skin. A Coke tasted ambrosial and froze in my throat. Wandering dogs held forth on various subjects. A guy with red hair and beard intoned Longfellow and was Longfellow. "Longfellow, Longfellow!" I called to him, and his beard got redder.

Hitching out to an armory dance in Phenix City the night before, I met a girl named Reba. At the dance, the LSD tab was in my jeans, but I held off. She offered to meet up at the park the next day, and I thought of her face in black-light hues as I wandered the outskirts of the concert crowd. She'd taken me for the friendly stranger and she was right. By the time I found her, everyone knew her. Her face was still purple. She was beautiful and led me away and I was wavy like eighth notes on a cellophane scroll.

She sat me down on a slope away from the crowd, but the music was still curling around the trees. She was talking about something, nothing, sitting next to me, and her name was this strange country wildflower growing between my feet.

I picked one of her sisters out of the ground and with botanical precision pulled it apart. Reba cooed the latest news in my ear. Her love played out like a stock ticker, though I noticed nothing. Piles of love-tickertape were gathering on the hill. Pretty purple-skinned Reba, singing her news to me, and I was lost to a wildflower.

SAYABOURY

LONG AGO MY Uncle John, Lunday's middle brother, sent me a compilation of home movies he'd had my cousin Brandon transfer to a VHS tape. The earliest clips are from the 1930s. In those brief scenes, my father's father poses proudly in his frumpy army uniform. He and others march back and forth on a parade field. In another clip, an infant is bathed in a galvanized tub, the water like an amber rain sprinkling over his amazed face. My grandmother, the second wife and my father's stepmother, thin and young, raven-haired and with deep-set eyes, walks coyly toward the camera, smiling, pausing at the end of an invisible tether. Her boys and the neighborhood kids do the same thing: move toward the camera, smiling and curious, haunting their futures.

Years ago, at Houston's Contemporary Art Museum, I saw a video installation called "Tall Ships" by Gary Hill. In a series of video loops, solitary figures appear in a black space, small in the distance, approaching until they are your own size, close enough to touch if they were real. They look at you, as if you share the same present as they. I was so haunted by the exhibit—art world meets fun house—I went back several times before the exhibit closed. How often is a museum exhibit as candy-like as a carnival?

In the Lunday home movies, that baby in the tub was my first father. Some grow up to be soldiers. The infant's eyes are shocked by the world, have yet to see anything but shadow and glare. In baby pictures, you see we all start out stunned, surprised, and gaping. Gradually details appear, we learn the names of things, make choices. Between the self and the world, a character takes shape: the me and you, a negotiation. Do we love people or patterns? Where do we become distinct from each other? My first father's face was so much like mine at certain ages, though his developed that sharp, jaded, killer's stare.

Some of Lunday's eight months in Laos in 1962 were spent training Royal Laotian forces in a place called Sayaboury. In the spring of that year, an article by correspondent Jacques Nevard called "Laos Army Balks at Attack on Reds"[1] appeared in *The New York Times*. Nevard depicts the challenges of counterinsurgency due to various conditions, focusing largely on the reluctance and naivete of the government troops and the frustration of the American advisors. The Royal Laotian command itself rejected the Americans' more-aggressive plan of attack because "it would get people killed." Then Nevard focuses on Lunday, first verbally pictured hovering over a map as he ponders the problems of success:

> Lieutenant Lunday, who is 28 years old, heads a six-man United States Army Special Forces team assigned to Sayaboury to improve the fighting capability of three volunteer battalions of Right-wing troops.
>
> Since the pro-Communist Pathet Lao movement broke the year-old cease-fire in the Laotian civil war and captured Nam Tha on May 6, the morale of the Pathet Lao guerillas in this province rose sharply, Lieutenant Lunday said.
>
> They began shelling Sayaboury Province from mortar positions on the east bank of the Mekong but the shells fell in the forests and there were no casualties.
>
> "I guess their shooting is not very accurate either," the slight, wiry United States officer said.

"These are decent, honest people," Lunday says a bit later in Nevard's account. "They are the most unwarlike people I have ever seen." Lunday remarks philosophically on the adverse influence their peaceful nature has on the training effort. The troops are given landmines, for instance, to help in their defenses, but they place them in the way of their own retreat.

"If they are attacked and run, they will have to go right through their own minefield," Lieutenant Lunday said.

I have a few lines in a book by a Native American Special Forces sergeant, Lionel Pinn,[2] who, besides his WWII, Korean War, and Vietnam service, spent a few months on the same team in Laos. Pinn calls Lunday slim and even-tempered and says he had a sense of humor.

The Laos mission was four years after Lunday had quit the army band and had put away his valve trombone to go to Officer Candidate School. Special Forces training, a lot of skydiving, a year in South Korea, and a lot of philandering came between. My mother had to petition Lunday's superiors to garnish his paycheck while he was stationed in Korea—he stopped sending money back home, he was having so much fun. The marriage sputtered along about a year and a half more after he got back from Laos.

Various Laotian, Cambodian, and Vietnamese objects Lunday had brought back were hung on the walls of the guest room in his parents' Nashville home. When we visited Nashville, I'd stare at the bow and quill full of arrows and the rice-paddy hat while I lay on the foldaway cot next to the bed. The wood and reed were of an eerie hue and texture, pieces of a different world. They couldn't be domesticated and made the bedroom wall a holograph of that far-off jungle in my eyes. My first father also was exotic.

We had a small library that followed us: a bible with pretty pictures of Jesus patting white kids on their heads beside a picket fence; some umpteenth edition of *The Army Wife*, another bible; Norman Vincent Peale; various well-worn children's books; and a picture book of France that made me feel I'd been there because I looked at it so many times.

On the same cheap but ancient chest-high bookcase that has moved with her for sixty-something years, along with two or three other battered bits of furniture, my mother still keeps a handful of those books, including three small paperback editions of Tom Dooley's memoirs. Dooley[3] was a navy doctor and humanitarian who wrote of his time in Vietnam and Laos between 1954 and 1959. The books had black-and-white pictures of young Americans treating horribly sick Southeast Asians, before-and-after photos, and in the after-shots the patients were always smiling at the friendly and helpful Americans.

In the early days, Dooley was the singular face of America in Indochina: decent, heroic, smart, and fun. I assumed my father was doing the same kinds of things: helping sick children, joshing with old crones whose last two teeth were solid black from betel nuts. Dooley turned out to be complicated. He was accused of exaggeration, rampant self-promotion, and ambiguous sexuality. Also, of course, he worked for the CIA. He died and was largely forgotten before the American war in Vietnam had begun. But I was taken with the idea of American greatness—whatever "America" was, somewhere in the distance from where I rode my red tricycle on an American sidewalk. Youthful, strapping, intellectual, pipe-smoking men. President Kennedy, First Lieutenant Lunday, and all the other men with bright smiles and rolled-up sleeves: they were doing good on the other side of the Earth, and that's why my father had to be gone.

For no reason I Googled the *Times* correspondent who'd met my father. Perhaps I imagined some serendipitous spark from their crossing paths. There is, after all, a smidgen of empathy in his report. After retiring as a correspondent, Mr. Jacques Nevard worked for the New York City Police Department, then the Transit Authority (TA). In 1977, after reports of financial shenanigans in the TA, he leaped from a balcony despite his apparent lack of connection to the scandal.

Nevard's death[4] was a few days after my father's death in his glider. Two men met in a jungle, then, in a bad week years later, fell from the sky. We're figures of happenstance, and the criss-crossings that score our surfaces are a magical, unreadable script.

When Lunday died in the glider crash in 1977, the cover of the *New Yorker* on the stands that week featured a ghostly aircraft hovering in a dark-blue sky. Significance was all around. I tore off the magazine cover and kept it in a picture frame. Lunday's buried in Section 25, Site 553 of the Barrancas National Cemetery in Pensacola, Florida.

I AM THE GRASS

H. BRUCE FRANKLIN[1] published a study of the MIA issue in the aftermath of the Vietnam conflict, finding that the focus on missing servicemen supposedly held captive by the communists was "pseudo-history compounded of self-deception, amateur research, anecdotes, half-truths, phony evidence, slick political and media manipulation, downright lies, and near-religious fervor." The book provides a detailed accounting of cases, categories of missing (such as pilots shot down over Vietnam, Laos, Cambodia, and the South China Sea), until virtually every possibly missing man seems, in Franklin's assessment, accounted for—making the MIA conspiracies, the political maneuvering, the protests, and the action movies into specimens of American mythmaking and paranoia. It's "families no longer looking for an accounting, but a resurrection," he says.

So why did some veterans, families of the missing and the dead, and some politicians press the issue, for so long? Franklin says: "Both the military and the religious career demand the whole man; that is, each of them projects the whole life upon a special plane." I think it was on some level an effort to win the postwar war—stupidly, with overwrought emotionalism, and by the same mode of lying and self-deception that got us into the war in the first place.

More recently, Michael J. Allen[2] revisited the accounting in his 2012 study *Until the Last Man Comes Home: POWs, MIAs, and the Unending Vietnam War*, wherein he considers the societal and psychological contexts of the MIA/POW movement to date. The numbers are complicated: The North Vietnamese returned more bodies and prisoners, overall, than the US government knew of in its own accounting. This was mainly because many airmen in particular had been listed as KIA. A few were alive and came home at war's end. The communists reported many who had supposedly died in captivity. So, continuing suspicion should probably focus on those claims. How many of those men were still alive, secretly imprisoned?

Around 300,000 Vietnamese from the North and among the Viet Cong are missing. No one knows how many from the South went missing during the war.

In Washington, DC, in the late 1980s, I often walked down Wisconsin Street through Georgetown and to the Mall, haunting the Smithsonian museums of an afternoon. Sometimes I'd go to the Vietnam Veterans Memorial to watch people trace names and leave things at the base of the wall. There are phone-book-sized directories for calling up the names of the dead with the tip of your finger, telling you which section of stone bears the name you want. I located the name of Michael F. Folland, a Medal of Honor winner who threw his body on a grenade to save Lewis. After the disappearance, searching the chest of drawers with Lewis's effects, I discovered a newspaper clipping about Folland's posthumous decoration. Lewis must have carried it for years but left it behind when he disappeared.

The Vietnam Memorial, the wall part of it, offended some veterans. James Young,[3] referring to "survivor outrage," says their experience inclines them toward wanting something more representational in a war monument—something more to the point. That says something about the power of abstraction in art. Walls, obelisks, pits in the Earth—how to achieve the balance between remembrance and erasure?

I'm reminded of the mad man on whose salmon trawler I worked before my trip back home in 1982. He asked me after we were out to sea, "Why the hell do you wanna do this kind a work, anyway?" and I said, "I'm a writer; I just want to write about it." He got angry—one of several warning signs on that voyage—then commanded, jabbing a finger, "Just be sure you don't tell any *lies!*" I think I get it. That experience, for me a flimsy attempt at adventure, was his life. It was what it was, nothing more or less. How could my words do anything but distort it?

On the Vietnam Veterans Memorial, on the wall, there are many names—58,318 at last count—but none for the missing, the scarred, or the soul-dead. The Vietnamese and others who died on both sides aren't named there. But you—*you're* there: the black marble reflects your face as if from a void beneath the lace of names. Maybe the most-famous poem about it is Yusef Komunyakaa's "Facing It."[4] It starts:

> My black face fades,
> hiding inside the black granite.
> I said I wouldn't
> dammit: No tears.
> I'm stone. I'm flesh.

He sees himself, then he sees others, past and present, in the shining surface. The blackness, the mirror-nature of it—here and there, then and now intermingle.

In some alternate dimension, such structures are along a no-street in a no-town, populated by no-people whose chiseled names are all that remain. It's not people who have names in that strange place, but the spaces between people: Vista, Shadow, Turn-Corner, Fog.

After the Great War, Carl Sandburg wrote these lines:

> Pile the bodies high at Austerlitz and Waterloo.
> Shovel them under and let me work—
> > > I am the grass; I cover all.[5]

Lyric can be memorial, but this is a memorial from that other side. So is the Vietnam Veterans Memorial, at least sometimes. The wall at its vee is a portal. Get drunk enough and you'll feel you might slip through, into the world beyond, though the beyond is just a creased and folded sense of here and now. Viet Thanh Nguyen, in his meditation on the wall in *Nothing Ever Dies*,[6] sees in the wall a framing of classic double consciousness, connecting it to W. E. B. DuBois's conception in *The Souls of Black Folk.* "While minorities may experience double consciousness regularly, even daily," writes Nguyen, "the power of the black wall is that it conveys that sense to individuals who are not used to experiencing it."

Above the Vietnam Veterans Memorial is a neat, green lawn. Give each blade of grass a name and you have a memorial to the enemy, the irksome allies, the delayed-dead, the altered futures. Grass has to be cut, but it always comes back.

THE BOY SCOUT HANDBOOK

I WAS BOTH a good and a poor Boy Scout. I loved the woods and campfires but hated uniforms and was no team player. The whole business chafed from the start, but I liked collecting the marks of progress. There should be more circular cloth badges and tiny brass pins in life.

After gaining seniority, I discovered that I was good at telling other kids what to do, though it was against my natural inclination to absorb rather than emit. I took to it because it pleased Lewis and kept him at bay. "You look pretty sharp in that uniform, Bobby," he'd tell me before a Scout meeting. Lewis didn't show interest in taking part, though. It wasn't lack of interest, and I wouldn't say being an adult Scout leader or taking part in campouts with me would have made him a better father. I'm pretty sure in his mind this was as close as I'd come to the rough ways of his own youth.

It was good as well to be told what to do through a handbook. The *Boy Scout Handbook*,[1] or at least the one from fifty-two years ago, offers a narrative of midcentury, American-male fulfillment remarkably comprehensive. More ambitious than a how-to manual, more useful outdoors than Emily Post, the *Boy Scout Handbook* was larger than the activity as I experienced and understood it. I liked reading the handbook more than I liked Scouting itself.

It was half reading and half daydreaming, as with most picture books. In my edition—seventh, first printed in 1965—the illustrations were an important part of that dream life. They were both practical and idealized, and in the consistent, detailed progression across nearly every page, they comprised a world one might choose already mapped yet virgin and wild. There was no stated author to this wisdom. Even the artist is unnamed, as if the whole thing were distillation.

The boys drawn throughout are entirely white. On the front cover, in color, are three white boys; on the back, another white boy is joined by a Black, East Asian, and Latino-looking lad. That's the Boy Scouts of America's framing of diversity circa 1965.

You won't find, leafing through this antique edition, any mention of women except in a few small illustrations: a proud, attending mom; a praying mom; and a mom letting her Scout son pull out her chair. One finds an extensive hygiene section, some nice drawings of athletic, shirtless Scouts, and even one naked Scout in a shower. Beyond that, all the eroticism of the handbook was cloaked in the knots chapter or the page on live wires.

I'm browsing the instructions on swimming. After I learned, it was the lakes at summer camp I loved. Lake water was alive and sexual. It embodied death as an appealing thing. I had no words, no archetypes to define it: the mysterious subterranean, the lulling motions, the deceptive draw toward deeper waters; days when the lake lay still under a gray sky, distant voices on shore, and the somber pines above the miniature bodies; the somnolent weight of things, and the unseen, gentle hand drawing you farther from land. One might sleep and settle into the amniotic bath, the great lathe turning slowly above, and you could feel its crystal needle scoring you.

But none of that was in the handbook. It's quintessentially mythic-American. Paul Fussell, in his essay "The Boy Scout Handbook,"[2] grounds the ethics of the handbook in the ancient Greeks and Romans; despite "the handbook's adhesions to the motif of scenic beauty," Fussell says, "it reads as if the Romantic movement had never taken place." But there's no avoiding the Romantic weave, particularly in Scouting's valorization of Indigenous cultures. Darkness, though, if not completely eradicated, is reduced to firm, clear lines. We're offered no Blakean shadow, but Rockwellian light of day that allows us to tell good from evil, or pretend so.

The handbook was for clear-cut and reachable achievement, as if all life and wisdom could be merit-badged into you. I liked at least that part of it: a system, simplistic maybe, but cataloging life in little round circles. The more I stayed with it, the more it mattered to Lewis that I saw it through: Eagle Scout, all the way, even if I was thirty before I finished. My preferred strategy was to fade, eventualities ever on the horizon, blanching into might-have-beens like large, distant mountain ranges. But to my dismay he would not let me fade, and I had to finish what I'd started. "You want my help getting your learner's permit? You want to drive my car?" he lectured me when I suggested I'd outgrown Scouting. "You don't get your driver's license, kid, until you finish what you started."

I approached the task in what I considered an intellectual, distancing manner, made a checklist, got it done item by item, with little emotion, and quit one day after my ceremony. It was Lewis's achievement more than my own.

I go back now and then to relearn what little of a language I used to know, an instrument I played, a handiwork my hands had warmed to. Rope lore has lately become an attractive cultivation, a kind of literacy and ethics. Every few years I pull out a knots manual and try once more to learn them. I like the choreography of knot-tying, though I almost never have anything I need to tie down. The knot knowledge fades again like all unpracticed habits. A square knot has to do for everything, and that's no way to go through life.

They sent us to the woods so it could absorb our natural foolishness. Capture the flag, dispersals and collisions, shouts and complaints all through the dangerous dark; rules unraveling and trampled outright, all ending with an injury to bring the men out of their tents in anger, a humbling scold and whispered recriminations back and forth as we packed it in and fought off sleep. Wildness peaked in the most expansive weariness, erasing everything but the essential.

At a place called Little Grand Canyon in southern Georgia, we spent a Friday night with our tents pitched on the edge of a precipice. In the dark it was a sky beneath us, deepening the one overhead but without stars. We ran around grab-assing all night, probably within inches of the abyss, sensed subtly by a change in air. Not a push back, but a slight tug toward the abyss. Asleep in the tent, I felt its promise of immensity and the urge to leap.

CIRCLES

IN MY FAMILY'S journeying I never saw anyone but my own siblings grow up around me, because each move put us among strangers who might have been always as we found them. No one really changed but us. A relationship works by our contending with change. In high school all you are is metamorphosis, so I made friends who were more important than family. Or it seemed so, but I barely remember them now.

After Omaha, in 1972, we moved back to Fort Benning. It was a joy to live on-post again, but the military high-schoolers that year were sent to off-post schools in Columbus according to race: white kids to a formerly all-Black school, Spencer High, and Black kids to a formerly all-white school, Baker. Some Black children whose fathers were officers petitioned to attend Spencer to stay with their peers by rank. Hispanic and Asian students went to Spencer.

At the civilian high school, racial distinctions were only slightly different from what the military kids had experienced in long-integrated on-post schools. The Black students who welcomed the military kids seemed quietly circumspect. Classes, clubs, sports teams, and even cliques mixed slightly, or not. My yearbook in its photo montages seems to tell both stories. The football team stayed mostly Black; the cross-country team, of which I was a lackluster member, stayed mostly white.

Spencer was in an old part of Columbus, industrial, split by highways, with public housing across the street from the school. The mainly unspoken rule for the white kids was not to linger too long after band practice and such, not to wander too far off the school grounds: that generalized, racialized sense of fear that defines whiteness.

Army buses returned late afternoon to shuttle kids back to Fort Benning after our extracurricular activities. Once I missed the later bus and knocked on a door at the apartment building across the street from school. I had the vague sense that any adult would feel obliged to help a child, and when a woman answered the door I asked if I could use her phone to call my mother for a ride home. The woman sized me up—a small, skinny white kid, long-haired, maybe a bit nervous—and opened her door just enough to let me in. "The phone's there," she said, pointing at a side table. "Leave a nickel."

At Benning we lived on Bjornstad Street, named for a general in the Great War, stretched out across a few modest blocks of cheap duplexes for junior officers. Our block faced an enormous parade-green three football fields wide. Hundreds of yards away was a wooded hillside, a gradual crest terraced with white elephants: large, old, southern homes for senior officers.

I don't recall seeing people in the field during the day. Surely families in the neighborhood must have used it, and the army on many occasions, but I remember it as blank, waiting, and all mine. At night, after homework and TV, I liked to run into the field because the dark folded in behind me. It was black enough to make the stars closer than the street, and the houses reduced to their laugh tracks and dishes clinking in sinks. The stars came right down into my head; it was better than drugs.

I knew in the dark that the field was a giant square, but the enforced blindness, with the faintest houselights or streetlights at a distance, seemed to round it off. The roundness was my mind. It was a circle of which my mind was the center and at the same time its circumference. When I think back to the almost-psychedelic experience of that field, it's like being inside a thought instead of thoughts in me. Both must be true. Said Goethe: "The center thinks the circle."[1]

Van Gogh wrote that life is most likely round, and Karl Jaspers[2] that being itself is round. This roundness was all-openness, the compass of potentiality. Equanimity, the roundness of the world (not the planet, but the totality of choices) was the self's fragile, beautiful bubble. A thing could be so perfectly round that it transcended thingness altogether.

That time, circa 1972, seems now like the precise border between childhood and the rest of life. Calling it adolescence doesn't capture the intensity I remember of childish things competing inside me with the appetites of the man. Daydreaming, wandering, and discovering were still important, but more often the searching was in books.

I was a timid teenager. When I had rebellious thoughts, Lewis's likely punishments gave me pause. But for about six months, around the time I was obsessively hitchhiking, I snuck out sometimes at night, because I was crazy about a girl named Ulla. What a crystalline moment it was when she showed interest in me! It would be brief because I was awkward and charmless.

Sure enough, Ulla broke up with me soon. We drove around with friends one night as she held my hand out of pity. We were a little high and I was dragging out the breakup. Her name was a duchy in my brain, though I lack evidence she existed.

On a bridge I was anguished and flung the door open to jump. It was not wanting to go over the side but off the page. I was halfway between falling and soaring. Ulla was distraught, so I felt remorse as she yanked me back into the car. She was elegant, whatever elegance might have seemed to a tenth grader: deep Marlene Dietrich voice, melancholy eyes, a practiced, weary pose.

Her crying was more stunning than sex. Being dumped is one of life's most exhilarating experiences.

Probably train tracks down there, or the Chattahoochee River.

Strawberry perfume, cigarette smoke in her sweater, flesh, hormones, hair, saliva. Autumn disappearing into winter. Even years later, in my early twenties in New York, a change in the wind might draw me back and she'd be in the crowd up ahead or turning a corner. At a fair, a ball game, a rally, or in the rush-hour press of bodies struggling to get home, how hard it was to track the one I thought I knew. She'd morph into a different person, disappear again, descend into subways, climb flights of stairs, turn corners into solid walls.

THE VERGE

DOUBLES HAUNTED ME at the edge of childhood. It was the effect, climaxing at that point in my life, of the many moves, the many streets, neighborhoods, schools, and circles of friends. Something in me felt the world was both bigger and smaller than it seemed; that the number of faces passing me by was infinite, but that some were the same and kept coming back around; and that I frequently missed my own figure turning a corner up ahead, hiding behind a tree nearby, a me a little older, who could clear some present-day confusion if he'd just turn around and speak.

One night I woke to rustling sounds. I got out of bed and looked out the window, spying someone near the well. Concentrating for a moment, I was sure I heard breathing. Reservedly I woke Lewis, who grabbed a pistol and went out and around toward the woods behind the house. Something had clicked and he was back in patrol mode, charged and alive. He came back to report nobody there, gave me a skeptical look, and sent everyone back to bed.

But the dark pushed in for several minutes on my window, and I felt the lurker still there. This was the last phantom of my childhood. They were always there, but like most people I'd block them by not believing in them. There's always suffering or hatred somewhere near, and if you concentrate you can catch a little of the malice or misery; and your brain squeezes out a golem, and it bears your face. Sometimes it's a future self. That night, it was my older self who would not be welcomed back into that home: not evil, but far from innocent, soiled by the score of cities and countries of my later passages. It was tempter and savior, composite of everyone whose friendship I'd crave or whose contempt would burn me. Lewis, the Missing Man, stealthily moves between my sleep and my waking, tracks the apparition, and keeps it at bay: not yet, not yet for this one.

Says Kafka[1] in one of his aphorisms: "With a very strong light, one can make the world disappear. Before weak eyes it will become solid; before still weaker eyes, it will acquire fists; and to eyes yet weaker, it will be embarrassed and punch the face of anyone who dares to look at it." Kafka's aphorisms are only loosely so. This one reaches beyond gnomic into narrative. It might work as a prologue to a story by D. H. Lawrence called "A Fly in the Ointment."[2]

Spending his day caught in floral, romantic dreams, at the school among the boys he teaches, with letters sent and received from his lover, and now on the edge of sleep, the narrator stumbles into his darkened kitchen. There he senses the presence of the intruder: a young man, a feral creature, curled in a corner. The speaker asks the creature why he's there.

Lawrence's narrator is still woven into his own sensibility and life, a dream-life, a life of words and flowers, which are themselves interchangeable. The man-beast responds fearfully, with threats and raw feelings so alien to the narrator's delicate, polychromatic openness. Still, as the story continues, he draws our empathy, as if he were the natural boundary to the narrator's world.

The narrator calms the fellow down with his teacher's authority. He looks into the mangled yard, the night that surrounds them both with its coldness and lack of feeling. The conversation between them is as one between a minor god and some mortal storm-tossed into the sacred spaces.

But the comedy is that both are human, dreaming entirely different dreams. "You loaf at the street corner till you go rotten," the speaker tells the creature, neither as prophecy nor curse: it's a report on the spiritual weather that surrounds the feral one, and little more, though an entire life might be lived inside that sentence. The narrator orders the wretch out: "'You'd better go. But for God's sake steal in different streets.' I rose, feeling he had beaten me. He could affect and alter me, I could not affect nor alter him."

The creature shambles off, and the speaker returns to the second story of his house, darkened, as if a shadow had crossed his body and left an indelible stain.

Elsewhere in Lawrence[3] one finds: "I can become one with God, consummated into eternity, by taking the road down the senses into the utter darkness of power, till I am one with the darkness of initial power, beyond knowledge of any opposite." I hear either of the two men in these words. Every stranger is us, and none is stranger than he is to himself.

Jay Scott Morgan, in his essay "The Mystery of Goya's Saturn,"[4] sees two sides of the Titan in Goya's "Saturn Devouring His Sons": "Cover the right side of the face, and we see a Titan caught in the act, defying anyone to stop him. The bulging left eye staring wildly at some unseen witness to his savagery. . . . Cover his left eye, and we are confronted by a being in pain, the dark pupil gazing down in horror at his own uncontrolled murderousness . . . asking, 'Why am I compelled to do this?'" One aspect will have its opposite, adversary, prior, successor, or varied degrees. We carry our potentials, we chase or evade, like Poe's William Wilson, our malignancies or better angels. Probability allows us to continue more or less as this person. It's generally not something required or absolute. That these different selves will be opposed is simply to understand their mutual distinction.

Two photographs of Lunday frame the distance between a soldier's innocence and experience. In one, the eyes are soft and moist. They smile and they welcome everyone to the moment of the image. Lunday is perhaps twenty-two, when my parents were stationed in France, where Lunday played in the army band. In the other, from several years later, he stands in a T-shirt in someone's living room back in the States, steel-eyed and menacing, as if the war were just out of the frame. Is it to be too much in the body, or too much out of it? Tethered, maybe, still the homunculus in charge, but floating.

For Lewis, I don't know when he might have moved from a look of innocence to experience. His childhood photos are of a sweet lad, surely. The several of adolescence already show that sharpness in the eyes, and it might come from having taken on the burdens of supporting his mother and baby sister after his own father, Jimmy, absconded. Or it might have been his essential force coming on:

not that he was shaped by circumstances, but that *he* shaped *them.* Though his later images are often of that man with the steely gaze, he does flicker back and forth across the album between serious and something else: impish, mainly. Lewis liked to joke around, teasing our mother playfully, joshing with his sons—but he could flip without warning, so those happier images still carry his edge.

A few years ago, my brother Kevin gave me an aviation magazine from the early nineties. On the cover was a small, high-winged six-seater, taxiing. You could barely see the pilot inside, but he had the thick-faced, no-neck, close-cut head of Lewis—the right age for that time, too. An article inside mentioned the place and name of the charter company in Washington. I did a little research, but they were long out of business. I didn't go further: too long ago, too unlikely. Why would Lewis have wound up exactly the opposite end of the continent from where he'd said he was going that day he drove away? It's yet another diagonal, though: traced onto the map of his possible destinations. The magazine cover is another relic and I can't discard it.

Anyone of a reflective nature will consider the uncanniness of here-and-now existence, the tentative nature of identity: that echo we sometimes sense, a semiautonomous shadow we almost glimpse. Most of us shake it off before it's cooked into actual thought.

Once we look, we find our doubles everywhere. They help visor reality, which means they keep it out as well as let it in. It's a lifelong balancing act, handing off the baton as the self makes its journey. Shadows must be the first doubles—sooner than mirror images: flickering, partial shadows on walls and other surfaces, even before we get outdoors, which is a menagerie of shadows. In Mary McGarry Morris's novel *Vanished,*[5] a dim-witted man, Aubrey Wallace, at the start of the tale, is a laborer who sees himself: "He has been watching his shadow work. He likes his shadow. He likes his afternoon shadow best, the way it stretches long and lean with the sinking sun. Sometimes he imagines there are two parts of him—two Aubrey Wallaces: the one they are grinning at now and this quick, dark one with its sure silent step." The doubling is already there when we're brought into the world. It's the projection of the natural recursion of thought that wraps around and around, creating sickness where the recursions get stalled or knotted, but taking shape, forming knobs of self, developing a physiognomy as a projection of brain, of thought, or the continuous personality slicing like a keel through the rush of time.

When I was six, walking on a sidewalk toward home, in Fayetteville, in summer, in jeans and a striped shirt buttoned to the neck, feeling the cars drive by, feeling the air and how it connected me to other humans, I paused, and I remember clearly pausing, on the sidewalk—the Great Sidewalk that wraps around the Town of the World where that six-year-old still lives—stopping in my tracks to question the arrangement: Was I alone human, aware, and weren't the others, walking further ahead of me, those who'd passed me by and must still exist out of my sight, those driving by, the family I was going home to? Weren't they senseless beings, obstacles and diversions to populate my world? They were robots, and I was the only one alive. Could that be? I paused briefly, asked the question, then walked on—either answering in the negative: that they *must* be aware, like me; that seemed the easiest answer—or perhaps letting it drop altogether. I think I respected the unanswerability of it.

Maybe to live, to be an ego, is to defer the problem indefinitely, but as life demands, to *act* as if others are human. Even now most people seem to me so much more in possession of their personalities. I can't so well remember when it became unlikely I was the Messiah, or a secret Superman, or even a future president. These were not cast-off futures but sloughed skins and outgrown carapaces.

We must all have had a sense of the time before we existed when we were children and must have felt either a dense solidity or an endless, weightless atmosphere around this sharp point of self. Standing on that sidewalk (where I still walk), my child-self felt the immensity of the past without me. I think I felt nothing of the immensity of the future, though like most I was a creature with eyes mostly forward. Where was the future other than in the anticipations, appetites, and apprehensions that defined me in the moment? Now, though it's so densely populated—with only the thinnest border between my own life and all the narratives of history—the past seems tight and small. The future is riddled with wormholes: all the unfinished travels of the past, tangled in a formless mass before me. Dostoevsky's[6] Ridiculous Man sees nothingness ahead of himself: "as soon as my consciousness is extinguished the whole world will vanish too"—*après moi le déluge*. Such a human has already succumbed to his sense of nothingness, and his solipsism is a brief bubble, a blister on the surface, rather than a true protest.

The Boulevard du Temple image taken by Louis Daguerre circa 1838 seems to depict a deserted street, but the vehicles and people rushing about there have been made to disappear through the ten-minute exposure. Outside of time, two small figures are hidden in the shadows: one man standing still while another shines his shoes. Disappearance, Jean Baudrillard[7] says, might be a way of describing our desire to observe the world in our absence. That's how I think about being an adult: to see into the world where my presence isn't needed. *Homo absconditus*.

In its third season, *Star Trek* offered an episode titled "Wink of the Eye," which was one of those that stayed in my mind for many years. In the early seventies, when the series would play on whatever late-afternoon UHF channel, I would look for my favorites, but this one in particular. It features a near-extinct race of aliens called the Scalosians who, due to radiation on their planet, have become hyper-accelerated. They live at a rate of movement far faster than the human eye can detect, registering only as the occasional insect-buzz when the ship's landing party descends to investigate a distress message.

It was striking to imagine that beings could exist not only on another world, or in another time, or in another dimension (whatever that might mean), but also at a different speed. Then I saw *The Incredible Shrinking Man* and had to add life at different scales. The Shrinking Man accepts his escape into the infinitesimal, for "to God there is no zero."

All the sudden reading I did when I was ten was a rush of catching up to some slightly older version of myself. I discovered Ray Bradbury's "Fire and Ice," a story about people trapped on a world where generations are born, live, and die within the span of seven days. What might the intensity of life be at such scales? What would the self be? What emotions might we feel? Life seemed so slow when I had lived only a decade. It wasn't so much that other people might not be human, but that they all knew things I didn't. The more I read, the more I felt so.

Sometimes we blink out. Some humans stay here longer than others. The frame might seem to hold them, but a malevolence, a cruel neglect pulls them beyond. Perhaps most people spend a certain amount of life, both waking and dreaming, lurking about the frame. Sartre[8] wrote of Baudelaire that he saw things only through watching himself see. Thus, the things he saw were "paler, smaller, and less touching as though seen through an eyeglass." An enfolded distance is the typical condition of most thinking people. At will they enter and exit the space of absence, from there encountering the essential falsehood, or if you prefer, the playfulness of the scene.

The point in my life when I discovered the magnetic compass seems now conjoined with that point in history when Homo sapiens, my shadow, discovered the same. I have done considerably less with it, but it has saved me at times. It's been a faithful if erring friend; a pet, really, or a djinn, who seems to serve me, but instead serves some ancient geophysical drama. The compass has metamorphosed into many other things, disguised in other devices and attitudes—for a magnetized existence is essentially a cosmic attitude—but I still have one of those actual early compasses, my Scout compass, and its needle still stutters "North" like a telling of the time of time.

Melanie Klein's[9] object-relations theory proposes that small children develop relations first not to whole things but only to parts of things. Furthermore, the child must "split" the world into good and bad categories to find their proper connection to the good—at least until the child's cognitive development allows tolerance of contradiction, complexity, and uncertainty that will not threaten their sense of self too drastically. So, getting older allows us to realize wholes: things in the real world that incorporate both the good and the bad.

The ideal dies or becomes an object of nostalgia. "Existence is the fragile and mortal result of a disequilibrium," argues Ilya Prigogine.[10] Extrapolating wildly from that insight, I say that a child confirms their existence when they sense that the good and the bad comingle in the things of the world: essential form of disequilibrium.

When I was five, walking down a street, perhaps a mere two streets away from our house, I saw a snarling, rabid dog at the end of my sight. I couldn't see its eyes, but it *was* an eye. Something enormous inhabited the world, but I could see only its mad-dog eye. I knew I was inside a myth, though all I knew was fairy tales: magic, horror, fate. The dog was one-headed. *Come this way*, it said, *so I can devour you.*

When my parents divorced in 1964, the news of it was a storm, distant, approaching. It seemed to render invalid my childhood to that point. It displaced me, displaced place altogether—the floating sense of place of our military, nomadic family, now no longer the same family—so how could I be the same?

In a photograph taken in Tennessee, when my sister and I were on a visit to our Lunday grandparents, the two of us are posed with our cousin Brenda around the gravestone of an ancestor named John: my sister with an appropriately mournful expression—she was an actress!—my cousin and I, younger and oblivious to such meanings, squinting and smiling into the camera.

The gravestone is jagged, uneven at the top, as if on its way to becoming a natural object again. It's someone's semirural yard, a lawn but no sidewalk, a drainage ditch and then the road. A fifties-style bungalow sits in the background across the street. A scrawl on the photo puts John's death in 1812.

In another image from the same year, 1964, we sit in a creek atop a waterfall, a smallish one, as if to plunge down and through into the stream of things. Soon after on that day, my parents walked up ahead.

They were serious about something. Sensing it, I tried to draw closer. I was barefoot, and the sticker burrs attacked the soles and sides of my feet with a vengeance. When I wore shoes, the burrs clotted my shoelaces, and it was an extended meditation to sit and pluck them out.

The burrs were everywhere, but I took them as a personal insult. They were the inverse of fireflies that languidly declined your grasp after dusk; a random pleasure in the brief life of a summer nightfall, tracking away, but a few always falling into the jar for a moment of theater before release.

Their evil twins were these burrs, creatures of the summer sun, always and everywhere as the fireflies were brief and native to the air.

I couldn't keep up with the somber adults, and it was a dream-scape, the biting weeds, separating me from my family. I panicked and wailed. Nanny, my grandmother, held me back. She wasn't of a mind to coddle me. It meant that something was wrong. I could hear the disquieting buzz.

My first father just disappeared, and we never spoke of it, as if he'd always been gone. A few times he did come back, unannounced, making a gift of himself.

VITA ACTIVA

"ACTION, THE ONLY activity that goes on directly between men without the intermediary of things or matter," writes Hannah Arendt,[1] "corresponds to the human condition of plurality, to the fact that men, not Man, live on the earth and inhabit the world." Our living together necessitates the political, or the call to action—but it's the *Vita Contemplativa* that grounds our action: such was the classical/medieval model. Studying the tradition, Arendt observes that truth revealed itself to the mind in stillness.

Modernity inverts this: Action comes first. The American form of self-discovery has generally been conceived as immersion in experience rather than contemplative withdrawal. The more reality one's experience encompasses, the nearer one comes to self-definition.

Louis-Ferdinand Céline, anti-Semite, veteran of the Great War, asks in *Journey to the Edge of Night*:[2] Isn't bravery the problem, and cowardice the solution? William James[3] said that heroism is the attitude one takes when honestly confronting pain and wrong and death; when going against "freezing, drowning, entombment alive, wild beasts, worse men, and hideous diseases." Heroism is entering into the world with more than "phrases of neatness, coziness, and comfort." The world, says James, is all our theater of heroism, and a man's heroism is "the fact that consecrates him forever."

We were told many times growing up that Lewis, at age five, hopped a freight train and rode it clear to El Paso. His mother got a call from the authorities, so the little boy knew his name and hometown. She drove 700 miles to retrieve him. When we were told that tale, the moral was that the rail-riding kindergartner "got his fanny tanned good." It was a way of keeping us in the neighborhood.

The story is ridiculous, but I believe it. I never bothered, later in life, to confirm it with my stepfather or his mother. I don't even know, and prefer not to check, what train line it might have been, how long a 700-mile journey would have taken, or, in 1945 or 1946, just how likely it was that a five-year-old could have climbed aboard a freight train and stayed unnoticed for hours and miles.

This and other accounts of Lewis's extraordinary qualities defined an idealized range of behavior for me. In the back of my mind, that five-year-old (though the image is a miniature of the fearsome, grizzled, adult Lewis) still rode the train somewhere in space, on some loop of eternal return.

We were also told that Lewis had joined the National Guard at fourteen. When I read Lewis's military records, I discovered that he was, in fact, five months shy of his fourteenth birthday. We were also told that Lewis's mother, rather than go immediately to retrieve her son, let him stay in uniform five full months. Driving to San Antonio, she then asked the sergeants, "Do you know how old that boy is?" They got thin-lipped and sheepish, admitting that Private Lewis might have lied about his age. "That boy there," Lewis's mother replied, "is *fourteen years old.*" At a more reasonable seventeen, Lewis lied again about his age and joined the regular army.

As a teen I often lay on the living-room carpet by our Phillips stereo console we'd shipped back from West Germany, listening to jazz fusion or acid rock. Mother might be in the kitchen doing dishes while my little brothers played or fought in their bedroom. Lewis often worked late. His dinner would be waiting on the table after our plates had been taken away. I tried to be done with my music-hour before he got home. The living room was his, always with the La-Z-Boy and the standing ashtray it was my duty to empty.

One night I dreamed too long, and Lewis came in, still in his fatigues, tired, already peeved at whatever had displeased him. He flicked on the light with a violence and growled, "There *IS* no 'deep truth,' Dickhead!" followed by a pause while he breathed like a bull. My heart leaped and the record skipped—Roy Harper's *Lifemask.* "Keep the goddam light on!" he added, as if he meant always, everywhere, in the room and in my life.

DISEQUILIBRIA

SOMETIMES MY MOTHER asked one of us to wake Lewis for dinner or to help him get up out of his La-Z-Boy and go to bed. It was a dicey project. You could shove him from all directions before he'd stir. But then, when he was just about back among the living, he'd throw a quick, wide punch at what specter was haunting him. If you didn't step back fast, you'd get tagged. It made me think of propping a plane, pushing down the big blade that could fan on and cut you to slaw if you weren't alert.

Lewis tried to get me into boxing when I was fourteen. He'd been an amateur slugger himself as an enlisted man. Steering me that way was an effort to give what final shaping I could take. It was a miserable experiment. I loathed hitting someone even more than getting hit.

I sparred a couple of times, disgusted everyone, and was left alone. But I'd discovered the gym. Left to myself, I found my own rituals of physical culture. Aside from the weights, I developed a fascination with the speed bag, the bouncing loops I could make in its little alcove, its rhythm the pattern of my own nerves. It was doodling, drawing the same cloverleaf over and over, getting it right.

Sports were an existential puzzle. Why try to win when next week, next season, you'll probably lose—as if to lose the present is also to lose all previous wins? I missed the point, not only in sports but in life. There were victories, a few, some wins I held dear. But I was merely forgetting what I already knew of the pointlessness of things.

In high school I became a cross-country runner. Cross-country seemed to escape tensions and contradictions of sport as I saw it. We could cross the finish line one before the other, but we were a team, our points combined, and we won or lost together. On the other hand, each runner ran alone. He tested his time against all times before and raced mainly with himself.

There was a pleasure in winning, but the pleasure was more in the chase: increasing the distance with those behind me, closing it with those ahead, sometimes winning the pure open field in front, which was worth more to me than the finish line.

The cross-country races tended to be through woods, fields, along creeks, down farm roads. It was a lot like reading. When I ran, I played a fast song in my head, whatever was on the radio at the time. I'd run to it, run after it, letting the pursuit take my mind away from the pain of pushing limits.

Havelock Ellis[1] said the personal freedom of Sir Thomas Browne led to splendor and that of Samuel Pepys to clarity. How can we see the world without tension between the two? The ratio of thought and action determines our character. The ancient warrior's way was keener, like the hawk's: soaring, diving, grappling with talons of steel.

The machines of war are everything that makes us. The grinding process starts at birth. Mary McCarthy,[2] after visiting American POWs in Hanoi, wrote, with little sympathy for the Americans: "If these men had been robotized, I felt, it had been an insensible process starting in grade school and finished off by the Army, which had passed them for duty as high-precision instruments, equipped with survival kits and the rudiments of reading and writing. Far from being an elite or members of an 'establishment,' they were somewhat pathetic cases of mental malnutrition." McCarthy offers slight fellowship further on, even admiration mixed with pity. But it's her construction of distance that I mark: ideological, intellectual, and moral distance from her countrymen. Anyone familiar with the military mien will see that she misreads the officers. Their psychic frame is altogether different from hers. What has been the measure and the balance of their lives is so different—how could they communicate with her, even in more relaxed settings? It was somewhat like the distance I felt between me and my stepfather.

"Living, of course, is rather the opposite of expressing," says Camus.[3] But the ratio—to *form*, rather than survive only—we don't make, we don't sculpt life every instant from some authentic core: There is none. We're pulled through unseen vortices into other worlds.

Henry Adams,[4] deeply aware of his status as non-soldier, defines warriors as "men who sprang from the soil to power," wary around others, sometimes even their own kind; perpetually in need of stimulation. Those men McCarthy met in Hanoi were deprived of their stimulant—not only from being prisoners, but also from the loss of a world view, loss of connection to their birth-ground.

The vortex takes away shape or form. It's immediacy, reality without frame, without sufficient distance for the mind to do what it must do: hover just slightly above. Karl Marlantes, in *What It Is Like to Go to War*,[5] says of his combat experience: "I had no framework or guidance to help me put combat's terror, exhilaration, horror, guilt and pain into some larger framework that would have helped me find meaning in them later." The field wasn't there—the bonds, the meanings, weren't present, and they did not coalesce later. The vortex was always there, always waiting to suck the man through. Why does it take longer for some than others?

Soldiering instills in some a strong desire to return to old ways, but in many it does the opposite—stirs restlessness that makes those old ways unpalatable. Said Alfred Schuetz,[6] studying the soldiers of the Second World War as they were still returning: "We cannot be astonished . . . that a United States War Department survey of June, 1944, showed that 40 per cent of the discharged veterans being sent back to civilian life through eastern 'separation centers' did not want their old jobs back and did not want even to return to their old communities."

Thus, we had the mid-twentieth-century migrations, disaffections, fashionable existentialism, subterranean and tumescent countercultures, biker gangs, casual alcoholism, ulcers, Valium, seven-year itches, along with the spurting skyscrapers, men in gray flannel suits, the busy sounds of industry, paranoia, and aliens from outer space. Missingness is normative amid it all. Men and women will light out for the territories, past the pink-and-purple haze.

A British ex-soldier, Barry Davies,[7] has written a how-to guide on disappearing that zeroes in on his fellow war vets. It seems a competent-enough guide to escape, self-effacement, starting over, or chasing one's fantasy—which, in this soldier's sensibility, is occupied by the ideal sort of woman: she's young, Thai, and in love with Western manhood. The prospect of that possession—of taking to oneself the Siamese beauty—seems, as subtext to Davies's how-to, the very goal of disappearance. Do the missing seek timelessness, agelessness? Is it sometimes a narcissism?

Some disappear slowly. This is Davies's advice. Build and test your plan, sever contacts one at a time. Give no hints, create a cover story. Visit the country you'll go to, look into changing your name.

Meanwhile, take a survival course. Consider joining a nongovernmental organization (NGO), becoming a hobo, going to sea, joining a foreign army or a private security firm. Enter a religious order.

Wherever you go, stay below the radar. Be committed, Davies says, avoid accidents and criminal activity (shouldn't we all?), steer clear of foreign nationals, stay away from the embassy. Trust no one.

A soldier who survives combat must be shadowed by those who didn't. "It is a mystery," writes Tobias Wolff in *In Pharaoh's Army*,[8] "why one man dies while another lives." The mystery carries over to the life now ancillary to that receding intensity. In battle or driving down the highway or sitting in one's living room, we have no reliable forecast of the next moment. I wonder how intense that mystery is when death can come from so many angles, when the weight of one's own death or of the death of one's fellow or of one's foe seems to fill every pocket of space and time. Those who die, as Wolff describes it, seem to have been killed in place of the still-living.

Other Vietnam veterans have written about living and dying in ways that suggest the doubling: in Ron Kovic's *Born on the Fourth of July*,[9] the author remembers another soldier, a corporal from Georgia, whose existence seems especially close to the third figure of death that follows and leads them. Kovic observes the corporal at times during patrols, as if seeing a ghost. The corporal's death later in the book seems to intensify Kovic's own near-death that leaves him a paraplegic, and to provide a fulcrum between the knowable and unknowable aspects of death within a space so charged with violence. Tim O'Brien's Jorgenson in *The Things They Carried*[10] constructs an apparition within the theater of his revenge.

In O'Brien's writing, this doubling effect occurs often and in varied forms. Even before departing for his tour, the new soldier depicted in O'Brien's[11] memoir senses it: "The war and my person seemed like twins as I went around the town's lake. Twins grafted together and forever together, as if a separation would kill them both." The disembodied feeling births these projections of alternate selves, of companions and fellows, of those closer or nearer the death-sun that warms us all. The doubling makes the space of the individual: without two, there can't be the one, which doesn't cast a psychic shadow, or seek its reflection in the water or other flashing surfaces, but instead forwards our existence, flickering as it goes.

It's among the many patterns of nature—mostly, a branching. Sometimes that branching or bifurcating carries a recognizable emotional or moral resonance. O'Brien's pattern in his memoir seems more rayonnant than branching: "You liken dead friends to the pure vision of the eternal dead soldier. You liken living friends to the mass of dusty troops who have swarmed the world forever." This sunburst of the living and the dead becomes an unendurable burden on the living. But it can be transcendence. Elsewhere, O'Brien describes it: "The man to the front is civilization. He is the United States of America and every friend you have ever known; he is Erik and blond girls and a mother and a father. He is your life. And, for the man stumbling along behind you, you alone are his torch."

That it was to escape growing old, the slowing-down, the broadening and softening—unfit for warrior status, unable to keep up, much less to lead. "And even if one must die," cries Musset, "what did it matter? Death itself was so beautiful, so noble, so illustrious, in his battle-scarred purple! It borrowed the color of hope, it reaped so many ripening harvests that it became young, and there was no more old age." Thus, the poet rhapsodizes the Emperor of his infancy.

As for the soldier, and others like him, that choice, or that being-chosen, or that perdition, or that ascendance, is the triangulated leap. Says Sophocles's *Antigone*:[12]

It was not war
Nor the deep sea that overtook him,
But something invisible and strange
Caught him up—or down—
Into a space unseen.

A veteran interviewed in *Soldiers in Hiding*, an eighties documentary, tells the interviewer: "At some point in Vietnam I became 10,000 years old and I died." It sounds not so much like a figure of speech but a simple truth. These woods he's in are the anagoge. In his Vietnam novel *Meditations in Green*,[13] Stephen Wright's protagonist tells us: "The leaves sighed. I could feel myself slowly emptying, the rushes, the bubbles, the shakes, until I was as blank as a stone Buddha."

During the Great War, men fell into the mud and disappeared. Flesh was ground back into earth: bomb-shredded, track-flattened, boot-softened, hoof-mashed, rain-melted. Major Dellaplane, in Bertrand Tavernier's *Life and Nothing But*, is a French officer at war's end tasked with identifying bodies dead and alive. He works in one scene with blank, amnesiac, or catatonic survivors. "I need signs, scars, warts, tattoos!" he calls out to his staff in the hospital. Bits seep out: a snatch of sea shanty or work song, a profane lyric from one he therefore deems a priest. Later, to a wife-or-widow seeking her husband, he pulls out binders of pantographs, drawings organized by physiognomic patterns in noses, heads, chins, and eyes. It's disturbing only in the first few pages; "then, it's like a herbarium," he advises. Out on the barbed wire that remains near battlefields still giving up their corpses, parents and wives have tied bottles with messages for the missing. The bottles, which have nowhere to float but on currents of time, bobble like living creatures as the wire coils respond to touch along their length.

My friend Marta found an old stereoscope at an estate sale. It's finely wrought in wood, still loaded with an image series from a battlefield of the Great War. She keeps it atop her upright piano. When I visit, I peer through the eyepiece at the images: a wobbly cart, stoic mule in front, overloaded with rib cages; their chevron arcs, the order of each, within the chaotic pile of trapped air and hell-marrow; the desultory but obedient mule, waiting to haul the bones toward oblivion.

Images like those occur in Erich Maria Remarque's writing—especially in the novel after *All Quiet on the Western Front*, called *The Road Back*: "Our hands are earth, our bodies clay and our eyes are pools of rain. We do not know whether we still live." The pastoral rises to great ecstasy as the returning soldier leaves his body, fusing with the elements of nature:

> My body, now even my body is passing into the meadow. Its boundaries are becoming uncertain; it is no longer apart, the light breaks down its contours and at the edges it is beginning to be unsure. Above the leather of my shoes rises the breath of the grasses; into the woolen pores of my clothing presses the odor of the earth; through my hair blows the moving sky, which is wind; and the blood knocks against the skin, it rises to meet the incoming thing, the nerve ends are erect and quivering.[14]

Too soon our grandest adventures seem behind us. Our mind's fires burn less brightly. Our bodies are past their prime. We'll make choices that narrow our essential being. The owner of that life will no longer fit into the world as before, may no longer fit into the world at all. Life has its folds, but we don't disappear for very long—not long enough, usually, to be noticed, to be reported to the police, to have our faces on Missing posters.

The Missing One, indeterminately alive or dead, is a mirage or a strobic projection. Some absconders seem to be aiming for the creation of a self-projection—an image to leave on the eyeballs of others.

Maybe for some absconders, the idea is to find an exit ramp before death. According to his daughter Helen, Ambrose Bierce wanted "to go quickly and with none of his friends near to look upon his face afterward."[15] The author slipped over the border with Mexico during the Revolution in 1913. But even that isn't certain, nor is it clear he accompanied Pancho Villa's army, though he wrote one letter claiming to have witnessed a battle.

Bierce fought four years in the American Civil War and carried that experience deeply. It shaped his anti-imperialism and his cynicism about the Spanish-American War. His own war stories, of a piece with and sometimes overlapping his tales of the weird, suggest a sensibility that shapes combat as an ecstatic experience. Bierce's supposed quest into the end of his life might have been suicide, or more broadly a renewal of that ecstatic moment, that anonymity.

Carlos Fuentes's version of Bierce in *The Old Gringo*[16] relives his war experiences as visions deeply woven into his own fictions. Fuentes sends the old man galloping against a machine-gun post of Federales, himself a vision of supernatural, Yahweh-like terror to those soldiers, while also blazing as a Soldier in the Sky above their heads—an image from Bierce's like-named tale of the Civil War in which a sentry rides against his own father, an enemy general— and, having been waked by an angel from a treacherous sleep while on duty, shoots the glaring image of his father, or rather, the horse beneath him, sending horse and rider plummeting into the abyss.

Bierce's most famous fiction, "An Occurrence at Owl Creek Bridge," tells of the protagonist's great expansion of mind, a virtual life lived fully within the final moments of life. Kazantzakis gives his Christ a similar expansion, and I read it as an alternative strategy of redemption: that consciousness is enfolded, that we move inward as much as forward in time. Our life is their ratio.

A BEAUTIFUL DEATH

THAT SUMMER OF 1982, before Lewis's vanishing, I went home without a plan for getting back into the world. Two years out of college I
had floated about, literally, two weeks before heading to Fayetteville,
on a salmon trawler as a deckhand of no worth. Prior to my one-week
fishing trip, I'd stayed in a bungalow on a cliff above the ocean with
the poet Vijay Seshadri, who'd been working on trawlers for years.
Out on the waves, the young captain I worked for, who'd spent his
whole life on the sea, sang Beatles songs in the most menacing way.
I've never heard "Love Me Do" interpreted with such grimness. My
ineptitude as a deckhand offended the mad captain so much I was
sure he'd kill me: bash my head with the handle of the gaffe hook as
he did the salmon. How easy it would have been to drop my body
into the Pacific and claim I'd fallen overboard, as a few times I almost
did. Such paranoid thoughts helped me pass the time while I stood
manning the lines in the pit, sunup to sundown for several days. I
had put a great deal of time and energy into traveling from New York
to Oregon for that adventure, and when the first jaunt was over, I
walked woozily away without collecting my earnings.

My parents had recently bought a house on the outskirts of
Fort Bragg, just on the other side of its wilderness zone. Occasional
artillery fire in the distance rattled the windows of the new home,
and it was comforting. Fayetteville is on a broad sand hill, making it
just a few degrees hotter than the rest of the region. The yard of this
latest family home was another competition between grass and white
sand. The house was new and comfortable. It had a big backyard with
a cedar fence, and in the living room a raised fireplace with a rock
chimney.

"You should apply for one of those openings, Bobby," Lewis ordered-encouraged, after Reagan had the air-traffic controllers fired. "I'll take you downtown for the exam myself." I complied, but I didn't do well on the exam, though I tried. After a month or so, Lewis brought home some recruiting brochures for three of the armed forces and left them on the kitchen counter. It was broadminded of him to include the air force and navy as well as the army. He left the marines out of it.

By early October I was a clerk at a mall bookshop, selling romances, westerns, soldier pulp, puzzle books. The soldiers, mostly away from home for the first time, arrived in haughty, huddled, close-cropped groups, sometimes in black T-shirts espousing how much blood and gore of a generic enemy they were prepared to spill. They wore this sixties protest irony, appropriated in the eighties as a pro-war slogan, irony removed, or perhaps doubled on itself:

JOIN THE ARMY
go to distant, beautiful, exotic places,
meet interesting people,
and kill them.

You couldn't buy those shirts in the mall, though. You had to go to the military-surplus stores on Bragg Boulevard.

My middle brother, Donny, had gone off to basic training in the air force. Kevin, the youngest, was in high school, tagging along with his dad when school was out, learning to fly planes and jump out of them at a local airfield where Lewis, recently retired, flew jumpers.

Every once in a while, if Kevin spoke pertly to his mother or committed some other infraction, his father would bully him up and down the hallway, smack him enough to make him scared and humiliated. He had knocked all the boys around, but this extended bullying and taunting was peculiar to his treatment of Kevin: my brother's special warrant, I suppose, as the blood son, or at least as the youngest and most salvageable male.

In a way, it meant Lewis respected Kevin more. He believed he could take it and be tempered by the rougher treatment. But it was not a pretty sight.

By October it was clear Lewis was stalled and slowly sinking. One night, what turned out to be the Last Night, Mom and Kevin had gone to bed while Lewis and I watched a ball game on TV, mostly in silence.

After the game finished, as I rose to say goodnight, he moved to the breakfast table and waved me over. "Let's talk," he said. He had more order-suggestions for my next step in life, I thought. Maybe I needed to get moving, he was going to tell me.

The request-command surprised me. Once before, in Omaha when I was twelve, Lewis had sat me down when it was time for the obligatory birds-and-bees talk. We sat on the bed in my parents' room. The talk was awkward and mainly involved the wily ways of a wicked hypothetical girl named Suzy. I remember none of the advice. This after-the-game talk was the second time ever Lewis sat me down for a heart-to-heart.

In my mind's eye I look at his face that night and see flickers from his past. I see them as best I can, having never seen the physical realities those images, in their fragmented form, must have represented. Someone like that survived the war. Others died in it, quickly, whereas many more lived for years, decaying slowly.

His eyes were distant. I'd seen that look often since coming home a few months earlier, and in later years, I realized I'd seen it in him numerous times in his post-Vietnam career, before I went to college.

Lewis did not, as a rule, tell war stories. When he did, they were meant to be funny: the time he was leading a long-range reconnaissance patrol (LRRP) through the jungle, and each man stepped over a log on the trail, until the last man, the biggest, stepped on the log rather than over it. The log moved, because the log was an iguana, and the big man ran screaming, heedless of the enemy, through the bush.

"Let me tell you something. You know—" he trailed off. I waited. The round breakfast table was an old Formica item we'd moved around for years. The chrome edge was a little rusted in spots, and two of the seats had cigarette burns. Even though I hadn't lived with my parents for a few years, details like those were fixed in me.

Lewis lit a Salem. He was finishing his third pack. When he ran out of cigarettes, it had been my job, for years, to run for a new pack from the cartons in the bedside table in my parents' bedroom—a task that fell to Donny after I left, then Kevin.

"We were on a patrol, one time," he continued after a long pause. "Another officer was up ahead—a new guy, from a different platoon; we were on a joint operation." Then he pointed at his ashtray, and I knew to fetch it for him.

"This guy, this young officer, was about twenty steps ahead. He stopped all of a sudden, so I waved everyone behind to halt. The man turned around, looked back at me—this is about a second, maybe two—I could tell from his eyes he'd tripped a wire." I listened, looked at Lewis's eyes, but he was looking at his Salem, which he'd rested in the ashtray.

Lewis talked some more. I forgot I was his son, became a visitor in his life, and listened. "Now, we're talking about a *second*, maybe two. He just looked at me. I looked backed at him, and maybe I started to tell him something—*jump, dickhead!*—but I didn't. I could tell the kid had already made up his mind, in a second—a *second*—made up his mind to just stand there."

Lewis looked at me for a moment, as if I were the young officer. I tried to imagine what it would be like to trip a wire, to give up in a split second, on some trail.

Then Lewis picked up his Salem and dragged, exhaled. "Gave up! Anyway—it went off. The guy got torn in half."

He chewed his lip for a few seconds, picked something out of his teeth. Then he curled in his lips the way I remember when he was angry. It always gave me chills. "It PISSED me OFF" he almost shouted, pulling back as the words came out, because Mom and Kevin were asleep. "It pissed me off," he echoed, as he stabbed the air with the crimson tip of his Salem. "You know? He didn't try anything. He didn't jump off, didn't crouch down, didn't get angry, didn't even look scared. He just stood there."

Lewis stubbed out the cigarette half-smoked, as always. He thought it was healthier to smoke just half a cigarette.

I had no idea what to say. I just looked at him, as if there might be more: more cursing the dead, more to the story. But we were done. Lewis looked at the pack of Salems, slumped in his chair, then seemed to get angry at something. I hoped he wasn't angry at me and my say-nothingness. But he just grunted and stood up, pack in hand, to go to bed.

He told me he loved me and went down the hallway. After a few minutes, I felt the heaviness lift and went to my room, too.

Other than his quick goodbye the next morning, that story was the last contact I had with Lewis. For years I've wondered what made him tell it—to me, on that night, knowing whatever he knew about the actions he was about to take. Was his anger at the young officer parallel to some disappointment in me? Was it about the choice Lewis was making—opposed, in some way, to the young officer's passive acceptance? Was it so? Was it a giving up, as Lewis seemed to say? The man had turned to look back. In the second he had left, he looked back at Lewis. They locked eyes; then the man balled up and died. Did the story mean: *Never look back?* Is that one edge of Lewis's own vanishing?

Jean-Pierre Vernant[1] wrote of the beautiful death of the ancient Greek warriors, which was to die in the fullness of their masculine nature; to die at the peak of their power and virtue. From such a death, they're freed from the need to be continually measured against another warrior's virtue or excellence. Of that the poets sing, a state of glory.

But the *Iliad* shows that the beautiful death can be denied the warrior who falls in battle—his body torn by dogs, dragged by the heels behind horses. The imbalance, the monstrosity of excess, such as the poem shows in Achilles's grief and vengeance on the body of Hector, is the shocking brilliance of the poem. "In the belly of beasts that have devoured him," says Vernant of the dishonored dead, "he becomes the flesh and blood of wild animals, and there is no longer the slightest appearance or trace of humanity."

I wonder how that officer on the trail might fit some conception of the beautiful death. I believe Lewis had such a conception. He wasn't a Greek warrior, but he saw himself among their line down to this time. Among his reading material were some serial novels by Barry Sadler, of "Ballad of the Green Beret" fame, about a warrior named Casca, condemned to be reborn through the ages and fight in war after war. Light reading. Lewis ate it up. I think he believed he'd missed his own beautiful death, and he didn't want the inglorious, debilitating death that comes with getting old.

I don't know if that journey was a conscious attempt to die. I think the story he told me was his effort to pose the question—for himself, and for that man he saw curl up inside the blast—as if to accept death in the instant, with an instant's gesture. I wonder if an entire life wasn't compacted into such a gesture. It would have more grace and lightness than any other moment because you would pull the world inside you.

So, move toward strength, or strong-mindedness. Be pragmatic. Maybe it works, except when the tightrope becomes a tripwire. As allegory, it seems self-contradictory. If we're mostly in false positions, from where does "any truth" arrive? Maybe a fragment of it, which is all we have at any given time, and all we have room for, anyway. But we need that magical thinking, the skittering between the real and the virtual, just to survive the jagged, honest edges.

Since I can't ask Lewis what he meant by his story, I've let the possibilities slow-cook inside me. For years, with many years between any conscious questioning, and yet with periods in my life when I obsess over it—generally, when I go through another intense, nights-long period of dreaming about Lewis's return.

At some point over many years the story of the young officer on the trail, in the instant before the blast, became allegory to me. The officer was anyone, at any moment of a life. At any moment, a blast might occur. If we know we've tripped a wire, if we hear the click, what's contained in that instant before annihilation? Does any instant contain the whole of a person?

Near the end of *Walden*, Thoreau writes: "For the most part, we are not where we are, but in a false position. Through an infinity of our natures, we suppose a case, and put ourselves into it, and hence are in two cases at the same time, and it is doubly difficult to get out. During sane moments, we regard only the facts, the case that is. Say what you have to say, not what you ought. Any truth is better than make-believe."

Dreams, for me, are fine laboratories for exploring the messy but often-interesting clashes of make-believe with reality. In a recent dream, Lewis has returned and, as always, he's the same age as when he left on his last tour of Vietnam. Our house is a warehouse filled with boxes, random appliances, papers. A large radio, something like a 1980s boom box, sits on a shelf. It has a chassis, so that from that angle in the dream, it's a finned, two-toned 1950s automobile, dominant red. A chimerical thing: fusions of the decade of his youth with the decade of his disappearance. I reach to the shelf, trying to take the radio down. It slips and a piece of it breaks off. Lewis is behind me, and I can feel his vexation. But when I turn to look up at him (as if I, too, were returned to my age fifty years ago), I see that we both understand it's only a dream, and nothing can really be broken, because everything is already broken. That's what it is to be a thing.

John Wolfe, in his essay "A Different Species of Time,"[2] writes of his experience in Vietnam and after, recuperating from serious wounds. "It is as if, when the world was created," says Wolfe, "allowances were made for special zones, non-homogenous with the rest of the world, redolent with supernatural mystery where man could experience the full expression of his darker side." The strangeness of place infects him. After being wounded, Wolf spends months recovering, and the strangeness frames his broader sense of the world. A psychiatrist starts paying him visits. Instead of the shrink, says Wolfe, "I'd have preferred a shaman, a Dantesque chaperone to help me navigate this dimension now intruding into my consciousness, someone who could posit me, sanity intact, back in my own milieu."

Later, Wolfe finds himself in the same room as a soldier who's lost all four limbs. Without speaking, they acknowledge their shared reality: "And then we both started to laugh hysterically. Neither of us expected to meet another human in the private dream to which we had been transported." Wolfe's own perceptions become more disorienting, "Bosch-like"—he tries to let go and accept the visions—"to adopt a totally passive attitude about my surreal visions. I'd resist nothing and I'd be open to everything. I literally surrendered body and soul. But, as one horror piled upon the next, the density of despair became unbearable. Shattered, I felt beyond reintegration or reconstruction, and I prayed for a speedy doom."

That morning after breakfast Lewis kissed his wife goodbye, said goodbye to his sons, then got in his white Ford Fiesta with a briefcase full of flight maps and a kit bag. "I'll be home in two days," he said. He backed out of the driveway in that Fiesta—a ridiculous car for such a man—and was out of sight.

Pat Conroy wrote the definitive novel of the warrior dad. *The Great Santini*[3] is a mainly episodic story of an early 1960s Marine Corps family in coastal South Carolina—much of it based on Conroy's own family and childhood, and a larger-than-life, abusive, hard-drinking, tough guy at home. In the novel's closing scenes, the father, "Bull" Meacham, dies flying his military jet, delaying a bailout until he's flown far enough from a populated area—too late to escape the inevitable explosion.

We've followed the trials of Meacham's teenage son, Ben, oldest of the brood. All take their father's abuse or neglect to varying degrees, though none more than the mother. After they learn of the father's death, Ben confesses to his mother that he hated his father. She denies it in her keep-up-appearances, Southern-belle manner, but Ben insists. "I used to pray for his plane to crash," Ben confesses tearfully. "I used to pray for it all the time. I'm scared that one of those prayers was up there floating around lost and he accidentally ran into on the way back from Key West."

His mother, a Catholic, tells him, "God wanted your father with him." But why is the first sort of magical thinking better than the second? Ben goes on to confess his recurring fantasy: that he would go to college, join the marines, become a pilot, a better one than his father, then quit, and be free of the man, free of his own demon. "Now I'll never be free of him," he says. "You don't have to be," his mother answers. About that, she's right. His recurring fantasy, though no more magical than his fatal prayer, is another life: not cut off, but opening some other, still-hidden path.

When I was small, I'd hated Lewis as Conroy's Ben hates Bull. I hated through the fear and practiced magical acts of mind to save myself, including when he was wounded in that last tour, and for a brief while the day my mother got the news, when we were unsure of his status. I remember, age ten, not so much wishing he were dead as wishing that one way or another it meant he wouldn't come back. I remember it that way—avoiding the sin, the enormity of wishing him dead—sensing that wishes, like prayers, could be deadly. By itself, I don't think it meant much. One allows, sometimes, brief play to abominable thoughts.

CHINA

15 Apr 69

Dearest Patsy:

Believe it or not I'm still on Radio Watch but I should get relieved when it gets light. I wanted to write and ask what kind of china you like (design on it) flower or plain with gold or silver rim? I like plain because it is proper wherever you are (country) also it comes in settings for 12 persons. 151 pcs. or 96 pcs. Let me know which you like! OK? Type and # of pieces.

Also do you want silver or bronze ware to use with it? It comes with service for 12 or 8, that is, 118 pcs or 80 pcs for 8—what do you think & want? It would be sent to the States from Japan PX.

Also it comes with design and modern. Let me know which of it you want!

I guess you can tell that I'm looking at a PX catalogue! I want to get something for you. I don't really know which size we need 8 or 12 because it's formal type dinner ware.

There is no big hurry on it because I have plenty of time to order it.

This was just a note, but I had the chance to write, and wanted to tell you that I love you more each second.

Jim

The china: by its name, an emblem of home and of the faraway. Lewis will connect his own fate to its purchase: to talk of buying it and to use that talk as purchase on his world.

We live in a series of inflections. The base form of feeling, which might be love, converts to many alternate hues: feelings about ourselves, about the world overall, even more than they're feelings about the one who went missing. That bud of worry might flower into alarm, diffusing one's immediate space with the throb of anxiety.

Nineteen eighty-two. Days turned to weeks. The September bills: Lewis and my mother would sit down together at the dining table, the neatly opened envelopes, receipts and invoices, and the account book my mother kept all on the table before them. Now the stack of papers waited on the table for a month before my mother dealt with it.

When Lewis disappeared, we had the feeling for many years that our experience was unique: that we alone had a husband/father who had gone missing, who was neither alive nor dead. People reacted oddly, not knowing how to react, when my mother told them of her situation. They could not console and had no established language for response.

In the digital age, some cases get more attention than others. Social media make certain factors viral or feed certain shared obsessions. Instead of the embarrassed silence, something opposite seems more likely—that some cases will become cultural milestones, urban legends, virtual clubhouses for people in need of a hobby. Andrew Devendorff's brother Matt disappeared in 2017.[1] Andrew says the help or consolation offered by friends has seemed like obligation; few follow up with serious assistance. Other people, acquaintances and outright strangers, just want to get close to a dramatic situation.

The perverse, intense influence of social media has created new dimensions to missingness. The lore of the missing forms a peculiar data set as well as another deconstruction of the self—the self at either end, both the missing and the searching. Through streaming-video programming—the proliferation of subgenres in series and miniseries; through Facebook and other social-media platforms; documentaries, Reddit, Websleuths, blogs, podcasts, hybrid literary forms—missing people and those who want to find them, or cosplay at finding them, create a hall of mirrors.

Freud,[2] in "Mourning and Melancholia," notes the near-identical relationship between grief and melancholy. We don't see grief as pathological but rather as a natural course. A key difference, he says, is that the melancholic experiences a blow to self-regard not evident in the one who grieves. But one who grieves for a missing person frequently experiences diminished self-regard. The loss is like the unconsciousness of the melancholic because it's not situated in a real place. "In mourning it is the world which has become poor and empty; in melancholia it is the ego itself."

Grief for the missing stays heavy for years. If it fades, there was perhaps a moment when one chose to let go—to abandon the missing person to an imagined death that can't ever be an event but becomes a state of being. "Ambiguous loss makes us feel incompetent," says Pauline Boss.[3] "It erodes our sense of mastery and destroys our belief in the world as a fair, orderly and manageable place." The ambiguity might be a disbelief that something happened or the difficulty of putting a name on the nonevent. Coping is forgetting: letting days go back to being days.

"For some people," Boss says later, "mastery means controlling what is internal—perceptions, feelings, emotions or memories— while for others it means controlling what is external—other people, a situation, or the environment." When I think of my mother's long journey to acceptance, to wholeness, it seems to me she had realized— at least by the time she sought help on the death declaration—that it was only the internal matters she could control.

In missingness, one's pose becomes exhausting. "Ambiguity destroys the customary markers of life or death," according to Boss, "so a person's distress is never validated. The community loses patience with the lack of closure, and families become isolated." In such a condition, the world's no longer a place where security or understanding seem possible.

In the April 29 letter, Lewis elaborates on the china:

> Should I go ahead and order the china & silver or wait until after R&R? I think that we should wait, and then I would still have (6) months to order & make sure it's delivered OK! It will cost about $160 for both and when it's delivered you will have to pay duty on it, about $15.00! That's not a bad deal, because it will be worth about $700.00 in U.S.

Then, in his May 1 letter, Lewis passes on some tragic news:

> Honey, do you remember CPT Bob Young (Bde)? Well, he was killed last month, and I just found out; I really hate that. He was an outstanding person.

A few lines down he returns to the china:

> If I can get to rear, I'm going to order the china & silverware ASAP so that it will get there NO SWEAT. Total for the (2) checks will be $186.00.
> I feel that I should go ahead and order it.

The other man's death, a weapon, aims at Lewis. His own continuance is in preserving what's homelike in his life. The talk about bills, paychecks, loans, expenses, getting things fixed around the house, corralling the kids—tactical and strategic choices, as much as combat.

And one of those must be to order the china.

THE SWERVE

"WHAT VANISHED ONCE keeps vanishing," says Maria Flook,[1] who lost and found a sister. There's a beauty to it, the way one imagines the precise moment of leaving: a recursive blossoming, kaleidoscopic reproductions of the same last wave goodbye.

The narrator in Derek Marlowe's novel *Echoes of Celandine*,[2] whose wife vanishes from their apartment, observes: "Within a single hour her absence was opaque." As time passes through the first several days, remaining possessions become relics, talismans: "Her comb, I notice, still lies on the carpet by the door. I step over it as if it were the width of the Nile, then leave." The time, the new story that has yet to find a theme, that has an un-character as its star, plays through moments brainlessly: "And so I daydream and invent a story, play patience, close the shutters and cease to be."

Seneca[3] advises against both hope and fear because they're not of the present. But for Christians, hope signifies the eternal present. Hope is faith's continuum not backward but forward: of shining sides, mirroring our wide eyes. The loved one who hopes for a return of a missing one aims at a reunion in this world, but not confined to the calendar, which shreds and flies away page by page.

Hope is attenuated, barely pronounced in its thin line, like the horizon. It's irrational. But this is how it breathes within the waiting ones: there might be a rational explanation, but it's equally weighted in the indeterminate future between good and evil. We dread-hope that a body will be found, or that a living loved one will walk through the door. That irrationality is wiggle room. It's space enough for logic to be a cohort of superstition, and so psychics sometimes join forces with forensic specialists. Magical thinking runs parallel to detection.

"Life," says Simone de Beauvoir in *The Ethics of Ambiguity*,[4] "is occupied in both perpetuating and in surpassing itself; if all it does is maintain itself, then living is only not dying." I assume "perpetuating" involves more will, more energy, than maintaining; that the continuum between it and "surpassing" is a crucial space in which the true individual defines herself.

But the literal warrior, and various others who have suffered in surpassing themselves, become broken. Survival past the wars becomes a lifetime of not-dying.

Edward T. Hall wrote in *Beyond Culture*[5]: "I believe that man in the aggregate resists separations, that he has more things in his life to be separated from than he can ever achieve and that one of life's important strategies . . . has to do with what one is going to give up." Do we exist in our refinements, more in the outtakes than the remains?

"Everyone has an original right to everything," says Schopenhauer,[6] "but an exclusive right to nothing, yet can obtain an exclusive right to particular things by renouncing his right to all the rest." It's a fairy tale, but fairy tales are adult, sordid, bloody traces. Nothing's more real than that path through the dark woods. Some trace might have remained in the young officer on the trail—the man who tripped the wire and balled up inside himself instead of leaping.

The swerve, a sudden shift, a beam falling, a tire blowing. It occurs all the time, lacking grand consequence, at least as one's consciousness responds to the accident, the intrusion of some fragment of reality. The role of life, Henri Bergson,[7] wrote, is to insert indetermination into matter. Each is the vanishing point of the other.

A FERAL PRESENCE

THE ARTIST, JOHAN, in Ingmar Bergman's *Hour of the Wolf* suffers illusions so powerful they project outward, afflicting his wife, Alma, as well. The artist's disappearance at the end of the film is an expulsion from his own illusions. The wife muses to herself at the end, "If I'd loved him less, could I have protected him more. Or if I'd loved him more . . ."—adjustment, calibration: there must always be a gap, some room between two people, no matter how close they are. Her frame tale, thus the whole film, is a look over her shoulder at what's just passed before our eyes. His disappearance is the turning, the recursion at its smallest visible curve, where he tried one last time to look into himself. Loving is finding the precise distance along a moving timeline. Annihilation is possible at any random point. Disappearance is the point past which we don't know another person, sane or mad. Alma is where she is, but most of us are to ourselves at short distances, catching up.

Luigi Pirandello's novel *The Late Mattia Pascal*[1] follows a harried husband and father into his disappearance. Mattia Pascal absconds to Monte Carlo, winning big. Back home, an anonymous corpse is assumed to be his. He takes the mistake as a further opportunity to make permanent his escape. Pascal starts a new life not so much different from the first, loses most of his winnings, encounters new troubles much like the ones he'd escaped—and ends up trying to re-enter the first life, which he can do only as officially dead. He's left with the volatile matter of raw life.

Within the moment of his escape, triggered, it seems, by those outward events, those felicitous or fateful occurrences, Mattia Pascal thinks: "The immobility of my existence inspired me with sudden, strange thoughts, like flashes of madness. I sprang to my feet, as if to shake them off, and started walking along the shore; but then I had to look, there at the sand's edge, at the sea endlessly bringing its somnolent flaccid waves." Those waves, those seeming choices: If he'd taken a deep breath right inside that moment at the sand's edge, might a different choice have formed?

When he located the lost child Kevin Dye in 1971, searcher Michael Murphy said: "There is a mystical moment when you rescue someone whom you've been seeking for a long time. It's reverence. You don't want to approach him—for suddenly you have discovered how wonderful human life is."[2]

In *Missing: A Memoir*, Lindsay Harrison[3] describes the frenetic search for her mother, and after her mother's car is found in the Atlantic, the aftereffects of disappearance and death. Harrison writes of the worried conversations, the searching, gathering of evidence, shifting of emotions, transformation of normality; the succession of days and weeks, life going on in fits and starts; the occasional comparison of the uncanny moments with other forms of the uncanny, or with the so-called ordinary states of existence.

Harrison's mother had suffered mental illness in her life, but her end was not from chaos or a death wish. The death, when it coalesces, settles in as Harrison presents it with the same hard reality, the same fixedness, of all deaths. The missingness, in this case, is misplacedness. A person can veer into an alley, a wall, a pasture, or the ocean in the same measure of distance.

Harrison, while sorting out her mother's affairs, protests: "That grieving required *feeling* so much seemed burden enough—that it demanded so much *doing* seemed wholly unfair." But the feeling and the doing intertwine, like the real and the virtual.

I imagine some experiences, such as combat, are so traumatizing because the already-unstable balance between outside and inside, doing and feeling, is jolted so forcefully. Veterans of war frequently compose it through such terms. Here's a passage from Stephen Wright's *Going Native*,[4] in which the experience of war dislodges past and present: "And each time he witnessed another raw incident like tonight's (the bodies by the road, the ragged line of blindfolded wounded prisoners shuffling from truck to cell) his past took on more and more of the insubstantial characteristics of fantasy. The war was real; he was not." Moments of intensity sometimes steal the self from the self. Our singular perspectives transplant one another, accumulate in memory, are plural, layered, non-Euclidean. The magical thinking sometimes helps, sometimes leads us deeper into loss. In Beth Gutcheon's *Still Missing*,[5] a novel about a child gone missing, the mother thinks to herself: "To have faith that Alex is alive—it has nothing to do with belief or thought. Do I *think* so? Do I think he's alive? To *think* or to *know* has nothing to do with it. I commit myself to his being alive, as an act of will." The facts themselves are like weeds in a field. Any might be significant, or none of them, but we pluck them, they are mostly anonymous, and they're endless once you look. We turn to belief because facts are dumb without some framework of belief. To believe is not counter to reasoning, but the mind looking for itself among facts.

Ambiorix, a Gallic chieftain in the first century, rebelled against Caesar. After a truce with the Romans, Ambiorix deceived them, hoping to remove the Roman legions from his part of northeastern Gaul, where we now find Belgium, who made Ambiorix a national hero. We have mainly the chronicles of Florus's and Caesar's own writings to tell of him: that he and his kinsmen were very brave; that it was the Romans' oath to destroy the Eburones, of whom he was a prince; and that, in a few years' time, after the Roman legions had succeeded in eradicating the Belgae, Ambiorix, accompanied by a few companions, fled across the Rhine never to be seen again.[6]

It's not so much that they were sought by their nemeses, or by survivors among their tribe; nor that the record has them vanishing mysteriously. The account in Florus, their "perpetual flight across the Rhine," renders the borders of the Gallic homeland something permeable and breathing. It's elegiac, a fold at the story's end to keep it from fraying. The vanishing is their legend.

Sometimes, a disappearance seems atavistic: something ancient but inside us, capable of pulling us back through time. Someone turns to a different but never-seen angle, steps around a tesseractic corner, moves offstage or offscreen, and we see it as a disappearance from the Earth.

After Gregor Samsa dies, in Kafka's[7] "The Metamorphosis," his father, mother, and sister go on a trip, abandoning their apartment (which Gregor had paid for), taking the tram, then walking freely in the countryside beyond the city. The sister, Grete, in her parents' eyes, seems to blossom, become lively, more womanly, full of color and beauty. She has the aura of fertility about her, as if drawing in the nature they've escaped to. Grete is the opposite of missing: growing into presence, goddess of her moment.

But this outside has been peeking into the story all along. "Window" occurs nearly two dozen times in "The Metamorphosis": they're closed, opened, worried about, but one of the last occurrences is at the most poignant moment of Gregor's tale—so long as we accept that we're inside *his* story. Gregor is dying, and his death is gradual, slow, graceful, even balletic, quiet, and calm: "In this state of vacant and peaceful meditation he remained until the tower clock struck three in the morning. The first broadening of light in the world outside the window entered his consciousness once more. Then his head sank to the floor of its own accord and from his nostrils came the last faint flicker of his breath." See the sacrifice: a gentle but powerful act of love for his family and for life itself. Sometimes I cry when I read it. Then I continue, following the three survivors as they reorder their lives and conclude the seeming-nightmare. They clean the house and take their little vacation. We who have been locked into Gregor's consciousness feel horror, dread, and pity when we pull our eyes away for a moment. We feel a new horror in the world carrying on so easily in his absence.

We wonder how far or near the missing might be, alive or dead: clear around the world, another state, another town, mere feet below the ground, somewhere walking-distance from home. By now, my stepfather's absence has been his most-stable quality. Maybe that's to forget, to drown in forgetfulness, to lose faith not in him but in ourselves. Antonio Porchia[8] says in one of his aphorisms: "I would rather grieve over your absence than over you." This might be how disappearance becomes many layers, many screens, of presence.

At some point for searchers, absence becomes a fetish. If the Missing One returns, the circumstances of missingness collapse from wave to particle—the particulars, that is, of *why*: what fate, what choices, in all its ugliness.

Think of Freud's idea of the screen memory: that each performance of a memory replaces the previous memory of an event, cloaked itself after the first act of memory. The missing person, too, becomes cloaked in all the ways we search for them, miss them, grieve ambiguously for them. Our effort to hold on to a personhood creates strata of absence. That absence, that missingness, forms a spirit in its own right.

When we seek the missing, we seek a return to what we remember as orderly or normal. Within the months and years of waiting, a feral presence forms. Missingness is becoming gone wrong, being thrown back on its prior states. That feral presence is neither the person waiting nor the one missing. It might be the malevolent force or figure behind the disappearance, but I think it's more—a deep, primal pull, a centrifugal reality that's always there, tugging bits of us away.

We play hide-and-seek all our lives, with more sophistication as we age. Peekaboo suffices for toddlers, and the awe of disappearance draws from its primal magic. In Margaret Atwood's *Surfacing*,[9] we find a haunting description of absence in a woman's memory from childhood of the one-armed woman in a country store: "Madame sold khaki-colored penny candies which we were forbidden to eat, but her main source of power was that she had only one hand. Her other arm ended in a soft pink snout like an elephant's trunk and she broke the parcel string by wrapping it around her stump and pulling. This arm devoid of a hand was for me a great mystery, almost as puzzling as Jesus." The impression is like Gregor's in *The Metamorphosis* when the old maid is instructed to clear out Gregor's room: "Above the table on which a collection of cloth samples was unpacked and spread out—Samsa was a commercial traveler—hung the picture which he had recently cut out of an illustrated magazine and put into a pretty gilt frame. It showed a lady, with a fur cap on and a fur stole, sitting upright and holding out to the spectator a huge fur muff into which the whole of her forearm had vanished!" That exclamation point belongs to the child, awed by reality—its beauty, its directness, its near-violence.

In a tribute to Antonio Machado, Rubén Darío[10] says:

> His gaze had such profundity
> That he himself went unseen

This is reminiscent of a moment in Paul Auster's *Oracle Night*,[11] when the writer Sidney Orr, working in his notebook, seems to his wife, when she peeks through the door of his room, to vanish. Coming back into the room later, she says:

> "When you didn't answer, I opened the door and peeked inside. But you weren't there."
> "Of course I was. I was sitting at my desk."
> "Well, I didn't see you. Maybe you were somewhere else. In the bathroom maybe."
> "I don't remember going to the bathroom. As far as I know, I was sitting at my desk the whole time."

Creative focus as an invisibility cloak: It's very low-key supernatural—Austerian, we might call it. Invisibility's a layer of thingness in itself—essential, I think, as part of what permits things to be here for us. In its general latency it has the quality of self-creation masking self-destruction.

The rawness manifests itself in strange loops of thought and action. Harrison in *Missing* describes her Uncle George, after her mother has disappeared, "saying the same things over and over to make it sound like there was more information than there really was." In Belinda Bauer's novel *Snap*[12], the daughter of a missing woman observes as the father sits in the kitchen, "obsessively reading and re-reading every word anyone knew or had guessed about his wife's disappearance"—eyes up close to the page "to glean more meaning, his lips moving and his fingers darkening with newsprint."

Canadian author Sheena Kamal's *The Lost Ones*[13] is deeply woven into the same energies and themes one finds in Stieg Larsson's Lisbeth Salander novels: a feral young woman skirting past the horrors, largely sexual and corporate, that have shaped her existence—against which she fights. In that struggle, the chief victory is the poetry of her own survival, for the evil she confronts goes on, remorseless and unconquerable.

Detective work in a novel like Kamal's, or Steig Larsson's series, is the singular power of the individual, deracinated, delegitimized in a corporate-controlled society, to redefine her individuality—to be free. In this story, the feral detective-girl Nora is hired by the victim's adoptive parents to search for Nora's own daughter, given up at birth after a pregnancy from rape. Mother and daughter, mother searching for the daughter, unraveling layers of mystery along the way that extend concentrically from the personal to the political, and ultimately to the environmental, defines the space beyond which missingness is our last magic: the way we lose power, the way we regain it. This passage seems to me to encode and encapsulate that range and its limits: "Nothing could be more indifferent to the caprices of human endeavor than the tides. Don't get me wrong—we can do a lot. We can move mountains if we really want to, or just blow them up, frack them, dislodge their innards, and ship their lifeblood down to the coast to open up new markets like the foolish little capitalists we have become, but no matter what we do, we don't have anything on the moon."

We have to live in the mystery itself and at the same time within the mundane order of our lives: finding a missing person, escaping violence, severing the many tentacles of a malevolent corporation—

and doing laundry (or not), eating, checking off the items on our to-do list for the day. Within the hour they weigh about the same. We're trying to reduce the metaphysics of our errands in life down to a practical checklist—one that involves moving our limbs in various ways, as we are meant to do.

Kate Crane's[14] father disappeared from his Baltimore truck-salvage lot in 1987. Police suspected his business partner but never proved anything. Eddy Crane became a bit of lore: allusions in crime dramas like *The Wire* and an occasional specter at the police department. Crane started digging in July 2007, when, she says, "an alarm clock went off in my gut." The waiting, she says, "instills a feral kind of patience." That summer she decided to act, though: "the patience evaporated, leaving only the feral."

I think of "feral" as the essential of *now*—survival, eat or be eaten, touching the immediate—a minimal contact with the virtual, the mythic, the symbolic. In Kate Crane's framing of information, we see the mind's tentative effort to be *more* than feral, even if it felt like a paring-down. We feel something more than a reaction to *now*—"piecing together," in its mixed metaphor with "murky vision"—and the recursions implied by "not only the crime but also of my dad himself"—from self-love and love of the memory of the parent, a sense through the connection of "crime" and "man" that the opposite is also true: that there was a man there, face-to-face with circumstance, alive in his postures.

Joan Didion's[15] experience of magical thinking is so strong that her husband, just deceased from a heart attack while their daughter lies comatose in the hospital, will return: even weeks after, having been gently advised to remove his clothing from the house, she stops short of discarding all his shoes, for the feeling that he will need them again is too strong. Confessions of such thoughts recur and are as emotionally real as they are absurd.

In a poem by Faith Shearin, "Disappearing Fathers,"[16] the lightness of the missing is given in terms perfectly balanced between allegorical and real. Shearin's survey of male morbidity makes lyric from a similar magical thinking. Statistical fact slides closely, poignantly through the surreal reductions. Some fathers "had heart attacks / during business dinners or while digging their shovels / into a late April snow" while others began forgetting things:

> their phone numbers, which neighborhoods belonged
> to them, which houses. They had a shortness of breath,
> the world's air suddenly too thin—

The fathers die as if from a plague of traditional manhood, "with suits / and briefcases," or fathers "who slipped down / rivers on fishing boats and the ones / who drank television and beer"—the poem lightens its passages with clichés almost cartoonlike in their portrayal of suburban masculinity. The lightness fine-tunes the adjustment of death with disappearance, conveying the way death can feel as unreal as vanishing:

> I kept imagining
> I would see them again: out walking their dogs
> on the roads near my childhood house,
> lighting cigars on their porches, waving to me
> from their canoes while I waited on shore.

This captures, particularly by its ending, how the vanishing has already been there. It's an atmosphere, a locus of indeterminate coordinates. If we think the missing walked or were taken away, we might wonder if the answer is more radical. They *vanished*—down to a point past which we simply could not see them.

Lyrical thinking, I should call it: not the mistakes of a grieving consciousness, but the mind's effort to see where the literal and the symbolic are inseparable. In that "waving to me" from across the water, I see the Pearl Poet's grieving father communicating with his dead daughter across the stream between life and death. I see so clearly the gesture and continuum of the missing as we contain them in ourselves—as we've lost them, though in a reverse motion, played out in dream or in lyric, how we find them again, how the losing and finding is exhalation, inhalation.

Time doesn't exist. The family resemblance to weather, "le temps," suggests lives proceed by storm, by drought, by shock of blue sky, by backward-falling snow—not by the ticking of clocks. Missingness is an alternative sense of time. A British soldier-scientist-philosopher named J. W. Dunne[17] believed that the human sense of linear time is an illusion caused by the limits of perception. Past, present, and future converged, Dunne thought, somewhere higher than this earthly plane. He believed one could explore those higher levels, living within the infinite regress of near-eternities: notice, again, the gentle contour of the asymptote.

Waiting or searching for a missing person, in Mona Simpson's novel *The Lost Father*,[18] is like "holding an empty glass jar waiting for the sky to fill it." So completely outside seems the sky, never coming down, though we enter it.

"The space they occupy," says Andrew O'Hagan,[19] "lies somewhere between what we know about the ways of being alive and what we hear about the ways of being dead." We're there in our deaths, in the cadavers themselves, in our gravestones, in the documents, bones and teeth, in the hat or coat we wore. When the poet Edwin Gallagher died, his friends hung his favorite vest and tweed jacket next to the podium at the memorial service. He'd worn those clothes, or versions of them, for many years. Headless, not-quite-motionless as the costume was, our friend was so nearly there, he was more than there. The gap, the subtle wind of him, magnified our memories.

DARK HEART

SOME YEARS AGO, a billboard down the rural road where I lived was plastered with the face of a missing young man named Johnathan Lee Hamilton. Hamilton was thirty years old, height 6'2", hair brown, last seen in Bastrop, TX, on 4/12/15. It was likely a driver's-license photo: neutral expression, slight beard, ruffled dark hair, and a glimpse of his off-centered shirt collar.

The background was blue—just a bit darker and more vivid than the sky behind it. A Gmail address was given in a bright-yellow stripe at the bottom, as if a giant hand could click to send. Johnathan's head, his dull eyes not quite making contact, didn't hover so much as lean against the sky.

Several months after the billboard came down, a human jawbone was found a few miles away at the Texas Colorado River.[1] Weeks later, DNA testing proved it to be the missing man's. The rest of him hasn't turned up yet. The river isn't deep, but it flows a long way to Matagorda Bay and the Gulf of Mexico. Between where he was last seen, some miles up the river toward town, and where the jawbone was found—near a popular swimming hole I've been to a few times—the matrix of the river might define what happened if one could find the other pieces of the man besides his jawbone.

On the Facebook page she created to help find her son, Hamilton's mother lashes out in broken sentences and paragraphs too filled with details that lack context. Her grief-driven anger is mainly at law enforcement, sometimes at a handful of possible suspects or reluctant witnesses the mother has painstakingly identified. Johnathan has gone from billboard to river to the long, underground stream of his mother's emotionally charged, stream-of-consciousness social-media feed. Though the jawbone might prove a death, a murder, can we say the young man was found?

Terkessa Wallace disappeared with her friend Shequenia Burnett in 2014, in Little Rock. A year or so later, Shequenia's leg was found floating in a river. More than a jawbone, as with Johnathan Hamilton, but is it any more indicative of death? I might say yes, but anything less than 100%, anything less than the whole woman might make for lingering, corrosive doubts for the rest of one's life.

As for Terkessa Wallace, she and her white Toyota Corolla are still missing. Finding the missing person's car is common and is usually considered a sign of foul play. Who but a kidnap victim abandons her car? For years, Wallace's cousin Tracey Holmes chased every white Corolla that went by. Holmes describes the feeling as being cemented to the ground—stuck in that particular day, holding her breath. It's a vortex: a perforation in reality that appears to violate fundamental law.

The missing become their posters, fliers, billboards, milk cartons, Facebook pages, websites, YouTube videos. Details of their disappearance become the corona of their existence.

In her sociopolitical study *Missing: Persons and Politics* Jenny Edkins[2] describes the long-lived posters of the missing of 9/11, worn and faded over many months. Leaving them up, ragged as they became, was stubborn hope, defiance. "Perhaps," supposes Edkins, "the persistence of the posters was like a collective scream, an open wound, a refusal to close over the trauma of loss, a refusal of the incorporation of the bodies of the missing as heroes of the state."

In the late seventies, when mothers organized in opposition to the forced disappearances of more than 30,000 Argentines, most of them young, they made large reproductions of the faces of the disappeared. In one event the faces filled the trees. When the mothers marched with large placards stamped with faces, with the names, ages, and dates when each son and daughter was taken, it was, Edkins says, as if the disappeared themselves had joined the march. During the court trials, years after, the mothers placed the posters in the courtroom, in the gallery chairs, mute witnesses.

Eric Carlson's *I Remember Julia*[3] collects details of the disappeared in the years of the Argentine junta, with the life and supposed afterlife of one woman, given the name "Julia," as its unifying spirit. Carlson, through the voices of Julia's family and friends, offers myriad fragments in a collage of missingness. An orthodontist tells Carlson he keeps three sets of records: one set for current patients, another for patients who have died or moved away, and a third for the patients who have been disappeared.

In Nathan Englander's novel *The Ministry of Special Cases*,[4] about the Argentine disappeared, Lillian, mother of a missing son, obsesses about time itself. The hours stack up since her son, Pato, went missing. "Every instant, she knew, could move him farther, bury him deeper, place Pato in endless ways more distant from home." More disastrously, missingness is a new kind of time—measured by "a clock that ticked both forward and back." It makes her world deeper, heavier: "From then on, Lillian breathed twice as heavy, felt twice as hungry, and swore to fight twice as hard."

In Jodi Picoult's novel *Leaving Time*,[5] a girl named Jenna devotes her days to searching for her missing mother, gone ten years. Triangulating the real and the virtual, she seeks help, eventually, from a retired detective and a psychic. The most insightful image about missingness has to do with its effects on the sense of time. "Sometimes," Jenna muses, "I think of my life as two train cars hitched together at the moment of my mom's disappearance—but when I try to see how they connect there's a jarring on the tracks that jerks my head back around."

Fin Kennedy,[6] inspired by a 1980s nuts-and-bolts guide to disappearing by Doug Richmond, wrote a play with the same title: *How to Disappear Completely and Never Be Found*. The guidebook promises method, but Kennedy's play explodes method. Disappearance becomes a form of live burial. Charlie, a businessman, exits his life, entering a metaphysical space where his name is Adam. Adam/Charlie winds up in conversation with the pathologist, Sophie (perhaps for her wisdom, for her lower-angelic presence), at work on his cadaver. Through her work, Sophie searches for her missing dad, whose disappearance might be why she's a pathologist. She tells Charlie/ Adam about her work, about the states of flesh, the gruesome circumstances of dying and being dead. "I think your job might be getting to you," he tells her. "It's the endless possibilities that kill you," she replies. "It's the endless possibilities that keep me alive," says he.

It's a gruesome fantasia Kennedy constructs of Sophie juggling Charlie/Adam's innards. The difference between the two characters marks the boundary between the virtual and the real. Charlie/Adam is a corpse because we're all corpses. That's the starting point of a life, as well as its end. It's the lies we tell with every breath—to ourselves, to others—that break the way between.

In Aimee Liu's *Flash House*,[7] a wife travels hundreds of miles across West Asia in search of her husband, a journalist and spy in the early days of the Cold War. At one point she's given a letter from the husband. In her hands the envelope is a living thing. Later, she asks a courier returning West if he's seen the husband. Looking at the photo she has given him, he answers affirmatively. "*Yes*," she repeats to herself; "the single syllable shimmered, elastic and dubious as a soap bubble."

Didion writes of the "vortex effect"—emotions coming on so suddenly, so strongly, from any sort of trigger, that we're pulled into a storm. Such is the gravity of someone's presence or absence. The vortex, too, is a reliquary, a charmed space. Absence and presence are always in a dance of actual/potential. We go away, and faith sustains us between appearances.

In Chang-Rae Lee's novel *Aloft*,[8] the mother of a soldier lost in Vietnam keeps the bedroom fixed in time. She won't even allow renovations, so the rain ruins everything. The bedroom is "a lab lesson in the varieties of fungi and molds, green-gray splotches on the walls, grayish shadings on the windowpanes, and then a cottony white fur growing in and out of his old sneakers and shoes."

Bedrooms freeze in time: mummification, some psychologists call it. Andrew O'Hagan, in his memoir/meditation *The Missing*, looks at the case of fifteen-year-old Lee Boxell, a South London lad who disappeared in 1988. His parents kept the room preserved. His homework was on his desk and the school uniform hung ready. The sex-symbol posters were faded after several years, and the sports figures alongside them were mostly retired. The CDs had become oldies.

The father, Peter Boxell, wrote a song about his son. Then he learned to sing so he could perform the song, which had come to him in a dream. In Britain, missingness has become a more layered cultural experience than in the States. There's more involvement of government beyond the law-enforcement paradigm, more coloring of and by culture—a Missing People Choir, for example, with whom Mr. Boxell performed his dream-song in concert several years ago, decades after his son's disappearance.

Anna, the disappearing lady in Michelangelo Antonioni's *L'Avventura*, returns from an impetuous leap off the side of a yacht into the Tyrrhenian Sea, crying "shark!" then laughing because it's a lie. Later she disappears when the party explores one of the many rocky islands.

Anna's friend, Claudia, wears Anna's blouses, drawing the notice of Anna's father, a distracted diplomat, when he helicopters in to search for his daughter. Claudia wears a dark wig and someone remarks, "you look like someone else"—not "you look like Anna," though the wig is dark like Anna's hair.

The movie is more about Anna when Anna's gone. Early in the film she rushes off in a fast car to join her lover on the yacht; then their departure from the busy world, from land, then Anna's impetuous swim, the escape from the nonexistent shark; then the vanishing itself, then the long fade from the plot, from the concern of the yacht party, even from the minds of her lover, Sandro, and her friend, Claudia, who begin an affair as they search for her. Then they aren't searching for her.

In a 1933 movie called *Bureau of Missing Persons*, vanishing is a phenomenon of daily urban life. In the opening shot, crowds of seekers push against the receptionist's desk, clamoring for an audience.

(Such scenes have the verve and urban quickness one finds in *The Front Page*, also starring Pat O'Brien.) The captain of the bureau is a kindly old gray-hair in a dapper suit who makes firm but sensitive judgments. There's something *moral* about every disappearance, yet it's pragmatic *common sense* that always solves the problem. The seeker must somewhat adjust their sight. The missing, once found, must both accept their lot and celebrate it.

The film is based on a nonfiction book of the previous year by Captain John H. Ayers[9] of the true-life New York City Police Department, Bureau of Missing Persons. In his cowritten work, Ayers comes out very much like the avuncular gentleman of the film, describing himself as "psychologist, analyst, humanitarian and policeman." The center of his humane craft is the "diagnosis"—a reading of what ails the missing person, and the couple or family involved. "There is no deeper satisfaction I know of," says Captain Ayers, "than to bring a person who has lost his moorings back to his proper place in society." That blending of the moral and the rational—"proper place"—is a particularly American form of bait and switch. It's the way, for a time, we danced between old-world religion and new-world commerce, technology, systems, organized violence, smash-bang, fisticuffs, face slaps, forced smooches, hair-mussing, the show must go on; then into bed, wake up, repeat. That's our reality, our pursuit of happiness. Some of us trying sometimes to abscond from that is part of the game; being disappeared from it, though—some invisible hand forcibly removing you from the game, robbing you of the pursuit itself—those are the real crimes. That is the true darkness of missing persons.

Weldon Kees parked his Plymouth on the Golden Gate Bridge and jumped. Or Kees went to Mexico or somewhere else. The three possibilities triangulate the whole life if you're willing to enter the territory yourself. You could continue crossing the bridge, fly or drive to Tijuana, but could you drop from the bridge in pursuit? It's not a path but an act. Sit behind the wheel of that Plymouth, adjust the rearview mirror: you might see the long chain of missing persons winding its purgatorial path through the mists.

James Reidel[10] argues that Kees "did not have the patience such an afterlife required." A missing man, particularly where a choice has been made, is emblematic of the Third Man, the conjured presence that haunts some people in extreme circumstances. The Third One might always be near: your sense of you, then one other (Doppelgänger, guardian angel, *daimon*), then the one outside that circle of two, observing the arc as it closes. That Third One pairs with the other two, and over its shoulder another, always some watcher, receding from where you are toward infinity.

Sightings are the comet's tail of a disappearance. They're spread far and wide and seem random, though patterns occur to the discerning eye: the long-distance of news and, over time, the depth and reach of a single mythic figure. Pete Hamill reported sitting down with Kees in Mexico. Kee's parents, sailing into the harbor at Sydney, Australia, spotted a man much like their son standing on the deck of a passing ship. The mother waved and called to him, but the wind sheared her voice away.

In 1969 Donald Crowhurst,[11] yachtsman and entrepreneur, got in over his head in a race to sail the world. He faked his position for months, hiding out near Brazil while he radioed positions toward Cape Hope and beyond. His trimaran in the Atlantic was found with two sets of logs: a fake document and the true, too-true, and strangely poetic version. He also left film and audiotape documenting his madness. The sea was sleep, and forgetfulness, and maybe forgiveness. He'd lived eight months alone, then stepped ashore five hundred miles out.

A man named Dick Conant, as Ben McGrath[12] describes him, was one who felt beholden to no one, living well enough on the edge where his paranoia had lodged him, making it the river of rivers, paddling its length as far as it would take him. Conant, steering waterways from Canada to Georgia, disappeared en route. Only an upturned canoe marks where he last touched Earth. Earlier, Conant had said to McGrath: "I have been denied what our men are supposed to do. So I do what I want, which is to navigate."

In Paul Muldoon's "Why Brownlee Left,"[13] a farmer vanishes from his land and from the community. The poem's speaker, chorus-like, a representative of the community, comments on the causal confusion of the status quo:

> Why Brownlee left, and where he went,
> Is a mystery even now.
> For if a man should have been content
> It was him . . .

This is followed by an inventory of rural wealth no sane man would have left behind. The first of two stanzas concludes with the passive voice, the blankness and distance of evidentiary reality: "He was last seen going out to plough / On a March morning, bright and early." And why should an ordinary day stop being so, simply because some dark miracle has occurred? Auden's take on the Icarus myth, or rather his take on Breughel's take on it, frames a similar layering of realities: how neatly, like a simple pearl, a blank eye, a dumb beauty!—how neatly and quietly the miracle fits inside the folds of the plodding world, with each moment swallowing those that came before.

The man, Brownlee, becomes famous by noon, we're told: talked about—though for how long?—for that famous moment itself, the membrane of meaning (or aporia, the quiet pearl), disappears with the turning of the page. Oh, but it hovers, that moment: a good poem's a hall of mirrors with no entrance or exit:

> They had found all abandoned, with
> The last rig unbroken, his pair of black
> Horses, like man and wife,
> Shifting their weight from foot to
> Foot, and gazing into the future.

The membrane of rumor, the leaky sort of truth that always stars a cast of "they," can't change the bare truth of what survives the passage of moments. Here it's realized by the beautiful movie, a loop of two simple frames, in which the horses (two horses is a universe away from the apocalyptic four) move so slightly in place, and vector for us the knowledge, the image, let's say, of Brownlee stepping away into his fate. What direction, what apotheosis or abduction, with what gait he moved out of their sight: the pearl of it, the infinite muteness of it.

In the eighties movie *Eddie and the Cruisers*, the singer leads an orbital existence outside his own mystery—a mystery he seems to have constructed out of failure. The failure is a matter of timing: transcending rock 'n' roll to make something more progressive. In his fiery youth, the rock hero carries Rimbaud's *Illuminations*, proleptic of his own ascension. After the long-suppressed experimental recordings are released years later, a reporter tries to track the artist. She ultimately fails, but still we're given sight of him ourselves: he stands outside a shop window, bearded, smiling gnomically at the TV episode about his life and mystery. It's a trope of exile's permeability, as if the meaning of his life, its vindication, were in never stepping back inside our world, but pausing just outside before carrying on. But it's a movie: his outside is our inside.

In 1916, Arthur Cravan got himself knocked out by Jack Johnson in six rounds, earning enough to go Stateside. There he met Mina Loy and they married. Official papers were always a bother to Cravan. He preferred to keep moving and above all to stay out of uniform. Cravan and Loy left New York, heading south for Mexico City. From there, they moved to the coast: Veracruz, then the smaller Salina Cruz. Cravan set sail with other unpapered bohemians on a trial run for an escape to Chile. Loy waited on the beach, wrapped in his huge fur coat, but Cravan and the others didn't return.

"I am at my best when traveling," Cravan said. To disappear is the vanishing point of bests. He was an assemblage: of English parentage, French-speaking, Swiss-born, picking up what few documents he possessed from other nations along the way. Vanishing, which he did more than once, was expansion of this hybridity. Cravan was believed by some to have gone back to Paris, making forgeries of works by his uncle, Oscar Wilde. "Wherever one went with him one was sure to arrive sooner or later in some forbidden spot," Loy said of her husband. "So intuitively did he separate himself from the accepted places."[14]

In 1938, nuclear physicist Ettore Majorana took a ferry out of Palermo and disappeared. He'd written letters to family and friends that might have been suicide notes, but he took his savings and passport with him when he vanished. The novelist and journalist Leonardo Sciascia[15] believed Majorana's work with Fermi led to the vanishing. Sciascia proposed that Majorana saw into the fission of the atom and chose to run away from the enormity.

Giorgio Agamben[16] also connects Majorana's vanishing to the indeterminacies he and his colleagues were studying. Agamben imagines the disappearance as the extension of a thought experiment: that his vanishing was a true-life version of Schrödinger's cat. Some scientists, including Majorana himself, have wondered how quantum realities might play out at larger scales. But Agamben's hypothesis is sleight of hand: "if quantum mechanics relies on the convention that reality must be eclipsed by probability, then disappearance is the only way in which the real can peremptorily be affirmed as such and avoid the grasp of calculation." It's a long way of saying *non lo sappiamo*: we don't know.

Connie Converse was an unsung singer in the fifties and sixties. An artist of promise, she did some demo recording but never signed a contract. She traveled from New Hampshire to Greenwich Village, composing and performing for several years. Converse grew disheartened and moved to Ann Arbor, where she became a writer and editor.

Years after leaving her New York life, she made it known to family that she was leaving, period. She didn't say where she was going, didn't mention suicide. It was just Connie going away for a while. "I've watched the elegant, energetic people of Ann Arbor," she wrote in her last letter, "going about their daily business on the streets and in the buildings, and have felt a detached admiration for the energy and elegance. If I ever was a member of this species, perhaps it was a social accident that has been canceled."

Such is the elegant profile to her leaving. I find captivating her sense of detachment, as when observing her fellow humans, no matter what depressive feeling lies behind it. The words themselves aren't sad. The language and syntax draw a circle around those people, as if Converse is already outside it.[17]

In Ian McEwan's *The Child in Time*,[18] the father of a child abducted at the supermarket imagines her in various ways over the years. Stephen Lewis sees his daughter Kate's spirit as it "might hover high above London, how it might resemble some kind of brilliantly colored dragonfly, capable of unimaginable speeds and yet remaining perfectly still as it waited to descend." Her disappearance is a fold in time, but Stephen, as his grief unfolds, as his marriage withers, finds other folds. A friend, Charles, goes back to a state of childlike simplicity and refuses to return from it. From outside a window, Stephen sees his parents in a tavern when they were young, when his mother has just learned she's pregnant with the child Stephen will become. The paramount effect of these folds is immobility within the violent forward movement of time, in which feeling becomes something we're inside of rather than the opposite. Stephen's sadness is "centuries, millennia old," he realizes, and it travels through him "like the wind through a field of grass."

In Hans Koppel's *Never Coming Back*,[19] a woman named Ylva causes another young woman's death when they are teenagers. Years later, after she's become a wife and mother, Ylva is kidnapped by the dead girl's brother to be held captive in a locked room. On a monitor, she's forced to watch her husband and children live without her. Ylva's imprisonment captures the true interaction with omnipotence and omniscience. Her family are an arm's length away, unreachable.

Magical thinking is crucial to the carrying-over of the self. It's a stall, an attempt at levitation in a moment that won't resolve rationally into the next. In Krabbé's *The Vanishing*,[20] as Rex waits for Saskia, at the rest stop inside the store where they agreed to rendezvous, he tells himself that he'll wait until the second hand on the clock circles one more time. Soon he falls into the vortex: "A hollow emptiness spread through his belly, as if he were sitting on a swing that did not stop going down." The virtual takes over completely—the real has pulled away.

The horror of missingness is that we have no definable boundary for return. When might we stop waiting? The missing have an indeterminate longevity that mocks our idea of death as conclusion. Horror, our sense that the worst has not occurred, has no middle distance.

The simplest actions are given cosmic force, as when, in Stewart O'Nan's *Songs for the Missing*,[21] one of the neighbor-children of the missing girl proposes a karmic rule to herself: find her neighbor's cat, the child thinks, and then someone will find the missing girl. In Maria Flook's *My Sister Life*,[22] Karen, the older sister, tells the young Maria she's going to the corner store. Flook remembers asking herself: "Perhaps, if I had asked Karen to bring me one little cake, she might have returned home. She might never have disappeared."

The emphasis is usually on a bifurcation: this way, that way—one or the other, a swerve. These are alternative worlds, splitting at remembered choices that were not really choices at all, but inflections. Magic overlaps with rational thinking because neither is purely one or the other.

Democracy, said Tocqueville, forces the individual "forever upon himself alone and threatens in the end to confine him entirely within the solitude of his own heart."[23] The next phase of society, Kobo Abe writes in an essay[24], will be "when a community is made that is so free that disappearance is impossible, or rather disappearance has no meaning."

In Emma Healey's *Elizabeth is Missing*,[25] and in the film version with Glenda Jackson, an old woman named Maud conflates the absence of her friend Elizabeth with the decades-old missingness of her sister Sukey. Both novel and film work through an interplay of past and present in Maud's failing mind. We participate in Maud's dementia—really an exaggerated version of everyone's irreality. Jackson's portrayal brings the confusion powerfully to life, capturing the jagged edges, the two-way violence of dementia, making missing-ness an urgency beyond time.

Maud's search for her friend Elizabeth is a refraction of the way her sister is seeking Maud herself, across the years. Sukey's death is a tangential matter. The will persists somewhere, perhaps in the way the missing persons put their touch on us. This passage from the novel captures that persistence: "I used to want to be Sukey, and I saw her everywhere: in the precise movement of a shopgirl as she pressed powder to her nose, or the dancing step of an impatient housewife in a grocer's queue. I carried on seeing her in other people long after I was married and settled, and a mother. She was still in the smudge of a face seen from a car."

We feel the recurring forgetfulness of which reading itself is a battleground. The clues—mainly, the overlap of place, time, and con-nection—come from the garden in Elizabeth's home, which had been Maud and Sukey's home many years earlier. Maud's long-suffering daughter finally accepts the virtuality of her mother's insistent claims. She brings Maud to the house and digs. In finding her sister Sukey's remains, she's reunited with herself, her past with her present, and an essential virtuality with her scattered, waking dreams.

THE VORTEX

SOMEONE WITHOUT CELEBRITY, disappearing before the digital age, is unlikely to have much internet presence. The disappearance itself might be in a database, with uploaded dental records, fingerprints, the missing-persons police record, DNA from confirmed relatives, all that can be scanned—as in NamUs, the FBI-sponsored online database in the US for missing persons and unidentified remains. Without those details to reconstitute the person, the analogue missing are missing also from the digital world.

Some people never *go* missing because they weren't noticed in the first place: The missing missing, including children born to sex-trafficked women or other lost people. Sometimes, such births are never recorded.

People of color go missing more often—especially Indigenous women—but receive far less attention from law enforcement and the media. Missing-person statistics are a reflection of larger social truths. A disproportionate number of the missing in America, around 33 percent, are Black. Indigenous women in some states, especially the Northwest and northern Midwest, as in Canada, account for alarmingly high percentages. In the United States, 40 percent of missing persons are nonwhite. Sometimes the people who are most likely to go missing are those whom others don't see even before they disappear.

Native women fall victim to the concomitants of poverty—alcohol and drug use, violence, and despair—but an essential problem is the removal, decades ago, of tribal jurisdiction on Native lands in cases involving non-Native suspects. Essentially, non-Native men, who account for nearly all suspected cases of violence against Native women in some lands, do what they wish with impunity. Many

Indigenous women go missing, in other words, because the violence against them is itself invisible.

Harmeet Kaur,[1] in a 2019 article on missing people of color, lists several reasons for the disparity. Lacking trust in the police, many Black Americans fear negative consequences of reporting someone missing. Families often lack the same resources as white families for searching or getting media attention. Some missing youths of color are already in dire straits: homeless or caught up in the foster-care system. Going missing is seen by many as an extension of such circumstances. If it doesn't seem mysterious, it isn't newsworthy.

The lack of media attention is self-asserting. Some news professionals argue that the public isn't interested, but the lack of coverage helps reinforce the sense that the subject isn't worthy of interest.

The media focus more frequently, and with greater intensity, on the victims who fit a script: white, young, female, pretty, and seemingly innocent. The assumption, as Rebecca Wanzo[2] sees it, is that what happened to them must be dark and mysterious—anomalous, therefore pointing to villainy that will prove, when uncovered, to be distinctly other. Wanzo argues that "Lost White Girls" are an "event": a recurring, fearful legend that allows the believer to ignore more complicated societal realities. If missing persons are of a marginalized group not considered *eventful*—Black or Indigenous women, poor white women, anyone with a history of drug problems—they expose inherently corruptive systems we prefer not to see.

In North Dakota, Lissa Yellowbird-Chase started her calling in 2012 as a searcher by digging into the case of a white oil-field worker. She became so obsessed with the case—befriending the man's mother, alienating officials and friends, scouring the land as assiduously and intuitively as she scoured social media. That's what solved the case, though the body was never found. Since then, she's focused on Indigenous people, mainly women, who have disappeared. She's developed her system, but she still relies mainly on *obsession*—still alienating people, starting with the family members of the missing she's trying to find.

Missingness, if it's anywhere, if it has a locus, appears most often to the unrelenting eye. Some people understand that what they're looking for, as much as they're looking for a body, a person, is the recurring event-of-being itself: missingness as it pervades our world, our lives, daring us to persist as presences when oblivion is so near.

Yellowbird-Chase was the subject of a well-researched culture-and-character study by Sierra Crane Murdoch[3] a couple years ago. Murdoch followed Yellowbird-Chase closely enough to see how she saw the land composed by its detail: " a patch of grass marked with pink paint; the track of an excavator cutting through sagebrush; a wide ravine cluttered with oak; a juniper; a scrap of tarp; a meandering creek, the banks silted and green; the clavicle of a cow; and among signs more difficult to discern, a mark in the mud by an animal or a boot, a beaver stick that from a distance resembled bone, and a wheel rim stuck in a tree, hung there by either a person or a flood." These details reside somewhere between the eye and the environment, between human and other. That betweenness is not missingness per se but the proscenium of missingness: its concurrent existence with presence and annihilation, or spirit, as I think of it: something less than material but more than perception. Yellowbird-Chase wonders of human spirits "if they did not drift in the air as she once thought but instead took shelter in everyday objects—in doorknobs, hot dogs, cigarettes touched to lips. In needles sunken in the crooks of arms."

In Roberto Bolaño's massive novel 2666, within the complex interweaving of stories, places, characters, and situations, a long, seemingly detached accounting of the disappearances and murders of scores of women occurs. The hub of disappearance in the novel is Santa Teresa, a deferred name for the real-world Ciudad Juarez, where multinational, neoliberal capitalism has sprouted and sent tendrils through the world beyond the border—rendering borders permeable, parodic, vortical. Bolaño's detailed, intimate, and yet detached description of the many disappearances—of females from preadolescence to the prime of life—both repulses and absorbs the reader. The chapter, or "part," is one of five altogether, and the textures and depths of Bolaño's narration will have already obliged you to acculturate your attentions before the accounting of lives commences. But you will be inclined to skim, to fly like a drone somewhere above the pages as they turn—as you turn them, as they turn you. Your drone will spiral down, though, into the virtuality that is the collective life of disappearance.

Each case, woven into the outer narrative, is both the same as those before and after it, and yet different. The reader's saturation in the cases, in the lives of women, occurs mainly, I think, through the ways similarity and difference carefully play out within the mind. We want to see each one as individual—as possessing the integrity of the individual girl or woman who was kidnapped, raped, tortured, murdered, dismembered, scattered, abandoned. But we can't. So we saturate ourselves, we release our own individuality, into the carefully written gaps of difference between each person.

Santa Teresa is the vortex of all missingness, at least within Bolaño's work. It's the world of the powerless, the exploited, the oppressed, the abandoned; the physiognomy is feminine, but the vortex takes everyone: the mothers and fathers in Mexico, for example, who take steel rods into the desolate places, but also into neighborhoods in the cities and towns, into off-spaces that are not distant at all; probing the silent underworld with those rods, with T-handles that let you twist, opening the hole a bit to release the air trapped below, liberating the smell of death and decay that is the devolved child; that, besides memories, photographs, odd scraps of a life, might be all they'll have of that child ever again.

The violence, the endless pulse of violence, decenters the world, but those strange crosses, those delving poles, are tools to re-center it. They have the heft and spare profiles of bodies that defy missingness as fate.

In the United States, one form of decentering is found in the legal system. Law enforcement in our country is composed of thousands of agencies that don't coordinate effectively. Efforts to set standards for reporting missing and unidentified persons have mostly failed.

The internet provides a slight degree of unity. Most states, many countries, have missing-persons webpages for submitting and displaying reports, giving advice, lending a sympathetic ear, and so forth. Some are the work of individuals, volunteers, small groups—hobbyists, sometimes, or obsessed relatives and friends of a missing person. Others have more official status, with sponsorship or recognition from governmental and law-enforcement agencies, or private backing. Private organizations in the US, many local or statewide, do a lot of the work in organizing searches, maintaining information, putting out fliers, creating social-media pages, and other activities that are more centralized in other countries like the UK and Australia.

The flipside of the missing person is the unidentified person: a body more or less whole, or traces of tissue, bits of bone, some teeth, or DNA from hair, clothing, jewelry, or bloodstains.

There are no universal protocols for storing, handling, or processing remains. Each agency among the thousands at every jurisdictional level goes by its own standards. States have different laws for how long remains are kept. Some policies are not statewide or even specific to an agency, but due rather to the practices of a particular clerk or technician. It's conceivable that incomplete remains found in one envelope, bag, box, drawer, or on some shelf are from the same missing person represented by remains in another container, in another office, in another state.

The unidentified are unnamed and compacted beneath their wait for names. In the States, more than 40,000 sets of human remains are held by thousands of medical examiners and law-enforcement agencies.[4] Picture them all on shelves, in drawers, in basements and closets; then, imagine the remains and effects never found—below ground, scattered across terrain, down ravines, underwater, or disintegrated.

Imagine you're walking down a street. Each block is a year, and along the sidewalk are doorways and alleys leading to an impossible number of days, weeks, and months. Figures stare from windows;

sounds peal from radios, televisions, and speakers, mixing in the air. It's a cacophony until you slow and listen, straining. Then, you hear various passages that become new streets, with alleyways and doorways and further windows, and further sounds within those sounds. The endlessness makes your legs heavy. You keep walking, surveying, eavesdropping, sometimes pausing and tempted toward a shadow, but always moving.

In this way you walk through a version of history, already constructed, densely populated, colorful, messy, and enormously droll. You take it all in, and the sounds, the glimpses of violence, victory, defeat, progress, the rise and fall of institutions, the flowering and decay of sensibility and culture—all of it enters you, and you move faster still, until one block is a century, then a millennium. Before you get so far that the entire project fits a single stride, you find you're at the center of the city. You're beneath the great, triumphant arch that marks the middle of everything. It's as far from home as you've ever been, but all you did was stroll. All you did was keep going with no mind of turning back. You see that continuing down the boulevard opposite the way you came, or on one of the other great routes that lead to the plaza where you are now, would simply replay the same sights, sounds, and choices. You have pure sensibility: not knowledge, not wisdom, not anything else but tired legs and worn soles.

After a brief rest you go back the same way, immune to it all as the sights and sounds play backward, a history of the future commencing in twilight, grotesqueries, and burlesques as the night deepens: all the choices you'll avoid, neither winning nor losing, killing nor dying, never seduced nor repelled; also avoiding progress, enrichment, and delightful decadence, taking it all in, but in reverse, letting it fade behind you as you stroll. It's you: you're the Angel of History.

Our circumambience is how we move into the middle distance: not to be too enclosed, or too expansive, seeking annihilation in the infinite. Circumambience is the sensorium, the bubble of our consciousness not perfectly spherical, but warped by our inner irregularities, imperfections, sins, terrors, lusts, inclinations, or aversions. Circumambience is the *shape* of a moment. It's the self as reaching its limits, just as it recoils from them: going beyond, falling back, appreciating place, moment, connection, fellowship; loving, challenging rivals, seeking what it seeks.

The sense of our freedom, how we obey our own choices, depends on the health of our circumambience. Think of it also as the space of language, looking, gazing, searching: sounds come in, whole sentences, exclamations, threads leading out to whole lives, whole cultures. The intangible, inexpressible world within us, and the solid, overwhelming world down the street, come together in our circumambience as *atmosphere*—mind and world, melding.

FLITCRAFT'S FOLLY

ALONG THE WAY in Dashiell Hammett's *The Maltese Falcon*[1] we find the Flitcraft parable. Sam Spade has been caught up in a search for the eponymous bird of prey by the femme fatale, Brigid O'Shaughnessy, who has hired the detective under false pretenses, seeking protection from others—Joe Cairo and Casper Gutman—who also seek the falcon. Spade relates the Flitcraft anecdote to a nonplussed O'Shaughnessy while they wait for Cairo.

Flitcraft, we've been told, was a well-off real-estate broker. Nothing in his history, Spade says, suggested a disappearance from his Spokane job, home, and family. Most of the story is in the narrator's voice, but the color of it is Spade's. "He went like that," says the dick, "like a fist when you open your hand," and we see the miniature theater in between the words.

After a phone call from Cairo, Spade continues with his own involvement in the story. Having hired Spade to find her missing husband, Flitcraft's wife comes by Spade's office to report a sighting. Spade confirms that Flitcraft has been living as Charles Peirce in Seattle.

Finishing the story, Spade tells O'Shaughnessy he went to Seattle and interviewed Flitcraft. The absconder expresses no regrets. Walking at lunch one day near his work, says Flitcraft, a beam fell from above, scarring him slightly, but terrifying the broker with the sense that random forces always threaten. "He felt," says Spade, "like somebody had taken the lid off life and let him look at the works."

We don't know enough about Flitcraft. Was he a war veteran? If so, he'd have been showered in falling beams already, might have vanished long before, and gone farther. Though Flitcraft's parable seems random itself, it's layered into the larger story: Hammett, our narrator, Spade-as-storyteller, O'Shaughnessy, then you and me—or me, and now you. And back to the other end: Flitcraft, quick-maker, who authors a new persona, Charles Pierce, nineteenth-century American pragmatist-philosopher.

Flitcraft is an inversion of the warrior. Soldier-absconders seek renewal of that ecstasy, anonymity, insignificance, or annihilation. Flitcraft, such as we have him, has led an ordered, sheltered life. His life is real estate, not wilderness or battlefield. It doesn't take war to send him spiraling.

"Life could be ended for him at random by a falling beam: he would change his life at random," says our narrator, "by simply going away." But his new reality is virtually the same as the old: new job, new family, new town (not far or near—a new middle distance), but essentially the same. Spade takes his satisfaction from the way he understands Flitcraft's actions, from how the man's choices fit into a larger understanding of life. "But that's the part of it I always liked. He adjusted himself to beams falling, and then no more of them fell, and he adjusted himself to them not falling."

O'Shaughnessy, whom we might read as one of life's falling beams, calls the story fascinating in a blank tone. She turns the conversation immediately to the situation she's in—to the matter of our narrative—in which the beams fall on almost every page.

If we get anything from the C. S. Peirce allusion, it might be that randomness, even chaos, is essential to growth: "By thus admitting pure spontaneity or life as a character of the universe," says Peirce,[2] "acting always and everywhere though restrained within narrow bounds by law, producing infinitesimal departures from law continually, and great ones with infinite infrequency, I account for all the variety and diversity of the universe, in the only sense in which the really *sui generis* and new can be said to be accounted for." What an elegant translation of differential calculus into prose!—or so it seems to a nonmathematician like me. The nested frame, the form, is the message. A swerve enters, and we're face-to-face not with the virtual, but with something tearing through, however cool its calculations are from an Archimedean point outside.

In Auster's *Oracle Night*, the fictional author Sidney Orr, in the magical notebook given to him by his mentor John Trause, creates a second-level fictional author, Nick Bowen. Bowen realizes, early in Orr's novel, that his life is shockingly random. He absconds, goes West, meets a WWII vet named Ed Victory, and winds up locked in the bomb shelter where Victory has been collecting phone books and other materials that prove the existence of the world, while Victory dies of a heart attack in the hospital.

Victory had tried to bring order to randomness. But order alone isn't meaningfulness. The archive in the bomb shelter is a space without movement, without flow. Orr writes Bowen into that tough spot and stops. He can't, or won't, rewrite it, nor find a way to get him out, nor let him die what death. What's the level of horror in such an ending? Our ability to connect with the character, to suspend disbelief, is diminished by our knowledge that a fictional character has created this deeper fictional character. What does it mean to further suspend disbelief? It's more a disappointment than horror. Circumambience is zero. He'll run out of air. But Orr's failure of imagination is deadlier.

In David Ely's novel *Seconds*,[3] a middle-aged, unhappy banker named Wilson receives a call from a friend he thought dead. The friend tells him about a company that provides its clients with new bodies, new identities, new vocations, new homes. The banker visits the company and goes through the process of being reborn. Once in their grasp, he has no choice. The company is a racket, though with avuncular leadership and clean, sterile interiors.

In his initial interview with the company, Wilson doesn't know what he wants. He describes the phone call from his friend, Charlie, as a jolt: "all of my usual defenses against anything new and strange had been shattered"—because a voice from beyond the grave had reached out to him. That's the swerve: "The grooves had worn down, so to speak, and the slightest nudge was enough to send me off in a different direction with all of the old instincts of habit still spinning away."

In his new life under a blue, California sky, the openness swallows him, and he wishes he were huddled once again on his commuter train. Wilson escapes, visiting his daughter and then his wife as a supposed friend. Both encounters are dispiriting. You'd think the wife might recognize her husband: some look, some remnant. One has the sense she never knew the man, as he didn't know himself.

The company picks Wilson up and brings him in. Asked if he can recommend a client, he demurs. In the same clinical setting where he began his new life, Wilson is anesthetized and killed. Every new client needs a faked death or disappearance; fake deaths require real corpses. This harvesting is the company's true business.

Like Flitcraft, Wilson really doesn't want anything different from what he had. His older personality conflicts with the artist's life the company made for him. What kills Wilson is the idea that a life can be commodified. This is the company's essential, satanic nature: a cancellation of the randomness that makes life possible.

WAKEFIELDS

IN "WAKEFIELD,"[1] AN early tale, Nathaniel Hawthorne explores the inside of anonymity and the possibilities of self-abstraction. Perceiving one's own absence has a bodily feeling. But it's a complex of feelings, and the complexity of "Wakefield" is derived from life in the modern city. It's framed as we might understand love and marriage, but also, what it means to touch the heart—or to pull back from our opportunities to touch.

Wakefield leaves his home, takes up residence on the very next street, and spies on Mrs. Wakefield for twenty years. His exit is unplanned, or at least we are told of no prior planning. Midway through this non-quest, they bump into each other, but Mrs. Wakefield doesn't recognize her husband. His anonymity, his street face, throng face, is a complete encasement. But absence is not mere anonymity. One might feel the Missing One watches from some unseen angle of existence, spying on the present life. Wakefield in Hawthorne's supposition, then, is simply the face on that angle—a story, a sketch, but also a thought experiment.

Wakefield leaves his life in the city without leaving the city itself. His alienation plays out within blocks of his wife and his home, but the greatest distance is himself from himself. Setting off from home can be the self's definition: quest, ascension, achievement, transformation, return of the prodigal. It depends on what, at the start, one absconds from.

If Hawthorne's sketch is about the nature and consequences of anonymity, then the chief frame of that anonymity is an urban landscape two centuries ago. In such a place it was possible to go on a quest without leaving the domain. Space could be explored as it threatened annihilation of the self. One could test boundaries without being Odysseus or Galahad.

The depictions of city life, of a life bounded by throngs, by streets, show the self as one without sufficient room in the world. The world itself is cut down to labyrinthine tricks of movement. Thus, the middle distance is missing in such spaces. The self is not aware of its freedom, lacks circumambience, and so is not itself.

"Wakefield," situated in London, anchors us in the early nineteenth century, when missingness was becoming a palpable effect of the massive migrations from country to city. People had more-consistent identities as named, located, chartered, registered, law-bound beings. Naming practices were more standardized, identification papers were more common, and people were more likely to be marked by things we now take for granted: addresses, mail service, conscription, employment rolls, health records.

Hawthorne's sketch uses a spiral frame that seems to expand in the reader's imagination—or, the reiteration in successively more-elaborate versions dilates our minds, reaffirming itself and soliciting our acceptance of its "facts" as transmitted and natural. First the story is told in one sentence, then in one paragraph with a bit more detail, and finally in whole. So, as it begins the third time, we feel we've already traveled its curves, and the result is déjà vu. Later, the narrator muses: "Would that I had a folio to write"—to remind of the spiral, the outer edges of it that the sketch itself can't contain. We are Wakefield, "in the meridian of life"—but there is no *selva oscura* where Wakefield might seek his way. He has the city's labyrinthine ways, but every day for twenty years, the narrator tells us, he finds his way back, briefly, to his own home, to look in as if a stranger.

We're the chorus, the narrator, the author: "We know, each for himself, that none of us would perpetrate such a folly, yet feel as if some other might." It's a tale to the side, out of step, but more familiar in its sideways view. That offset line is the profile of Wakefield's anonymity: "We must hurry after him, along the street," says our narrator, "ere he lose his individuality, and melt into the great mass of London life." It reminds me of Virginia Woolf's suggestion of solitary freedom in her essay "Street Haunting"[2]—her London of a century after: "We are no longer quite ourselves. As we step out of the house on a fine evening between four and six, we shed the self our friends know us by and become part of that vast republican army of anonymous trampers, whose society is so agreeable after the solitude of one's own room—" Except Wakefield, so far as we can tell, has nothing of the artist's need for solitude, no need for peripatetic discovery of his thoughts. We have but the singular thought of his absolute gesture, the trick he plays on his wife with a "crafty smile" on the way out—much like the one he'll give her on his return, twenty years later. That smile is all his artistry—crafty in that sense, as well as the demonic: craft is all the Devil has against us, and craft is all we have when we abjure grace and mercy.

In Hawthorne's stories we often see phantasmagoric effects, tricks of light and shadow in the framing of a scene or narrative element I think of as pre-cinema: in Poe, in Emerson, in many Romantic poets, one finds the spark and glow of the movies before there were movies. But photography as prolepsis, as dream, is thousands of years old. Hawthorne frames Wakefield's departure and return as shadow-puppetry when he draws our eye to the crafty smile. Before his return, Wakefield sees "the red glow and the glimmer and fitful flash of a comfortable fire. On the ceiling appears a grotesque shadow of good Mrs. Wakefield." The sketch, the framing of it, its spiral projections, the pointlessness of the gesture that forms the midpart of a life, are explorations of the fine and dangerous edge between virtual and real. The real, in this case, is what the narrator calls "system" in the final paragraph: "Amid the seeming confusion of our mysterious world, individuals are so nicely adjusted to a system, and systems to one another, and to a whole, that, by stepping aside for a moment, a man exposes himself to a fearful risk of losing his place forever. Like Wakefield, he may become, as it were, the Outcast of the Universe."

Does Wakefield burn a new profile at some edge of his personhood, his individuality? Does he find his queerness, his adventure, his wonder, his courage, or even his failure? He's a flaneur without a cause, a cyborg too loose in his machine parts: he neither wears them nor is worn by them. He's not melded, his isn't new. Of men at sea, W. S. Sebald in *The Rings of Saturn*[3] says, "From such a place, it must seem better to have the world behind them, and before them nothing but emptiness." Such persons are as much astronauts as any outer-space traveler. Profile burns bright at the edge of space, no matter the altitude. A navigator is the point of risk between nothing and everything.

Is Wakefield's un-adventure a form of suicide—an experiment with self-slaughter, using the urban blankness as a laboratory to test his nonexistence? Wakefield's "moment" was an Odyssean span of twenty years, though without adventure. His quest was no more than "stepping aside." His return is from the impossible space of wandering the streets where, in another rendering of the tale, he might have explored his circumambient existence—that space of potential for discovery, communion, growth, serendipity, fellowship, or oneness with the environment.

The domestic also holds circumambience: Two or more share a space, a vision; they form a family of expectations. But from his own way of moving in the world, Wakefield's home-space has become a crypt. A labyrinth at least offers form. Lacking connection to others, where are you if you can't get lost?

Hawthorne perhaps worked from a true if spare account by Dr. William King[4] of an early eighteenth-century Londoner who stayed away seventeen years. He, too, lived very near and kept tabs on his wife. But his homecoming was due to the depletion of his savings. As in Hawthorne's tale, we get no contrition, forgiveness, or happily-ever-after. Each man returns to the life he abandoned. We're forced out of the scene without even knowing the wife's reaction, much less a clue as to the transformed lives they lead in the aftermath.

Dr. King reports: "that when we reformed from popery a few convents had been exempted from the general pillage, in which men of severe morals, or of a melancholy cast and turn of mind, might have found a retreat. But I have observed, what is perhaps peculiar to this island, that there are men wholly free from the spleen, or a lowness of spirits, in good health and good circumstances, and only actuated by some whimsical considerations, seek a retreat where they may forget their friends and relations, and be forgotten by them." It's a clean, tight circle: to forget, to be forgotten; there is purgation, oblivion as a small globe in the hand, becoming itself the hand that holds us.

Further nesting his tale, King ascribes it to the account of a Dr. Rose, who, King emphasizes, was prone to recount the tale on several occasions at a coffeehouse where they sometimes met. At this point in the anecdote, we enter into a niche in which a small social circle is engaged: an element to signify the fractal. Dr. Rose witnesses the wife's receipt of a letter from a stranger. In the letter, this stranger offers to meet her in St. James's Park, at the Birdcage Walk. Rose identifies the handwriting as that of Mr. Howe, the errant husband, at which the wife faints—adding another layer, another threshold.

The next day, the group make the rendezvous at the park, and the marriage is again joined. The anecdote ends with such a pull toward infinity, a happily-ever-after that, if it doesn't weaken the anecdotal nature of the tale, nonetheless gives it a blurry outline where folktales stir.

How do we compare it to a beam, or the crafty smile? Is there some broader geometry of choices, convergences, random particles, or waves, some formula whereby our own willful ways get woven into magic, physics, genetic forces; and then, of a moment, instead of a pivot and return to our routine, the momentum carries us a few inches out of our lives? Is Howe/Wakefield someone in a fugue state? Might it be not so much in the mind as in the Oort cloud, beyond the skin, beyond the range of senses, though remnants of our making?

The version in King works by careful framing of the situation. The mystery at its core—why did Mr. Howe (our original Wakefield) choose to disappear from his family and home?—is never solved, though it's acknowledged. The fastidious planning is impressive, as King recounts it. The narrative itself has several inverted folds, so that the overall tale, the experience of Mr. and Mrs. Howe and their intermediaries and observers, is a machine—an automaton, as I see it: it moves with human gestures though it has no soul.

Mr. Howe's overall departure and return is given in the first third of the account. What follows is something like the exploded-view depiction of the machine—its cogs, wheels, and springs. We learn that Mr. Howe had simply moved to a house nearby; that ten years into his absence, he made the acquaintance of a Mr. Salt, who lived near his old home, and dined with him regularly at a restaurant from which Howe could see into his dining room, where Mrs. Howe received company. He sat in church in his acquaintance Mr. Salt's seat, from where he could see his wife without being noticed himself.

A few years into his absence, the Howes' children died. Before that, Mrs. Howe petitioned the government for a settlement of her husband's estate. The petition was granted with little delay. From his short distance, in his newspaper, Mr. Howe "enjoyed the pleasure of reading the progress of it in the votes, in a little coffee-house, near his lodging, which he frequented."

The last few phrases of this sentence crystallize the experience. It's about perspective, or channels of movement through the larger self. If the self is a city, and the movements of bodies through the city streets, and the entering and exiting of buildings and parks, then the tale is an allegory of the mind. Those last few phrases measure out specific arcs of consciousness, as if the "abdication," as King calls it, were an attempt at creating a new blueprint of the self. The senseless abdication, then, is an experiment—not Howe's experiment so much as King's. The story is a probing of the new consciousness rising from the print-based world, finding just what kind of story would fit into the pages of a magazine, fitting new templates of mind in the urban environment. The new, periodical-based writing, its new sentences, new forms of myth, is reshaping the literate mind. "This act he suffered to be solicited and passed, and enjoyed the pleasure of reading the progress of it in the votes, in a little coffee-house, near his lodging, which he frequented." With its channeling and spacing, by its frequency, as in radio waves, the sentence seems to me a machine of consciousness. It comes from the very design of things: of the city, its streets, its traffic flows, its vistas, the newspaper he reads as a channel itself by which he sees into the machinations of law as they touch his life—rather, the life he's vacated. I've argued that the sentences, the tale overall, are a machine. More precisely, they're a kinetoscope. We see into the channels of movement, feeling, choice, and vision as we would through a carefully made panorama.

E. L. Doctorow's[5] take on the Wakefield story puts the husband in the suburbs—a space already angled toward disappearance, hiddenness. This latter-day Wakefield is a phenomenologist: "Now the entire neighborhood seemed to brim with an exaggerated presence. I was conscious of the arbitrariness of place. Why here rather than somewhere else? A very unsettling, disoriented feeling." His detachment is only partly located in the gradual distancing the story shows us between Wakefield and his wife, who's more animated with her own feelings—disappointment, mainly. His disappearance, were the story told in reverse, might be fantasy fulfillment.

Doctorow doesn't simply transfer urban disease out of town, but rather highlights the inexorability of nature's presence. When a man pulls just a bit out of his treadmill existence, the world itself in all its amplitude shows how unnecessary we are to its own persistence: "From the shadow of the garage, I beheld the back yard, with its Norwegian maples, the tilted white birches, the ancient apple tree whose branches touched the windows of the family room, and for the first time, it seemed, I understood the green glory of this acreage as something indifferent to human life and quite apart from the Victorian manse set upon it." Doctorow's Wakefield is more of a conscious philosopher than Hawthorne's, who seems a trickster in his own life, more demonic, more instinctual. Doctorow's husband is aware of the possible meaning of his act. He reads himself as a symbol, in a way one rarely does, as to be such a symbol, or rather a specimen, is to be less a real man. Or does it allow him to transcend the cruel game he's been obliged to take part in: the rat race back and forth on the commuter train, the dutiful father/husband, the citizen? As in the Flitcraft parable, we witness a swerve when one day the commuter train breaks down: "Well, it was an entirely unrelated mishap. I knew that, but when you're tired after a long day and trying to get home there's a kind of Doppler effect in the mind, and you think that these disconnects are the trajectory of a collapsing civilization."

As months go by, this Wakefield molders. Living in the dark attic above his garage, Wakefield's beard grows. He casts off friends, hygiene, credit cards. It might be too much editorial intrusion, but I think, rather, it's the true axis between narrator and character when Wakefield tells us: "After having lived dutifully by the rules, couldn't a man taken out of his routine and distracted by a noise in his back yard veer away from one door and into another as the first step in the transformation of his life?" He scrambles for food, becomes a pet project for two inmates at a home for "mentally deficient persons" nearby. Throughout, he reads signs of the encroaching wilderness. He becomes nocturnal; a raccoon becomes his future, furtive self. This Wakefield achieves a sort of enlightenment, or at least a heightened awareness. The raccoon is a sideways look at oneself: the swerve was deep inside the man all along.

In his novel *Mrs. Wakefield*, Eduardo Berti[6] explores the wife's own journey during those twenty years of her husband's absence. Berti gives his story more historical texture than other versions through references to the Luddites, breakers of looms who tried to keep modernity at bay. Mrs. Wakefield becomes peripherally involved, assisting one of her servants whose brother gets caught up in the movement, and though condemned to hang, is exiled to Australia.

This Mrs. Wakefield gets out of the house, testing the fabric of her new reality by probing the city as a conspirator in her husband's disappearance. She sees him spying on their home and finds the boardinghouse from which her errant husband ventures forth in disguise.

In her wandering, Mrs. Wakefield discovers herself in the city. It's labyrinthine and seems to double itself. On one occasion she comes before a house that seems her own, though she's journeyed into a different neighborhood.

The texture of Mrs. Wakefield's progress through her ordeal is the alternations of her searching and her involvement on the edges of the Luddite movement. The added history in Berti's account supplies some sense of Wakefield's machinations: that his own disappearance is a response to the changing world.

Mrs. Wakefield keeps a journal according to this rule: "She does not write in the notebook any thought which has not visited her at least three times. In this way, by consulting the pages, she faces certainties, not just vague ideas." So the notebook is a map of self—a triangulation of her movements through the streets and through the ghostly realm her husband's absence has revealed. She notes that his copy of *Don Quixote* is missing, and that he must have taken it along. This observation gives the city streets a hybrid quality: "The usual street corner suddenly becomes a border between the ordinary world and the extraordinary world that does not surround her house."

The Wakefields inhabit two worlds that overlap. Her thoughts and journal entries tend toward bifurcations—spare, divided choices that shape the world: "People are divided between those who fear God more than the devil and those who fear more the devil than God"; or, in the manner of Isaiah Berlin's Hedgehog and Fox: "People are divided between those who know only one thing deeply and who reduce the world to this vision, and those who without any depth know many questions."

As the Luddite controversy compounds, she wonders at the world that seems divided "between those who sympathize with Wellington and the followers of the Revolution." How this binary approach to the world defines Mrs. Wakefield herself, or her husband, is unclear—except, perhaps, that she's on one side, he the other, and his haunting of her reality is the shine of contact between. Like Hawthorne's man, this Wakefield returns after twenty years—but in Berti, the wayward husband soon dies in his sleep.

It's how missingness is latent in us all: not simply that we could get lost, but that being lost might unravel our personalities. Antonio Tabucchi[7] tells a short, lyric tale of a morgue worker who becomes obsessed with identifying a corpse. His friends wonder why he has become so obsessed. He argues to one:

> "And you?" Spino said. "Who are you to yourself? Do you realize that if you wanted to find that out one day you'd have to look for yourself all over the place, reconstruct yourself,

rummage in old drawers, get hold of evidence from other people, clues scattered here and there and lost? You'd be completely in the dark, you'd have to find your way."

That moment in Tabucchi's story dovetails with the situation of Patrick Modiano's hero in his novel *Missing Person*.[8] Guy Roland, as he has decided to call himself, is a classic fugue-sufferer, a man with amnesia whose remembered life goes back only so far. His job has been as assistant to a detective, who, retiring, sets the hero free to detect his past. The streets of Paris are the labyrinth in which meanings are gathered piece by piece—names, identities, somehow connected to the war and the Resistance. He interviews the people he finds, slowly gathering information on his past, in part by carefully impersonating himself—audaciously, especially in the earlier stages, given that he has so little of himself to go on. Gradually he becomes the man he thinks he is. But is he? His search is somewhat like a developing photograph, its image gradually materializing—though the end result might be a fiction. In such a nonlinear world, the past ripens alongside the present.

In the middle of this attenuated, nuanced tale, Modiano's narrator says: "I believe that the entrance-halls of buildings still retain the echo of footsteps of those who used to cross them and who have since vanished." The belief is advanced, perhaps, by the felicities of cinema: double exposures, slow motion, reverse motion, montage, and so forth. Post a camera at one of those entrance halls and capture a day's worth of foot traffic, then overlay—amazing that we all fit through, nor do I pretend to understand how someone's here one moment and gone the next. Sometimes I've stared at a place where I had rendez-voused with someone dear, years earlier, wishing for a brief while that they, that I, would appear there once more, laughing and young. We might have carried on in our shared journey a little longer than we did, on this arrow of time where I'm stranded. But today's foot traffic is ignorant of my nostalgia, not part of it, not tolerant of my hanging about. There's business to tend to—get on with it!

THE CIRCUMAMBIENT SELF

IN KOBO ABE'S *The Box Man*,[1] the so-named hero lives in a reduced form of the locked room: a cardboard box that is itself a compact iteration of the city. Within the box, the man has canceled out his choices, his circumambient flow. The cityscape constantly morphs, rendering circumambience sterile. In the early modern city where Hawthorne's Wakefield wanders, the streets and buildings are stable over time—at least, the city into which he vanishes is more or less the same from which he returns twenty years later. In far less time, postwar Tokyo changed beyond recognition.

The Box Man says, early in his confessions, that living in his box is a nakedness beyond mere nudity. It's a way to be a voyeur forever. "It was nothing at all to get out of the box. And since there was nothing to it, I felt no compulsive need to leave it." This velleity, this flatness of will, matches Wakefield's experiment in meaninglessness. We have from it two forms of invisibility, the next stages from anonymity, which both citizens have lived by and seek to escape—not through true action, but by sliding further beneath the surface of things, by melting into the throng. "In seeing there is love," says the Box Man, "in being seen there is abhorrence. One grins, trying to bear the pain of being seen."

The box is a camera obscura: "Instead of leaving the box, I shall enclose the world within it." The photographic virtuality, this reduction of circumambience to its barest dimensions, is an argument against the dominant virtuality of the city, of the state. "Actually," argues the Box Man, "a box, in appearance, is purely and simply a right-angled parallelepiped, but when you look at it from within it's a labyrinth of a hundred interconnecting puzzle rings." In it he avoids the middle distance: not to be too enclosed or too expansive, avoiding annihilation in the infinite. The megalopolis, the constantly changing, demolished/rebuilt city without form, larger than its sky, greater than its ground, causes the circumambient space, the organic sense of the individual connecting with his world, to implode.

"He turns into an apparition," says the Box Man of his ilk—for the Box Man is an analyst, after all. What's the box if not a laboratory just beyond the skin? He "turns into an apparition that is neither man nor box." It makes him a nuisance to the world, but inside his box he has "an entrance to another world"—though that other world remains abstract. It's atavism: a way to escape the city, its modernity, its crushing weight upon the body and the mind. Our essential self is an ancient creature, a troglodyte. He's a blockage in the throng, an un-flaneur.

Circumambience is the slight skip away from ourselves. It's the space of our struggle to be who we are, but not too much, not too little; the map of ourselves, just a little bigger or smaller than us, overlapping the maps of others. We cross each other's paths and nod, we miss altogether, or we annihilate each other through the slightest touch.

The Box Man's existence, in the end, is *deferral* of circumambience. His life is intersected by a woman—a nurse, he calls her. Through fragmented observations and confessions, we see the Box Man pursue his glimpses and fantasies of the nurse, along with bits and pieces of the city, of other box men. In the end, we have only his velleity: trapped with possibilities for escape, but in the end, no reason to escape.

In Abe's *Woman in the Dunes*[2], an amateur entomologist gets trapped in a sandpit with a peasant woman. His failed efforts to escape, thanks to the villagers above as well as the incessant shifting of the sands, lead him toward an acceptance of his fate; a fusion, really, of being lost and found. The novel ends with a missing-persons report in the outside world he's lost to: a piece of paper that reduces his existence, for the reader's benefit only, to a linear end point. But we know his erotic, dynamic life in the sands isn't ended. Is it horror? Or is it the balance of real and virtual, a life lived in direct contact with time: the shifting sands, inside the hourglass?

The Woman of the Dunes, angel of missingness, "had probably spent her whole life down here," thinks the Entomologist. The sand world is "a monotonous existence enclosed in an eye." Sand redirects consciousness continually as they tend to its movements, its stability, the water it contains, its effect on their skin. Even in sleep, sand dominates their dreams. When not digging or fighting with the sand, they eat together and bathe each other. Gradually they're lovers, but with a fitfulness: the man's desire is tangled with anger and fear. Their life in the sandpit is a missingness deeper than the man's own disappearance. They live with the ghosts of her prior family, with the loss of a purposeful life, of a future.

The sky alone is fixed for him. Compared to the Box Man, the Entomologist has more time to explore this condensed space—just outside himself, just inside the communal skin. "From the outside," observes this observer of microworlds, "this place seemed a tiny spot of earth, but when you were at the bottom of the hole you could see nothing but limitless sand and sky." The Entomologist comes to accept his fate. It's not like Kafka's K, not a hopeless struggle against the state. It's learning to live at scale. In the city, we live too far below or above our human measure. In the sand, digging away, sleeping at night with his woman, whole beneath the sky, the Entomologist is right in the middle of things, and that's his freedom.

SUBTERRANEAN

IN MAX FRISCH'S *I'm Not Stiller*,[1] a man denies who he is to his distraught wife, to the warden of the jail where he's confined for striking a policeman, to his lawyer, to the prosecutor, to himself. The novel is a series of notebooks Stiller keeps while jailed. Gradually they shape a staggered, sideways self-portrait around the man deflated by his supposed failures: failures as an artist, as a husband, and as a soldier in the International Brigade during the Spanish Civil War. "I'm sitting in my cell, staring at the wall, and I see the desert. For example the desert of Chihuahua. I see its vast arid expanse full of blossoming colors, where nothing else blossoms anymore, colors of blazing noon, colors of dusk, colors of the indescribable night." North America was his escape. In the notebooks he writes while in jail, he escapes through fabrications of his adventures as James White, into the beautiful desert of his Nature Theater: detailed, historical, grand as cinema.

This desert reframes the abstraction, the inexplicable abandonment, of Wakefield's twenty years of looking in on his own life with no other purpose: Stiller's/White's desert in Mexico and the States is a failed quest. It's the elliptical that shapes the biography into an immediate profile of the person as they might appear within reach—in the prison house of identity, of having papers, of acquiescing to the law. At the center of that relation is the connection that's most real, most ardent, most painful: the marriage, the spouse. The marriage is either who you are, or it's who you're not—in which case it must be denied, escaped, subtracted.

Stiller tells his jailer of life in the American desert: "how one summer morning on the prairie, feeling a bit fed-up with my everyday life as a cowboy"—this, a recursive or nested narrative element within the lie itself, for it is Stiller's outer abdication as the Swiss sculptor and husband the official record makes him out to be—"I rode further than usual, further than necessary." More than usual, more than was necessary: That, in its essential geometry, is Wakefield, and the testing of one's middle distance.

In his American excursion, Stiller/White finds a crack in the Earth through which a magnificent cavern appears. He explores, then returns to the ranch, returning with "Jim," another cowboy who will die during a second, hazardous exploration of the cavern. This second cowboy is the matter/antimatter of identity: One might survive or succumb to the danger. But why not both? Let it be that branching, that quantum movement within the field.

This is the cave of time, the cave we escaped from or must return to. White figures its history through speculations on earlier explorers, Coronado and Cabeza de Vaca. He finds the cavern in not finding it the second time, proving its worth in its hiddenness.

> My cavern in the rocks began to turn into a ghost that was impossible to find in reality, although I rode over the region several more times, each time equipped with a lantern and a lasso, one pocket full of carbide, the other full of provisions, and I had really ceased to believe in my discovery when one evening, when dusk was already falling and it was high time to ride back, I saw a cloud of bats. It was as though they were rising out of the ground. Millions of bats. They were coming from my cave!

It's a beautiful inversion of Plato's cave. With White/Stiller as our guide, we explore this Notre Dame of Dreams where our light falls on no floor, where the stars shine within the cavern, where everything, once our lantern has swung its arc, returns to darkness as if what was there in the fleeing light had never existed: did not exist before the light struck it, does not exist after; the cavern carved in eons of time by a river that's vanished into even greater depths; the cavern where a shining skeleton is our salvation, where a queen who never lived still reigns.

All the shapes the human psyche ever dreamed are preserved here in stone. The deeper you descend, the more luxuriant the shapes that rise from the floors of the caves, like coral; you tramp through forests of snow-covered firs, then again you see a pagoda, a goblin, an extinct fountain from Versailles, according to the angle from which you look—a strange Arcadia of the dead, a Hades such as Orpheus entered. There's no lack of stone ladies slowly swallowed by their pleated veils of amber, never to be freed again by any human love.

How wonderful to have escaped the cave of one's legal name, to have fled via passport to foreign lands, then flung the passport to the winds, then followed one's wandering nose down into the bowels of the Earth, where no nationhood, no identity, no name can hold you—only the captivating ladies of stone.

The end of Stiller's complicated ruse is grief, because by that point the story is one of great love—or a very simple but enduring love of the man for his dying wife, Julika. After traveling in time and space and mind, Stiller is back in his cell: "I try in vain to see her laughing face; I only know very vividly that whenever it laughs I want to take it in both hands like a gift from heaven that cannot be grasped with the hands, but only believed in." Stiller admits that failure can't be buried away. "This means," he says, "one must be capable of passing without spite through their confusion of identities, playing a part without ever confusing oneself with the part; but for this I must have a fixed point"—and for both Wakefield and Stiller, that fixed point is the wife. Even for Abe's Entomologist, the settlement is with the Angel of the Dunes, his common-law spouse. For Wakefield, though, it's the domestic space given form and temperature by Mrs. Wakefield, whereas for Stiller, it's the woman herself—her, and the possibility of losing her. Julika dies, and Stiller, now truly and only Stiller, is left alone with a grief deeper than his cavern-universe.

All we are in the end is love. Both he and Julika get there through great suffering. During a hearing, when everyone is still trying their best to prove to Stiller that he is Stiller, he asks Julika, "Do you love me, Julika, or don't you?"—without admitting the identity of "me." It's a gaping, precipitous cruelty, and she sobs. "I endeavored to explain to Julika," he records in his notebook, "why, as long as she really loved me, she needed no confession from me that I was her lost husband."

In the Myth of Er, at the end of Plato's *Republic*, a soldier killed in battle finds himself before the paths to the sky, and the paths belowground, where judges decide among the dead who will go where, and which souls will be returned to life. Those who return choose their next lives. Strangely, Odysseus chooses to return as a humble farmer. Perhaps he has taken a cue from the self-chastising words of Achilles's shade in hell: better to be the slave of a poor farmer on Earth than king of all the dead. Odysseus takes the middle way.

In that place is the Spindle of Necessity. Around the Spindle eight orbs move. It's a model, but only because what the dead souls see can be no more than a model: that's what it means to see something. This is as close as the real and the virtual come to convergence.

Elsewhere in the Republic, we have the Allegory of the Cave. The vividness of the scene is that we sit in darkness, flames behind, casting shadows of writhing, grappling, attenuated and distorted creatures on the wall before us. It's the skull itself. Someone—Hercules, Pandora, Orpheus, Prometheus, Persephone—gets up midmovie to have a smoke outside. There's something traumatic about that shift from night to day, from the closeness of the cave to the mash-up of rolling green hills and craggy white rocks, the distant peaks, the faint sound of the sea—and that pale-blue, wifty sky. You're not in your own skull anymore, are you?

The first thing I'd do, even before smoking my cigarette, would be to lie down in the grass and close my eyes: to see inside the cave again, but with the breeze sliding over my face and the insect-and-bird sounds that grow more intense as I breathe myself into that smaller version of the cave. Does it seem as vivid, as real? Can I control the writhing figures if I squeeze my mind hard enough? How long can I stay like that before something happens?—because something will always happen.

I know I'm being watched. Let them watch. I'm naked and proud. I wear no uniform or insignia. I've avoided the wars altogether. There's work to be done right here under these trees, near the mouth of the cave; I'll wait for my instructions.

SPIRIT RADIOS

"AN OBJECT, A being, a fugitive impression," writes Henri Lefebvre,[1] "thus receives the privilege of an unbearable, unbelievable, inexplicable burden of presence. A smile or a tear, a house or a tree become a whole world." The objects we preserve retain memory, shape, smell, contiguity. This clothing or this letter touched what we touched, retains skin, sweat, a tear- or blood-drop.

We still have a few of the cassette-tape letters sent back and forth in 1969–1970. Our mother sat us down at the kitchen table once a month to say a few words on them. She'd put the new tape into a care package with other items—cigarettes, cheese, crackers, smoked meats. Lewis would record over the tapes and send them back.

Kevin borrowed the remaining ones several years ago but couldn't bring himself to listen. He sent them to me. I felt the same hesitance, as if it would release spirits trapped for half a century.

It was startling to hear a young man's voice: Lewis's strong Texan accent, but with that clipped military edge. He speaks of our home life, gives the children orders, my mother instructions and advice, tells us he loves us, tells my mother he loves her again and again, yearning and not giving up in that part of his brain, below the soldier part, that wants to be home.

He says little of the war itself, of his environment, but he says enough to reconstruct some spare feeling for the momentary experiences that add up to history. Ambient noises—choppers, jets, mortar fire, machine-gun fire—draw occasional remarks about the war only yards away. Lewis's intimate knowledge of anything mechanical with wings is on display. After the sound of an aircraft, he tells us "that's an OV-10, flying low; Nightrider. When he finds Charlie, we go do 'em a job."

At some points, Lewis either forgets who he's talking to or lets the pillow talk get even closer: "Jim Perry, remember him? He's working for Paige Electric now. Yeah, he's a spook. Colonel Grieves?[2] He's run-ning the National Police—big-time spook. Another guy you didn't know, he's with RMK-BRJ—another spook. Well, enough of *that* . . ."

The disembodied voice, without face or image, seems to rise from the past itself. The magnetic tape is likely warped. The sound of his voice is a bit high-pitched, making him sound even younger than he was. But the machine imperfections only add to the magic of it, because I want to reach in and touch the past, change things—as if I knew what small changes my hands could make.

In *Dispatches*, Michael Herr[3] writes of the tension, as he calls it, between rot and genesis in the jungle. Maybe in such an environment it's compressed, sped up, thus more visible—more sensible overall, almost a body in itself. But that tension, or that recursion of what's essentially the same element, pervades the world—not only its jun-gles. It's the life, the voice behind the voices, on the tapes.

Lewis talks of the temperature and the mosquitoes and his back, which is being eaten away by jungle rot. "Everything's underwater," he says, and I see an unreal world. A Cobra passes overhead: "reassuring," he tells us, "if you have a radio." There's a good bit of mil-speak about his boys, their propensity for teamwork, for "playing ball," and the threats he makes as a loving father figure (as a newly made captain, he's the old man at twenty-nine to the average of nineteen).

Then, via tape, across the miles, he does more or less the same to us boys at home. If anything, the language for us is sterner. Masculinity is emphasized: he nixes the idea of getting a cat; asks us if we've had any boxing matches. "I understand you're not toeing the line," he warns my brothers, Don age six and Kevin age three; "I want you to understand that when I get home, there will be a chalk line drawn, and I'll hold formations on it."

He addresses each child: me, Don, Kevin, and Debi, the oldest. "I miss boxing with all of you," he says. I did not miss the boxing. He praises Don for the artwork he sent—but with moderation: "You won't be a Rembrandt, or a Picasso, Don, but keep at it!" Each audio-letter to the sons ends with orders to help Mom. To my brother

Kevin, he says: "You're getting to be four years old, now; it's time to stop acting like a baby."

Most of the tapes are meant for my mother. He expresses frustration at not getting mail for a few days. My mother wrote practically every day, but his mail arrived in batches. He talks of the coming R&R—as he does obsessively in the letters. There's an enemy sighting, he says, about half a klick away; we listen to the firing. "You express concern," he says to my mother, "that you don't hear from me for two or three days, but Honey, sometimes I go out there. I'm taking care of myself; you do the same. Be careful," he advises her, "with those diet pills." More sounds of automatic-weapons fire.

He spends the last minute or so on one tape, waiting for it to run out, simply repeating *love*—that he loves his family, loves his wife, again and again. I think of a Tim O'Brien essay, "The Vietnam in Me":[4] "For me, at least," O'Brien says, "Vietnam was partly love. With each step, each light-year of a second, a foot soldier is always almost dead, or so it feels, and in such circumstances you can't help but love. You love your mom and dad, the Vikings, hamburgers on the grill, your pulse, your future—everything that might be lost or never come to be. . . . Intimacy with death carries with it a corresponding new intimacy with life." And although it might simply be that Lewis really misses us—misses his wife, anyway—I think the same poetry of death O'Brien writes about was animating Lewis.

Of the several audio fragments remaining, one has my mother's voice on it. I'd not heard my stepfather's voice in decades; I'd expected that hearing it again would be eerie. But my mother's younger voice was equally strange: younger, more Southern, more innocent, though still her: passive, sweet, questioning. The intonations were meant only for her spouse, and I'd not heard that voice before—not in eavesdropping, not from behind paper-thin closed doors. The distance, the disembodiment, the yearning, the anxiety: making decisions with only Lewis's long-distance guidance (though frequent, specific, and insistent) must have been trying.

She talks of the things he says to her, the words he uses face-to-face, that she goes back to. "I'm sending very, very happy thoughts to you there." I think that's what saved him: her happy thoughts. "I know it must be awfully miserable," I hear her say. "It feels like years since you've been gone, not months." She talks about TV, that always-on presence in my childhood, and the news: the special report, interrupting the Emmy Awards, that President Nixon was authorizing the withdrawal of 2,500 troops, or was it 250,000 troops? "You know me and figures," she says apologetically.

"Mr. Hill [our landlord] has gotten things pretty well repaired," she assures Lewis. "The car has a crack in the window. Do you want me to bring it to the service station? Everything seems to be bigger when you're not here," she complains. "I know I let little things get all out of proportion." She, too, speaks excitedly of R&R, and complains of my teenaged sister Debi, and the trials of raising us all without a father.

As I listen, it becomes clearer that both my mother and my stepfather were operating at opposite ends of a continuum. Their realities were different, but the continuum was their virtual, shared space. That's where the life was, for two people so far apart but so in love—not in either Vietnam or Fayetteville, but in the space they'd made between.

LIGHTNESS

ON THE SPECTRUM of causes for Lewis's disappearance, we find many points where the linearity collapses into other dimensions. Let's lay out some possibilities:

(1a) Lewis knew all along that he'd never come back. He met a younger woman, and they went off together to live in a tropical paradise. Given his three-pack-a-day habit, he's long since died of lung cancer.

(1b) The new wife reformed him; he became a health nut and is living slim, sinewy and clean-lunged on a crystalline beach.

(2a) Lewis knew all along he'd never come back, but went off by himself: (2aa) to fight the good fight against Contras, communists, fascists, drug dealers, or other assorted bad guys; or, (2bb) to pick up and deliver some drugs himself, make a quick killing and then (2aaa) return to us refreshed and debt-free or (2bbb) carry on in his new life as a drug runner/freedom fighter, having long since died or (2aaaa) ended up in a South American prison or (2bbbb) something like (1b) above, but after the aforesaid adventures.

(3a) Lewis got knocked on the head and caught amnesia. In that case any of the above might apply, but also any other sort of life one can imagine for him, short of the one we know he didn't have: a return to us.

Possibly I should separate out (2bb) as a new number: he went somewhere (maybe not Vero Beach or maybe not to work for a small-aircraft dealer) to make some legitimate or less-than-legitimate money, then come home in quick order, his wife never knowing the worst of it.

These possibilities fan out further than I'm allowing here. If you start from any random fact or element of the man's life and character, pondering all the possibilities your mind is open to, innumerable lives grow like algae on a pond. Somewhere, the real man, still clinging in our memories, starts to lose his human face. He becomes a collage of American error, promise, comedy, or tragedy.

The body others see never gets beyond sight of its own surface. Mirrors attempt to swallow it, but it's indigestible—the body rebounds and a reflection is manifest: the second body, escaping consumption. It's this body that causes many to despair, particularly with age. For Lewis, it must have been an enemy to conquer, and his act, already gleaming with disappearance, was a tactical assault.

Paul Valéry[1] wrote of the three bodies: varied senses of what we are as a way toward thinking who we are. The first, the "my-body," is what we speak of to others as belonging to ourselves, though "it is not altogether a thing, and belongs to us less than we belong to it." It rests on the world, but equally true is the opposite feeling, that the world rests on the my-body, that the body is an event in the world, or again, that the world is a passing event in the body.

This my-body seems formless. Distances within the body are not the same as comparable distances external to the body. Distance, in fact, is meaningless within the body. But we tend to think we're living within that my-body. One part of it can be alien to another—particularly in certain events, as when one hand grasps the other, finding it alien and strange.

The second body is the body seen by others—in passing, or as eclipsing their own my-bodies at times. It also appears to us in reflections, which is so often a moment of despair—the moment, I suspect, when someone who will disappear starts to feel the varied bodies pull apart: for it will be some object and event we miss.

The third body is the dissected body: what we'd expect to find as evidence. But the fourth body Valéry proposes is transcendent of the other three, or contradicts them: real and imaginary, in and out, it's the locus of all forces. "My Fourth Body is neither more nor less distinct than is a whirlpool from the liquid in which it is formed." It's the incarnation of nonexistence, says Valéry.

I propose this Fourth Body as what we find when we enter missingness; that we might find this Fourth Body even when we never find the others.

J. H. van den Berg,[2] in defining the subconscious, said it's the index of nearness or remoteness in one's relationships with other people. Today it's common to call the unconscious mind the body itself: the cells' receptors, caught in chemical patterns. We're bracketed; we live inside a mise en abyme, falling into our future selves, who fall into our past selves.

In Milan Kundera's *The Unbearable Lightness of Being*,[3] the protagonist Tomas moves from the Nietzschean idea of eternal recurrence, and that "one time is never"—that meaning comes from this recurrence of experience—to the opposite idea that we have one life, one chance; and that we therefore have lightness of being, which is not merely the opposite of "Einmal est keinmal," "one time is never." That is, not "one time is enough," exactly, but rather something closer to "there is no one time"—that the counting of experience, of life in packaged form, is an illusion. So, to revise the adage further: "one time is not never"; or, live your life forward and backward.

This pull forward, like a vacuum: he has to be somewhere, seems not to be anywhere. This splitting, branching, or bifurcating—it seems dissipative, because we're looking at the person as whole. But we miss them in the first place, we suffer from missingness, because of the ways that person's behaviors had grafted into our own subjective sense—into our own experience, which in itself we can never share. We grieve, I think, for that.

The liminal zone between rational thinking and magical thinking widens and becomes itself normative: rationality intrudes but doesn't necessarily frame our lives in missingness. The supernatural realm, on the other hand, seems fickle as always, but that fickleness becomes more personal.

If I think of missingness as vigilance, then I'm persuaded that something important, and not merely something sordid and horrible, awaited Jim Lewis. Not a new life, not escape, but rather some further, sharper definition of who he was. Maybe it didn't include us. It was not a utopian space in the usual sense—a better place, an advancement of the rules Lewis might have wished were in effect. It might be a no-place, utopian in that older, more-accurate sense: a nowhere for dying apart from the faltering of manhood, from the doldrums of midlife.

What was it like to enter into this vigilance, never leaving it for years? For myself, ambivalence kept the searching at a distance from my daily life—and was off altogether for many years; though my dreams, at various periods, were plugged into the mystery, as I would find Jim Lewis coming through the door in various houses, various ways, as if nothing had been wrong.

For Kevin, the search for his father shaped his life. Kevin has idealized the man, choosing his own behaviors to some extent in an effort to be like his father—to recreate the circumstances and environment in which such a man would live. He is masculine, is respectful of the military, and has kept involved in the small-plane and skydiving communities all his life. But he's also searched records, chased after phantoms, interviewed aging soldiers and others, constructed possible narratives, and found the center of his emotional life to be this search.

One becomes a stalker of the missing. Anyone resembling the missing person walks up ahead, in the crowd; you follow, perhaps even embarrass yourself by confronting, and the stranger's affront is a farther distance from the Missing One.

FOOLISH DREAMS

A FEW YEARS ago I drove from Texas to North Carolina to visit my mother, passing through the Tennessee Hill Country south of Nashville, where my mother's ancestors lived back to the 1790s. I'd pinpointed a family cemetery where several are interred. On an earlier trip I'd not succeeded in finding the cemetery. Where it should have been I'd found an outcrop of stones in a disused pasture: uneven, random, dateless slabs of varied shapes.

Though close to cities—under an hour from Nashville, fifteen minutes to Murfreesboro—the area was uncannily old-fashioned-looking and silent. The houses were all prewar, or at least I was blind to newer ones. Even the vehicles seemed antique, and I noticed few traces of a world later than my mother's childhood. The only indications were yard signs: "No Sharia" and Trump placards.

On the second try my wife accompanied me. We visited Bell Buckle, the little town where my mother had been born. Yukiko bought a thrift-store dress, sleeveless with antique floral patterns. We drove around together, back along the deserted road near Jacobs Hollow, where I knew the cemetery had to be, and I realized my map pin from the earlier trip was on the wrong side of the road. I drove up a steep, rutted, gravel driveway on the other side. At the top was a bungalow with many windchimes. A pickup was parked outside, but no one answered my knock. Yukiko and I walked around together, she in the old dress, finding the cemetery behind the house.

The headstones are clustered in the middle and some at the corners, going back to the early nineteenth century, numerous in the mid-to-late nineteenth, less so in the early twentieth, and none past the 1960s. The names match those on my mother's family tree: Jacobs, Todd, Mankin, Summers. I took pictures, and Yukiko took several of me next to various stones. The day was sunny and warm, with just a little wind.

As we worked our way back toward the car, Yukiko paused and

shivered a bit. "Someone's grabbed my ankle," she said, with bother in her voice, but otherwise indicating that it was natural, even to be expected, since we'd lingered in a cemetery. She has at times served as a channel for spirits.

In the cemetery, in her antique dress, lovely and faded-floral, her hair long and still rusty at the ends from an impetuous dye job, Yukiko slowly moved her right leg over the grass, as if lifting something. She got to the end of the field, turned, and meditated as the breeze ruffled her hair. After several minutes, the ghost hand let go. We got in our car and drove on.

When I call that field to memory, it seems somewhere between the ancient outcropping on the opposite side of the road and any random graveyard. It fits between nature and the abstractions of culture and history. The gravestones seem always to have been there, like the ancient rocks. The ghostly hand seems as real as the breezes.

Why does it matter what happened? How does it alter our lives? This passage in Susan Griffin's *Chorus of Stones*[1] holds answers:

> I am beginning to believe that we know everything, that all history, including the history of each family, is part of us, such that, when we hear any secret revealed, a secret about a grandfather, or an uncle, or a secret about the battle of Dresden in 1945, our lives are made suddenly clearer to us, as the unnatural heaviness of unspoken truth is dispersed. For perhaps we are like stones; our own history and the history of the world embedded in us, we hold a sorrow deep within and cannot weep until that history is sung.

Again, the middle distance, that space between here and there, now and then, selves and not-selves: "After so many years of effort to find one's drift," wrote Henry Adams,[2] "the drift found the seeker, and slowly swept him forward and back, with a steady progress oceanwards." Let the ocean be the undercurrent of time that flows always below.

Edward Gaither Jacobs was my mother's sixth-great-grandfather. I can't find an online record of his grave. In my obsessive genealogical searches, I came across a petition for a pension written decades after the Revolutionary War, in which Mr. Jacobs had been a private. "In the year 1777 and in the month of July or August but cannot state which month," starts the narrative, "he was drafted in the militia of the state of Maryland, in the Company Commanded by Capt. Brisco of Montgomery County and recollects that Bazzel Gaither was an officer in the Company to which he belonged but cannot state positively whether he was 1st or 2nd lieutenant."[3] So it continues, with half-remembered names and places, of service first in Maryland for a few months. A few years later, after a move to North Carolina, he was conscripted again. His battle experiences are likewise vague: men running through woods, first this way then that, and perhaps an officer letting them know if they'd been victorious or routed. The feeling is of being caught in weather instead of war.

My mother's father, James Hudson Jacobs, was drafted in 1943, age thirty-eight. He served nearly three years in an artillery unit and was wounded when one of the howitzers hit him on recoil. Kevin found an incomplete set of military records for our grandfather: mostly health reports, and most of those are on his psychiatric care. Medics and MDs wrote notes on the state of his psyche, which from long before his service had been fragile. They recorded his lifelong battle with anxiety, hysteria, and "neurasthenia"—a quaint, catchall diagnostic term, the sickness of civilization. He told them of a breakdown when he was sixteen, working on his father's farm after he left school for good, and the many years of tiredness, emotional breakdowns, and alcoholism that afflicted him through his early adult life. All that, piles, and flat feet—that was his wartime experience while working the big guns.

One of the psychiatrists who talked to my grandfather refers to his "foolish dreams." It seems a particularly nonclinical term. From the account, I can't tell if it's the doctor or my grandfather who refers to them as such. They were dreams of home—foolish because home was so distant for everyone, including the doctor who typed the note. My grandfather, forty years old, was tired and sick, missed his kids, mourned his dead wife, and had never been so far from Tennessee.

In the *Aeneid*, Book VI, we go to the underworld. Aeneas passes into Dis, encountering Grief and Care, Old Age, Fear, Hunger, Pain, Disease—

> Death too, and sleep,
> The brother of death, and terror, and guilty pleasures
> That memory battens on. Also close by that doorway:
> The iron cells of the Furies, death-dealing
> War And fanatical Violence, her viper-tresses astream
> In a bloodstained tangle of ribbons.
> > Right in the middle
> Stands an elm, copious, darkly aflutter, old branches
> Spread wide like arms, and here, it is said,
> False dreams come to roost, clinging together
> On the undersides of the leaves.[4]

A quiet man not meant for war, broken down in youth by harsh work; a widower, his home and three small children far away: my grandfather might have experienced war with such impact. Pa Jacobs was on the grand scale of manhood somewhere in the middle, not great and strong, not shiftless or mean. He was a channel for that softness in the family line, however it comes to us—genes or nurture, blessing or curse.

My mother's brother had a breakdown in the marines, then spent his working life as a meter reader, retiring early in Florida. When I visited him, not long out of college, we went out to the garage so he could show me his masterwork: a huge plywood table carefully transformed into a small town, a quiet place, frozen somewhere in the middle of the last century. Descending onto my uncle's Lionel-train town, you'd find yourself in a lost world soaring, then diving toward a clapboard home with a broad porch that had not appeared until you were below cloud-height; then setting down in shadows, entering a deserted cottage within sight of the town's central steeple, to sit at a hearth that suddenly, magically flickers to life—because you, its focus and reflection, have settled in among the never-born.

OLD SOLDIERS NEVER DIE

SOMEWHERE LEWIS SLIDES along a subterranean track. He sees his mother, Mildred, who died after his disappearance, chiding him for his reckless wandering. Shades of those he killed in war, and others he didn't harm at all: men sliding through hell, or can we call it purgatory, a cosmic Skid Row—condemned to peck at each other, to be chided by the lost and the dead.

"Old soldiers never die, they just fade away," said General MacArthur at the end of his farewell speech, after Truman sacked him. If it's true, it's true of everyone. We wind up divorced from our original purposes. Best if the mark and the displacement combine as chiaroscuro for our flat, static characters. Decay is movement. Let's disappear in stages.

Some leave slowly and without chance of return, peel away into nowhere, leaving no remains, but only movement like a free flame or a bright thread winding out. Francis Ponge, poet of objects, writes in "Snails":[1] "As soon as it rests it withdraws deep into itself"—not dispersal but the terror of inwardness.

"Presences are descendants of souls; they are evoked rather than presented," writes Amélie Rorty.[2] Called forth, called on—from elsewhere, rendering tentative our *here*. Such is the reality of missing persons and those who miss them. They're not forgotten, because their exit vexes indefinitely. To keep them alive and hoped-for, we ourselves must be vexatious. We have to stir, disturb, call forth. In the end, it's magical thinking. No one is simply "there"—someone else must desire their presence.

Old soldiers never die because it's a way of life that disappears before the person. The process of making a warrior, the modern type of warrior, grafts the individual into the machine. Retirement can't undo that. The individual—especially someone like Lewis, who enlisted as a child—can't possibly rewind to that point of innocence. There's no self to resolve, for it has been grown over with rules, structures, work-arounds—with a virtuality that won't work outside the system it was made for.

I grew up in the military and never desired to be a soldier. Many brats grow up to enlist. I thought such a life would break me. Let it also be a dialectic posture: to seek within and outside myself the antipodes of such men as those who made and raised me. Hippie culture sprouting like daisies: It was both attractive and embarrassing. The attraction and embarrassment go together, as when lovers undress the first time. Counterculture in the sixties, when I was a preteen, was the near-exotic: sounds and sights of something fun outside the fortress. Protest was one chord, part of the zeitgeist, the sensibility. That light switch counteroffensive of Lewis's in the living room, a few years later, that was against the infiltration of sensibility, the longer locks of hair, the acid rock, the paisleys on my shirt—paisleys!—seed pods of dissent, madness, corruption.

A public-service television commercial circa 1970 showed several old men climbing a hill: politicians, diplomats, corporate executives, all in business suits. At the top of the hill, two of them take off their jackets and slug it out, pathetically. At the ad's conclusion, words appear on screen: "Wouldn't it be great if all wars were fought this way?"

Maybe they took it from Remarque's *All Quiet on the Western Front*:[3] "Kropp on the other hand is a thinker. He proposes that a declaration of war should be a kind of popular festival with entrance-tickets and bands, like a bull fight. Then in the arena the ministers and generals of the two countries, dressed in bathing-drawers and armed with clubs, can have it out among themselves. Whoever survives, his country wins. That would be much simpler and more just than this arrangement, where the wrong people do the fighting." That they'll fade away, before or after they die, is illustrated by the lives of warriors like Napoleon, of whom it was said that his mind let go increasingly, during exile, of reality—of the supreme virtuality, the virtuality of *virtu* in fact, that he'd shaped and commanded so winningly—"until in the end he became involved in a world of chimeras," as Guglielmo Ferrero[4] put it.

In college I kept a passage from one of John Adams's letters to Abigail[5] above my desk. It was a page out of a *TV Guide* advertising public television: "I must study politics and war, that my sons may have liberty to study mathematics and philosophy. My sons ought to study mathematics and philosophy, geography, natural history and naval architecture, navigation, commerce, and agriculture, in order to give their children a right to study painting, poetry, music, architecture, statuary, tapestry, and porcelain." Skipping, in my case, the math and engineering, and leaving the tapestry and architecture to my betters. Adams's words appealed to me, removed from context, because they seemed an argument against the warrior's way, or an argument against giving it more than provisional worth. I wasn't giving much thought to poetry's sometimes-bellicose history, and I wasn't too focused on the sense of sacrifice—or, on the meaning of that provisional existence to a single man or woman, or to the nation that was not yet. I don't see anything now but the provisional, operative states. The nation, possibly at risk more from within than without, is eternally contingent on so many contradictory elements—how can it be saved? How was it ever born?

Lewis was brave. He could be cruel or kind; but the bravery, the great heart—I felt it in him even when my fear was dominant.

Clausewitz[6] says: "FIRMNESS denotes the resistance of the will in relation to the force of a single blow, STAUNCHNESS in relation to a continuance of blows. Close as is the analogy between the two, and often as the one is used in place of the other, still there is a notable difference between them which cannot be mistaken, inasmuch as firmness against a single powerful impression may have its root in the mere strength of a feeling, but staunchness must be supported rather by the understanding." I like that for looking closer at who my stepfather was. "Staunchness"—it has the sense of something water-tight, solid, impermeable. But if we take staunchness as a strength that carries over through numerous blows, not from feeling but from *understanding*—there, I'm getting somewhere. If we want to find Lewis, we have to find out what he understood, and if he lost that understanding, or if it carried him through to where our own understanding couldn't take us.

This ratio between feeling and understanding might be the same as that of reality and actuality. Not direct correspondence, but a ratio: In a world out of balance, how do we find it? How do we maintain it? That's our journey into the middle distance. That's the risk of getting lost.

WORLDNESS

BARBARA NEWHALL FOLLETT published a magical novel at age twelve. At twenty-six she walked away from her husband and never returned. Follett's *The House Without Windows*[1] is the story of a child, Eepersip, whose desire to escape home and family is so powerful, so preternaturally willful, she *becomes* the wilderness. A few years into her escape, hearing that her parents have had another daughter, Eepersip slips back into the home to spirit the child away, though she returns her soon after.

It's an aggressive tale, posed sharply between its too-muchness and its innocence, like the best fairy tales. Follett's mother gave her daughter's papers to Columbia two decades later: a gesture at shaping the body of her daughter as a body of work, to "undo a disappearance" as Laura Smith sees it in *The Art of Vanishing*. [2]

Follet's father, Wilson Follett, published a mournful letter in *The Atlantic* a year or so after the disappearance.[3] "This sky, in the sector where you should be," he writes, "has now been misshapen for one whole round of the seasons; and by memory and reminder there has been telescoped into this single year all that I was ever able to have of you and share with you in the twenty-five before it."

The land of the missing in Maria Semple's *Where'd You Go, Bernadette*[4] is the purity of last resorts. The mother is a former architect who gave up work for motherhood. Years later she absconds to Antarctica: an escape as pursuit of scale to counter the sense of self that has shrunk in her dormancy. The lastness, vastness, and blankness are beautiful without proof. The round Earth has no end, but the continent of ice will suffice. Of its icebergs, Bee, the missing woman's daughter, says: "There was something unspeakably noble about their age, their scale, their lack of consciousness, their right to exist." Bee and her father find Bernadette by finding her missingness. The icebergs fill the heart with sadness and wonder. It's the sublime extremely chilled, taking us out of ourselves. Bee wants to "stretch it out as long as possible," bring missingness to the breaking point of possibility.

In *Mardi* Herman Melville[5] follows his protagonist's obsessive search for the missing Yillah, a mysterious princess/goddess of the South Seas. Yillah is human, divine, localized, environmental. Her disappearance fits a ritual timeline of which the protagonist knows nothing; yet his ecstatic lyricisms keep her present even as he seeks her body across ocean and islands.

The expansiveness of absence, particularly under the sky of love, makes the Missing One equal to the space we search. "Besides, what cared I now for the green groves and bright shore? Was not Yillah my shore and my grove? My meadow, my mead, my soft shady vine, and my arbor?" So also is Yillah doubled: "But so etherealized had she become from the wild conceits she nourished, that she verily believed herself a being of the lands of dreams. Her fabulous past was her present." The novel in this long section is threaded with repeated variations on the phrase "No Yillah was there" as the sailors wander: a rhythm in missingness that deepens the depths, broadens the expanse, enriches the adventure.

In a world where divinity is distance under broad, round skies, vanishing is the wave of some divine hand: a flick of the bangled wrist, a blink of the all-seeing eye. Yillah is horizon and the pull past horizons. Yillah is the widening of its circle into metaphysics. Later, her drowning is his despair already closing the horizon. His search beyond death is like the searching of Orpheus, Odysseus, and Aeneas.

When I was fourteen, I came upon a novel called *Walking Davis* by David Ely,[6] the author of *Seconds*. The titular hero, an Iowan, walks around the Earth, initially as a promotion for a local business. Davis abandons his purpose but keeps walking, entering the dimension of world-walkers, leaving this world behind—continually, as it were.

Davis has learned how different the walking-world is—how the trees and hills move and are as alive as we. He's been arrested, released, taken for a messiah, rejected and chased by his followers. He's walked across much of Britain on crutches, in a fugue state. He's been swallowed by an earthquake in Turkey and fallen in and out of love.

But Davis keeps walking. His steps are not merely forward. Each is a reason unto itself. For the world-walker, his middle distance is a coalescence of the cosmos. Here and there invade each other, cancel each other.

The world reveals its worldness to Walking Davis. After he's transcended the mundane challenges, Davis seems to enter into a different dimension—one in which the world offers wonders obscure to our ordinary existence. The world he walks on is alive. In the Gobi Desert, he senses a double, a shadow. An ex–world-walker who has graduated to stillness tells him the double is Death itself. Walking is mortal, the boulder man tells Davis. Simply standing is immortal.

"Motion," wrote Elias Canetti,[7] "is most likely a remedy for incipient paranoia." Pascal,[8] conversely, said that our miseries stem from our inability to remain quietly in a room. The stranger, the nomad, the hobo, the world-walker are pilgrims steering for a point both in and out of this world—"absorbing the sweet and far from meaningless Siren songs of the world," says Gerald Ladner,[9] "without being deflected from the right course."

"If wandering," asks Georg Simmel in "The Stranger,"[10] "is the liberation from every given point in space, and thus the conceptual opposite to fixation at such a point, the sociological form of the 'stranger' presents the unity, as it were, of these two characteristics." We're condensations, vectors, saliences. "Although he has not moved on," Simmel continues, "he has not quite overcome the freedom of coming and going." It's the stranger's potential for wandering that matters, and his possible importations: qualities he has borne, qualities that threaten the new group.

These are the traders, the immigrants, with new goods, new language, new blood. The stranger brings nearness and farness. The least common element of our humanity is the most essential and the most unnerving.

Cicero argues in the *Tusculan Disputations*[11] that there's no intermediate condition between existence and nonexistence. I say the intermediate condition is who we are.

Achilles's spirit dreads death more than slavery. Odysseus wants to return in his next life as a quiet man. It's our own choice, for no god or demon forces us to it. The middle distance is refusing to become either a beast or a god. Just to be a human—and from there, where next? Disappearance disturbs the careful balance between universal and particular. Is knowledge possible if the blinders, the brokenness, the fadedness, the perspective, the occult framing, be removed? We know what we know because of limits. How do we keep changing limits, without falling into the abyss?

One kind of missing-persons story is of people who disappear before one's very eyes. New England is a region rich with such lore. In a typical tale, the hiker walks over the crest of a hill, down the other side, followed by a hiking partner, who, upon reaching the same hill crest, sees no one on the trail ahead.

We have in the center of the narrative a resistance to physical law. It's important that it's in the story, this resistance. From the story we don't really know the event itself. We don't see the spot, we don't feel the perceptions and enter the awareness of the hikers. So it is in every narrative from true life. We have this whirlpool of mystery, however small: that someone walked ahead and vanished.

Ambrose Bierce liked to write sudden-disappearance stories. In each, someone walks or runs on a path or across a field, is perhaps observed from a distance, and vanishes—as if a wormhole opened and swallowed them, and the observers, looking, find no trace.

Sometimes such stories are given a frame of reportorial hearsay. Bierce used the frame somewhat, but others used his stories—especially "The Difficulty of Crossing a Field"[12]—as an ersatz origin story, though of questionable provenance. It's a trick of the press, flaring the boundary between news and lore.

In the abovenamed story, an Alabama slaveholder leaves his porch, crosses a road, and enters a field opposite. He vanishes—that is, the few who saw him enter the field claim to have seen and then not seen Williamson in the field. Williamson's wife, running out of the house after her vanished man, goes mad. At an inquest, the people working in the field, all enslaved, are reported not to have seen

Williamson at all (he, who didn't see their humanity). A neighbor, Wren, says what he didn't see, and that's all. Williamson is declared dead so his property can be dealt with.

The story, in Bierce's framing, is deceptively blank and reportorial—a swirl around a drain. Such stories might simply remind us of our smallness in space as well as time.

Such a story reads like the condensation or compression of slower vanishings, including those that are the speed of life, decay, and dying—that we're all here, then not, in this room, on this Earth. Live burials and locked-room mysteries are similar compressions, and so symbolic of the overall singularity of this life as gesture, as parabolic mark, rhyme of birth with death.

In 1925, Colonel Percy Fawcett disappeared on his sixth expedition into the Amazon. He was searching for the lost city he called Z. Ian Fleming's brother James took part in one of several search missions. "It had been great fun," Fleming[13] wrote, "and very funny. Reality is a commodity hard to come by: and, when found, not always easily recognizable." Within that slant of mind, the search itself goes missing.

The plot of V. S. Pritchett's 1937 adventure novel *Dead Man Leading*[14] resembles the true-life tale of Fawcett. Pritchett's novel follows three men, one the son of a British explorer who disappeared in the Amazon seventeen years earlier. The son, Johnson, finds the forest baffling, for it mirrors him in disconcerting ways. The trees are human, or concealed humans, "or animals, their eyes as fine and narrow as needles glinting with note taken of him." That life, human or animal, shows Johnson scenes of his own life: not hallucinations, but an amplitude of memories "breathed out thickly, heavy with brooding and weighted with significance"; the trees hold his thoughts, fears, and embarrassments, "so that looking back one would dread to return that way." The two men he travels with, each caught in their own purposes, are small as fleas—recursively, as if "the world was a gorgeous tiger"; that recursion is where place is formed between the everything of space and the anything of mind.

Johnson's father is everywhere around him. His father is "the man of the last seventeen years or more, the man they knew nothing about, a vacancy rather than a man. He was all the things one did not know." The son has grown up in that vacancy, and in the jungle he awaits his father's judgment.

B. Traven wrote of adventure and heroism in service to the Common Man—the Worker, the Revolutionary, the Exile. To do so, he found it necessary to hide himself from the world according to various stratagems: connecting with others through varied names; resisting notoriety by limiting as much as possible any connection to photographic evidence, quotation, or definitive biography; telling autobiographical lies; confusing the matter of his origins and nationality; and living abroad. Traven disappeared, in other words, into his work: his novels, and through the likely deployment of alter egos, their publication and translation into film.

You might call Traven the inverse of a missing person. Long dead, he still goes missing as one looks for him. The most likely name for Traven, prior to his self-creation as such, seems to have been Ret Marut, a writer, anarchist, and actor forced to run from the agents of the Kaiser. That name, too, might have been an alias.

The heroic act, the sacrifice, in Traven's case, we might define as actions against the state—the tendency, or rather the most-absolute fact of modern identity: that we all go by a name and carry identification; that we must admit to a definite, linear series of biographical facts.

Vanishing was itself the trail he followed. Biographer Karl Guthke[15] quotes Marut from just before the advent of Traven:

> As soon as I feel the hour of death approaching, I will crawl like an animal into the heart of the bush where no one can follow me. There, with great devotion and reverence, I will wait for infinite wisdom. I will then die without a sound, crossing over amid stillness and silence to the great unity from which I first came. And I will be thankful to the gods if they allow hungry vultures and outcast dogs to eat their fill on my corpse, so that not even a single white bone remains.

Such a proclamation to the self feels pure, or a reaching out to purity; a gesture beyond understanding. It was 1918 and the world was hinged to its destruction. It doesn't apply to the literal hour of death, but to the hour of death such as one carries it through life, a much-rubbed coin.

Recently a man whose body went unidentified for months was finally connected to his name. Vance Rodriguez, as a trail hiker, had taken the handle "Mostly Harmless." Hikers and web-sleuths solved the puzzle of his prior life by fanning out in digital rather than physical space. The most alluring stories are the ones with the details left out. Objects and faces can be prettier in the half light. We see a faint shape and add the lines and shadows we want. We hear one part of a story and add another part we hope might be true. But crowdsourcing, the hive mind, denies the gaps. Will the wilderness resist its digital translations of satellite imaging, data, surveillance, near-infinite triangulation, microchipping, heat-seeking, DNA divination, and more to come?

Rodriguez named himself with slight understatement. He turns out to have been a man with a dark side: if not a sociopath, then someone most detached from those who were closest. Going into the wilderness might have been to seek a cure, a punishment, or which came first.

Nicholas Thompson[16] interviewed one of the online searchers, asking if she was bothered by what she learned of the man named Rodriguez. "I don't think I was committed to Vance as a human," she answered. "I was committed to solving the case with others because it would be a great way to prove that people can do great things together." It was the internet proving itself. We're less its citizens than we are its synapses. The searcher was, in this case at least, an idealist, but only within the virtual. She kept the real Vance Rodriguez at a safe, digital distance.

In my default imaginary world, everything's a forest. Gradually clearings appear, then mountains farther off. The sound of a stream marks off a perceptible distance to my right. The remnants of a stone wall form a frozen stream under the trees. The mountains, the rumor of the water, the stone wall: all are the map of the place they form. In this mental woods, the map is the territory, and there's no life except on the map.

One can be unsure of one's location, Kenneth Hill[17] tells us, but still know how to become unlost. "'Knowing where you are,' Hill says, actually means 'knowing the way,' rather than being able to pinpoint your location on a map." This is fundamental the way language is fundamental: that we communicate through iterations of signal and noise, not sure of where we are in the instant, nor sure of what comes next.

In the desert wilderness our middle distance has the cast of geologic time. In the forest wilderness it's biologic time that shadows our movements. We find we're kin to everything, and everything makes demands. Everything beckons, tempts, threatens, enchants. In the desert we're inside a giant lens, enchanted by every cousin-atom of the air, by every stirring thing. Our circumambience attenuates and becomes mirage.

Roderick Nash[18] thought *wilderness* came from an ancient word that also led to *will*. Thus, wilderness is of the self-willed. When a willful human enters the wilderness, it's a test of wills. Wilderness was sanctuary from the sinful society. Wilderness was where one found and drew closer to God, a testing ground where a chosen people were purged, humbled, and made ready for the land of promise. Becoming wild is surviving, growing stronger and freer.

In Peter Weir's film adaptation of *Picnic at Hanging Rock*, the teenage girls trip toward a winding path into the massive stones towering above. They cross a stream between their waking lives and the dream about to swallow them whole. The camera slows. Each light leap across the stream takes a second longer than it should. More than a ribbon of water has been crossed. The disappearance has already announced itself. Unfathomable in human terms, it will never find solution. Yet it's also the most natural thing to occur if we forget they're human. It happens all the time, at varying speeds faster, slower, and perpendicular to our own. It happens all the time somewhere beyond a single human view, within others' lives shattered or rent by circumstance. A breeze or a hurricane swallows the sound of it. Evidence of the violence is swept away before we turn the corner and catch a glimpse. Whole lives, whole worlds escape our knowing.

From the rocks' point of view, how could the girls disappear if they were never there? In Lindsay's novel,[19] the threshold itself approaches: "Mr. Hussey was reduced to looking knowingly at the shadow of the Hanging Rock which ever since luncheon had been creeping down towards the Picnic Grounds on the flat." Or the threshold moves up—and one moves through it, all the same, by holding still: "The immediate impact of its soaring peaks induced a silence so impregnated with its powerful presence that even Edith was struck dumb." But it might also simply be a door, a birth channel, a port of vision, or an eye: "Irma at once discovered a sort of porthole in one of the rocks and was gazing down fascinated at the Picnic Grounds below."

Then, near the moment of disappearance, they experience again the fairy-tale sleep that signals passage into another world: "Suddenly overcome by an overpowering lassitude, all four girls flung themselves down on the gently sloping rock in the shelter of the monolith, and there fell into a sleep so deep that a horned lizard emerged from a crack to lie without fear in the hollow of Marion's outflung arm."

Albert, the young fellow who witnesses the girls' threshold-crossing at the brook, who falls in love with the eldest as she passes, spends a night alone at the Rock. His own crossing is aborted, though he suffers one night of bewilderment. He reflects further—channeling some deeper insight Lindsay wants us to receive through him: "A search with dogs and trackers and policemen was only one way of looking, perhaps not even the right way. It might even end, if it ever did end, in a sudden unexpected finding that had nothing to do with all this purposeful seeking." What's the other way of looking? If this narration comes from the verge of Albert's own growing awareness, it's all he brings back from his failed attempt to pass the threshold. We find something different from the thing we seek. He himself is all that remains of the girl Miranda, echoing her nonexistence, creating her backward within his and our imagination. The one thing to prove any of this is real is the Rock itself.

Disappearance consumes Weir's film. The characters, except for the Aboriginal who appears briefly in the search party, are a thin illusion by the end of the film, cast tentatively over the world of stones and insects and the endless dream-time that shapes the faces of the stones like ripples in murky water. The girls walk; their angle is upward, their clothes airy and sky-colored, their faces beatific.

Henry Green's novel *Concluding*[20] also takes place in a girl's school, though in some near-future England gone slightly authoritarian. As we wake one morning at the start of the novel, two girls are missing. Though there will be nothing supernatural about their fates as in *Picnic*, the missingness is still unreal: matters of atmosphere and tropic energy more than plot. The staff talk of the missing girls in a way that shows no purpose but to deny and delay. "And all the while a line of girls fetched their breakfasts, served themselves, the sleep from which they had just come a rosy moss upon their lips, the heavy tide of dreams on each in a flow of her eighteen summers, and which would ebb now only with their first cup." One girl, Merode (all the girls' names begin with M—for Missing?), is found early in the story, in a bed of weeds, disheveled, pajamas slightly torn. She's been offered back, somewhat like the spared girl, Irma, in *Picnic*.

A retired scientist, Mr. Rock, inhabits a cottage on the grounds with his daughter—his residence a reward for service to the nation. Mr. Rock is hard of hearing. His deafness frames a zone of ambiguity in the novel, though there are other, visual layers of indeterminacy. Rock is rationality, fixedness, but also haze. He's our lens into the natural frame that, as in *Picnic*, should be counted as main character of the story: its glare and spill, sudden sunlight and branching networks that seem a tangle to the mind.

"Disappearance," the Alaskan poet Sheila Nickerson[21] writes, "is the place we go when we are ready, or forced, to throw down language and measurement." Something there is that can't be measured or contained but only entered. Cabeza de Vaca, says Rebecca Solnit,[22] "ceased to be lost not by returning but by turning into something else." But we know Cabeza de Vaca did return, healer not conqueror, one of the children of the sun until, one more time, the state reabsorbed him. Missingness had been his salvation if he'd stayed in the desert.

Lew Welch, Beat poet, left a note of departure somewhere between suicide and pure exit. The exit might be to die. It might also be new life—a wandering, an apotheosis, though the negativity of the note to Gary Snyder does tilt toward self-destruction: "I never could make anything work out right and now I'm betraying my friends. I can't make anything out of it—never could. I had great visions but never could bring them together with reality. I used it all up. It's all gone." I have such feelings often, and sometimes I feel the fever of a desire for annihilation burning in the back of my skull. For me it's there instead of in the brow. After a few instructions as to his material effects monetary and otherwise ("I don't owe Allen G. anything yet nor my Mother"), Welch says, simply, "I went Southwest. Goodbye. Lew Welch." Into the Sierra Nevadas he went, with a revolver.[23]

Was it satori or breakdown? Was he driven out by the din of the tribe? Can we assume his missingness was the powerful will not to be found—to leave no body but the body of his work? Or is it the Earth's great appetite that has taken him away?

In Atwood's *Surfacing* the narrator's father, an anthropologist, has gone missing. She goes north with her husband and friends, alienated from the three companions and finally disappearing from them altogether. We only ever know her as She, and she speaks, sees the world, with feral directness. Remembering a scene from childhood, she describes her father playing hide-and-seek in the dark: "It was different from playing in the house, the space to hide in was endless; even when we knew which tree he had gone behind there was the fear that what would come out when you called would be someone else." The father has left drawings of Indigenous art—petroglyphs, though the young people don't know at first what they are. Without knowledge of the father's research, they see the drawings as an alienness out of the absent father's brain. But they're indeterminate, not alien. The outer layer of missingness is of an entire people, their trails lost in the seeming randomness of trees and rocks, their art tattooing the high rocks and floating in stillness on the lower rocks below the surface of the lake.

The absent father isn't far. It's like waiting for a knock on the door, for his presence is the life of the forest. Finding what secrets the wilderness tells is finding the father, whether his body returns or not. "Daddy! I'm here! I'm going to find you!" she shouts into the forest—as if a child, and his absence a game of hide-and-seek.

After the husband finds the first petrographs, high above the water, he falls and injures himself. His discovery is a sacrifice to the father, to the wilderness. The effort to return him and the others to civilization defines the isolation the daughter needs, on returning to the wilderness, to submerge herself and find evidence; to be the arrow that points at the discovery of the lost society. Her father's corpse, when she finds it while swimming, is pointed toward one of the rock drawings submerged beneath the lake's surface.

Why transform? Because, as Atwood says, the father has realized he was an intruder. The cabin, the fences, the fires and paths were violations. Now his own fence excludes him, as logic excludes love. "I say Father," she speaks to the wilderness. "He turns towards me and it's not my father. It is what my father saw, the thing you meet when you've stayed here too long alone." Wilderness is timelessness, as in dream, tangled and choked in the forest undergrowth. It's the immediacy of trauma. "I am not an animal or a tree, I am the thing in which the trees and animals move and grow, I am a place." She disappears, hides from her friends; injures herself, such that she can "feel the blood swelling out like sap"—so has she disappeared. The father has been found, not in his corpse, but in the way he found what he'd sought in the woods and waters.

"But nothing has died," she tells herself, "everything is alive, everything is waiting to become alive."

FLYING ON FUMES

"THE MARCH OF the mind is not direct," says Alfred de Vigny[1] in a journal entry from 1833, "for if its flight were in a straight line, it would lose itself in the infinite beyond." Travelers in a maze perceive their situation differently from someone flying above. In flight, viewing the wonderful design of things, we see our minds and escape anxiety. In flight, we see the confusion from above and laugh at how simple it really was.

Hammett's Flitcraft is a sort of aviator. He flits, but his craft is one without resistance to the actual forces in his life that he conflates with the dangerous disorder represented by the falling beam. Flitcraft has no resistance, thus no true direction either forward or backward; and no altitude, no way to be the beam, the airfoil—anything that torques, bends, threatens to break. There is no flying without the alternative tale of falling.

How high is too high? Chang-Rae Lee's hero in *Aloft*, Jerry Battle, is a man who takes to the air to feel "the shuddery lift of the wingtips in my hands" and to look down "just this middle distance on the world, this fetching, ever-mitigating length"—for that's the challenge: to manipulate the distances, to adjust one's nearness or farness from one's own life.

Flying, temporary escape, putting wings on the beam—it's hardly necessary in our time to abscond outright. Jerry Battle, in any case, is familiar with missingness, and somewhat later than the passage above, he confesses: "I am disappearing. But let me reveal a secret. I have been disappearing for years." This is more than the usual trope for alienation. Jerry's brother was MIA in Vietnam, a family tragedy that provides deep background to Jerry's own slow vanishing. An English adventurer, Sir Harold Clarkson-Ickes, floats at a few brief spots above the main narrative in his hot-air balloon, going missing in the news and in the periphery of Battle's own flights of detachment.

The flying body is lighter than our ground body. One thinks and feels a little differently, because perspective reflects a stronger sense of our smallness, but also of our potential—and because the middle distance is shown to be more than two-dimensional. Flow is all around us, including below. A tilt up or down tells our organs that the slightest change in elevation changes the world-path we're on.

It's a vision I've had In small planes rather than big jets. The frailty of a Piper Cub, its thin skin, the sexual power of the joystick, the sense, through the vibrations, that flying is a form of prayer: some of us feel it even in the jetliners, but in a small plane, faith has to do more of the work. Jane Mendelsohn's fictional aviator in *I Was Amelia Earhart*[2] muses of her aircraft: "Planes used to be vehicles for dreaming. They were strong and curvaceous, manly and womanly at the same time, simple, almost old-fashioned mechanical toys and vessels carrying the future."

As a mere passenger, I put that faith in Lewis's piloting skills—his knowledge, his keen senses, his grit and toughness that would see us through. Riding with him made me appreciate more his manner on the ground, though it had often chafed and bruised me in our grounded life. James Lewis in the air was more balanced between his solid and fluid selves. His mind and spirit led the way forward in air, instead of drawing in, grappling, binding with force toward his own dark center.

Lee's novel is a celebration of family. The balance of real and virtual is undisturbed at the end. Atwood's heroine goes totally wild, animal-like, pure; Auster's heroes slowly disappear, within nested disappearances that disappear. Lee's hero, though, discovers that there's no disappearing outside of death. Family, however damaged and hurting, gives us our coordinates: "This sprawly little realm as laden with situations not simply dangerous and baleful; it's the fact that no matter how fast or how high you might keep moving, the full array of those potentialities are constantly targeting your exact coordinates, and with extreme prejudice." After Jerry Battle has lost his daughter in that rarified air, but saved the baby she birthed and gathered his father and hapless brother and his brother's family under one roof, his resolve is simple: *I'll go solo no more, no more.*

What will Amelia Earhart's status be if they get a few millimeters closer to the truth—those who've spent so much time and money on their hobby? If they find her bones, her DNA, some definitive scrap of the plane, some evidence of her partner Fred Noonan: What will become of her if they solve the mystery? Has the mystery itself, the unsolved puzzle, become the person?

"Their disappearances," says Katrina Gulliver[3] of notable missing persons, "allow us to create a narrative, to get much closer to them than we ever did before by creating fates for them." After so many decades as Queen of the Missing, is it possible that Amelia Earhart can ever be found, no matter what evidence? Amelia Earhart is still aloft. The world is still rounded by her flying, but as much by her having flown into oblivion.

Mendelsohn's Earhart tells her story in first- and third-person—for Earhart sees herself from far away, we're told. It makes for an angle of perspective in which the reader, adding Noonan's character, can triangulate the missing couple's location—not in geographic space, but in the realm of possibility.

She makes a microworld, a world with edifices representing achievements like her own marvel of flight around the world: The Hoover Dam, the Eiffel Tower, there in the sand, in miniature. Was her flying escape or apotheosis? In Mendelsohn's fantasia, Earhart's eventual happiness—the trials of heat, hunger, anger, blame, boredom, madness—is a long path to Heaven, as they name their island. But it's not heaven. It's as perfectly middle as can be. "I'll only have Noonan and my Electra," says Earhart, "and I'll live on a desert island. And I'll be lost in the between, in the emptiness of the between, with the threats and the moments of radiant danger, the perfect days, the oases, the furious whisper of the night wind in the trees, the happiness, my fears, the imminent dawn."

Each of us is enlarged by the times if we get to high ground. The meaningful world we inhabit is bracketed by security and risk: home on one side, adventure on the other. But they can transpose, invert; one becomes the other. That's ecstasy, being-beyond, movement of the soul, without which our stable, stationed existence couldn't exist. Missingness is the baffle between.

Helen Macdonald's *Vesper Flights*[4] captures that transposition. The vesper flight is the swifts' high glide at dusk, perhaps while sleeping or half sleeping. "At this panoptic height," Macdonald writes, "they can see the scattered patterns of the stars overhead, and at the same time they can calibrate their magnetic compasses, getting their bearings according to the light-polarization patterns that are strongest and clearest in twilit skies." All of it—"stars, wind, polarized light, magnetic cues, the distant stacks of clouds a hundred miles out, clear cold air"—all of it, the totality of the world below, "tilting toward sleep or waking toward dawn," allows the swifts to "work out exactly where they are, to know what they should do next." But the mind does this all the time, prising moment from moment, here from here, thousands of times a day when we're free men and women, soaring to heights. When we're free.

"Three hundred and fifty miles can be no distance in a plane," says Beryl Markham in *West with the Night*,[5] "or it can be from where you are to the end of the earth." Markham, too, as Macdonald does in studying the swifts, notes well the importance of amplitude, of detail, of the variability of phenomena. "If it is night, it depends on the depth of the darkness and the height of the clouds, the speed of the wind, the stars, the fullness of the moon. It depends on you, if you fly alone—not only on your ability to steer your course or to keep your altitude, but upon the things that live in your mind while you swing suspended between the earth and the silent sky."

Lewis liked to fly on fumes. He crash-landed and swam away once that I know of, but a man who flew with him decades ago as an adolescent told Kevin that my stepfather let his fuel tanks get near-empty many times. I suppose it was a test of his skill, but how could he play that game with a passenger on board—a teenager, a child? I imagine someone who's come close to death, who's seen others die or nearly die, might develop a keener sense of the edges. The whole journey, in his mind, might have been on that edge.

Flying home to North Carolina after a visit to Texas, Lewis crashed in Lake Waco. He wrote a detailed account of the incident for his insurance company:

On June 19, 1976, I lost power in my 1946 Globe Swift after taking off from Madison/Cooper Airport in Waco, Texas. The engine was idling at 800–900 rpms. I went through the routine steps: pulled carburetor heat, and got on the wobble fuel pump, to no effect. The state of Texas is, for the most part, one large landing area, but I was over Lake Waco. The beach was full of people. I steered away from a houseboat and landed in the lake. The aircraft almost immediately began to sink. I got out through the window and was hit by the tail of the plane. I could swim, but the Swift could not.

Much of the man comes through in this report: facts, cool reason, requisite Texas pride, a parting joke. In fact, according to one news account,[6] he was twenty feet down before he got out of the plane. If we ever make a cenotaph, I vote we put these words on the plaque.

Robert MacFarlane,[7] writing of Antoine de St. Exupery's aerial aesthetics, gives us the sharp, gleaming, squared Greek word *katasco-pos*—which, in MacFarlane's usage, is a seeing from above. It's a release from trivialities, he says. That's what flying feels like, at least in a small plane: a sense of permeability, that there's more in a defined area than what our eyes see. Volo leads to flying and wishing. The wishing part is the membrane between magic and physics.

In a used-bookstore in Saratoga I found a small Penguin[8] paperback on the subject of flight. It was by an engineer, in a series published in the fifties with the purpose of explaining the modern technological world. It was very technical, but straightforward and unrelenting in its attempt to make its subject real in every possible detail.

I read it, as I do such books, for the deepest possible metaphors of whatever I could attach to the subject. It's my desire to find animated presence in what seem, rationally, to be abstract and random processes. Flight was meant to be. It's spirit and it has to do with more than levitation of bodies above the ground—for it was, earlier still, atmospheric and cosmic forces that shaped us. "Yet the pure physics of flight was still simple," wrote Norman Mailer,[9] "simple and pleased with itself as a Greek statue," granting the endeavor life as well as elegance. The elegance is its rightness.

People imagined flight long before they could fly. They dreamed of cinema and in the form of cinema long before the invention of moving pictures. The little Penguin book shows the decades before Bleriot and the Wright brothers were a long spell of busyness spent sorting the details. A few people knew what it would take to fly, but they had to fine-tune the physics, chemistry, metallurgy, mathematics.

Lewis was a muscular reader of various subjects, but mostly flight. When he met my mother, he was enrolled at the University of Maryland correspondence-school program. Around the house, on the side tables, nightstand, coffee table, kitchen table, in the bathroom, and piled in drawers were dozens of flying magazines, manuals, histories of flight, and other materials. The magazines were always folded and creased at a particular page, showing Lewis's progress at absorption of every word. No one moved the magazines without permission. Each one was a work in progress, all toward the advancement of his knowledge and passion. It was a performance in pure democracy.

For the second time, barely seventeen, Lewis enlisted, this time in the regular Army. He did his basic training at Fort Chaffee, Arkansas, in 1957 and started his skydiving career in April 1958 at Fort Campbell, Kentucky. He had his first freefall there in December 1959, and soon after he was one of the first people to freefall in combat gear.

The earliest memory I have of my stepfather is his model planes. They were small but very real, balsawood and paint, small struts and wings, intricate engines, acrid fuel. He carved with an X-Acto knife, assembled, painted, then flew them by himself, all of it himself, though we could watch. It was a lovely theater—in part because I could spy on my stepfather from a safe, sideways angle. He was intent and focused on his labors, narrowed into them, one with the materials. I admired his love of the materials and his purpose, though I couldn't yet integrate that feeling with my fear of the man. But it drew me in, and I imagined riding in that small plane, as I did ride years later in the planes Lewis learned to fly.

The bright-red model dominated the dining table for weeks, and my mother dared not complain. We ate off TV trays. That balsa-wood plane was a toy. But it had such intense being, such shimmering reality and personhood. Its weight, though I could never touch or hold it; its various smells—of the bare wood, then the varnish, and the oil and fuel it consumed; even its interiority—that no one could inhabit its cabin, that it flew for itself, made it heavy with life.

I've read that the invention of the wheel might have come about through the construction of a toy by a mother to occupy the hands of her child. When I think of the model plane, and my stepfather's leap into real planes years later, I think he was creating himself. In Plato's *Laws*,[10] the Athenian says: "The soul of the child in his play should be guided to the love of that sort of excellence in which when he grows up to manhood he will have to be perfected." But it's not so linear. We're adult and child at the same time, each working back against the other.

The adventure movie *Flight of the Phoenix* puts a plane-load of oil-company employees down in the North African desert. Jimmy Stewart's the pilot—our balance between adventurous and familiar, fighter and father. In the elaborate effort to repair the damaged plane, a German engineer among the passengers leads the effort. The others think he's made real planes, but the most delightful moment of the film is not when the jury-rigged thing gets aloft, but a bit earlier, when the others realize the bespectacled fellow is a maker of toys.

In a small neighborhood park in Fayetteville in 1965, we watched Lewis fly the model plane he had painstakingly built. When we drove over to the neighborhood park, he let us watch as he set up the plane and managed the radio controls, flying above the trees. It crashed, and he was grim but silent as he gathered the pieces. Again we watched at the kitchen table as he rebuilt the plane.

By 1974, in the postwar doldrums of the all-volunteer army, Lewis was briefly put to pasture overseeing regional recruiting offices north of Charlotte, North Carolina. The job left him with spare time, so he finally got around to taking flying lessons. He spent almost all his waking hours in the air after he flew solo and got his first license.

Though planes had always been the idols in our house, skydiving was religion. Lewis had been a founding member of the Army Parachute Team. Jumping was how he made contact with the world as a young soldier, winning awards and trophies on four continents, shaking hands with statesmen and royals, getting his name and face in the newspapers.

Lunday was also a skydiver, so when Lewis entered the family, taking my father's place, it made sense that men spent their weekends jumping out of aircraft while their families waited, staring up at the sky from the edge of the field. Wives sat in folding chairs, craning their necks and visoring their eyes. Kids tracked around the drop zone, off toward its edges.

Lewis used me as a weight to keep his rig in place while he prepared the chute for folding and packing. I sat on the harness or stood with my back into it, leaning away from where he pleated the silk or untangled the lines. That continuum of cords, tight and alive, was where we trusted each other. His full canopy in the air above was proof I'd done my part.

Parachute silk was alive to the slightest wind. On the ground it looked like an alien thing, but in the sky, it was the better part of a man. When the men were aloft, time slowed, and the sound of their voices was held back. During an air show, a groundbreaking, or the Fourth of July, colored phosphorus smoke flumed from their ankles. Then at a certain altitude the voices came through. Men talked to the air, breaking through again to the ordinary world.

In the sky was a dot, slowly moving northward. The buzz was larger than the dot, though it was the dot making the sound. The buzzing, so near, made my ear seem larger than my eye. Lewis looked up at the dot, squinting his eyes, shading them with his meaty hand.

"That's a C-130. Wingspan 132 feet, capacity 42,000 pounds; 64 airborne troops, cruising speed 336 mph, range 2,000 miles; 40,000 total fuel capacity with the added tanks . . ." He knew everything about every type of plane. When he spooled out those stats, Lewis was in the air himself. I felt edified by his knowledge and his obsession. Flying was so much his passion and purpose, it seemed flight was the main measure of knowledge.

Planes cut their engines, then specks appeared from behind, floaters on the eye. The specks got larger and discharged fluidlike streams of color that swelled and rounded into domes. Below the domes, the specks grew limbs and heads. Soon you could tell one from the other, and the specks were men. I could hear their talk as they got closer to the ground: the distance up no different as a space of action from the distance across a field.

Then, at the target, the thud and roll, death of the silk, except on those blustery days when it threatened to drag them across the grass or sand. The chutes had to be pulled in, the last bit of sky pushed out of them. Then the jumpers, the silk and cord full and tangled in their arms, marched back, black-booted. The heat rippling the air turned them into ghosts.

On August 12, 1965, Lewis's one thousandth freefall was written up in the *Fayetteville Observer*.[11] He's listed as having seventy-seven world parachuting records and counting. On the team, he was a cutaway man, baton passer, tracker, and formation slot man. He was the eighteenth jumper to receive gold wings for one thousand freefalls.

In a *Pathé News* short from 1965, the camera records Lewis leaping backward out of a plane's open door. He wears a black jumpsuit, goggles, a white helmet with "Army" printed above the brow, boots, and the thick parachuting rig of that era. As he leaps out, facing us, we see his stern, determined face. His arms cross briefly before his chest, as if he's gesturing to us, sending a departing message—but he's moving one hand in to pull his ripcord, balancing his position with the other. We see the forked road below him, a few thousand feet: the splotched, flat, bare ground he's headed for. His thick form recedes, but he keeps looking at us for a few moments as the pilot chute trails out, and the main chute behind it, his body plummeting. Finally, he looks down, the narrator's voice describing the precision-landing exercises they're practicing. The body becomes a white point—the helmet, with a thin rim of black, the jumpsuit, and the thin wisp of not-yet-opened parachute above, capped by the blossomy pilot chute. As the shot concludes, the main chute explodes open.

My own skydiving career was short and meant to undo my step-father's disappointments in me. I made seven jumps my junior year of high school, then rested on my brief laurels. The most unnerving part of the first jump was not the leap out but the ride up: the takeoff from the dirty runway, a line of pines racing alongside in a blur, then the g-force pull on the stomach right after the plane was aloft. After that, you're far above the world and it isn't real.

The exit comes in machine silence after the engine's cut. When you step out, the wind hits you like a wall and wakes you to the instant. Every choice we make should be as real as that act of letting go.

The first time's a total blank. Up and down don't exist for an indeterminate moment, because time has also let go. The static line pulls the chute open and an invisible hand draws you from a birdlike pose into uprightness. Then the white silence, plane flown away; above and below more or less where they should be: patchwork landscapes, languid earth broad and democratic, fences and walls too small to keep you out. But you're falling, not flying. Look up into the belly of the chute to confirm it's full, voluptuous, and untrammeled by the lines that should lead straight down to you, point of the cone. Toggles on either side of the harness close manifolds, or openings in the canopy. If you pull one, it swings you around in the opposite direction. Pull both and you slow your fall to drop farther downfield. It all comes too quickly: the Earth hardly rises and seems just there, patiently waiting, as if you could choose not to return.

Soon enough sound rushes up, depth opens, shadows loom, and time has you in its weave again. You are, as it were, skydiving back into your life.

A balance of skill and chance marks any act of survival. We all do it every day driving a car, but too habitually to enjoy. Falling has a poetry all its own, and it's in the quick reckoning of altitude, direction, distance, and wind speed. It's in the simple meter of counting out before the pull of the ripcord and the trustful timing of impact.

Three other fellows made first jumps that day. They were all under thirty. Silent on the way up, each man screamed on the way out, and sensibly so. Perhaps it was a last chance to try their immortality. Maybe the mind gets it first, but then the body needs to test the theory for itself. It's not falling but the anticipation of falling that terrifies. Descent is the acceptance.

I was just trying to please my stepfather. I didn't believe I could die, but I did believe Lewis could kill me. There was only one way down and it wasn't the same as the way up, Heraclitus notwithstanding. I saw him falling so many times—the slow fall beneath the open canopy, the descent through spare sound, voices in the air, after the small, barely perceptible freefall. Freefall was his true home, his body in its full dimension.

I imagine if one could move more or less horizontally in this way—your invisible parachutes, or your conscious choices through the day to live, to move, which are the same—you pull them open as needed, you look up or back to see that they've done their job, that they appropriately billow; then, you look down or over at your target to see that it's there; then, you finish the long gesture you started, or that you entered—from whose hands?—and think of readiness: that the readiness is all.

JULY 3, 1969

LEWIS WAS TRANSFERRED in late June 1969 from M Company, 75th Infantry, back to command of D Company, 2nd Battalion, 3rd Infantry.

On July 3, 1969, his company was involved in a significant battle with the North Vietnamese 33rd Regiment. Bullets and grenade fragments in the chest, mouth, both arms. He lost several men, spent several days in the 24th Evac Hospital, got decorated, then went back into the thick of it right before his R&R.

While recuperating, starting right on the 4th, Lewis kept up housekeeping—on his fungus-infected back, strung with IVs, still 13,000 miles from our front door.

4 July 69
Dearest Patsy:
Well, Darling, I'm not as good as I thought I was. I was moving my company across very thick jungle, and ran smack into a NVA base camp. Snipers in the trees and MG's at ground level. I tried two attacks, and I got hit both times. It was a bear because you couldn't see over 6 ft. because of the undergrowth. I woke up on the Medevac and am not sure how many people I lost. I know of at least (4) KIA & 10 WIA.
   Patsy, I love you and the kids! I'm fine, I was hit 4 different places: mouth, chest, arms (2). I lucked out!
I love you, Patsy!
Jim

He followed with a synoptic second account that same day. I think he was out of it a bit, in the field hospital, in between surgeries, and writing home was the one urgent task he could handle.

4 July 69

Dearest Patsy:

Hello! My Darling. I found out that I'm not bullet proof, but anyhow, I'm fine. I lost 12 KIA and 20 WIA at last count. The kids did an outstanding job for me and I did my best, but it was not enough. I got frag from a grenade in my face and chest and 2 bullets took out a little meat on my right arm, and a small piece of frag also. No sweat! I will be out of the hospital in time to meet you for R&R. The Red Cross should not have told you because I told them not to. Send mail to D Co. 2/3 and they will bring it to me.

Baby, I'm OK! and must be in good shape because I've cussed out the whole world. I'm in the 24th Evac. Hosp. at Long Binh. My face is puffed all out of shape, and I'm missing a couple of teeth, but I should look just as ugly as ever after a week or so. But right now I look like King Kong, and feel like he did when he was shot off the Empire State Building.

The fight lasted over (8) hours. I was hit every time I got up an attack. I can't tell you how bad I feel about the dead and wounded.

Patsy, I love you so very much, and can't wait to see you. I'll write every day and let you know what is happening. Plan on meeting me on the 28th for R&R.

I love you, Patsy!

Jim

The next day he sent another letter, but the battle, its casualties, and his own condition come second. He goes first with domestic stuff, responding, no doubt, to complaints from my mother's recent letters and her own urgencies: mainly what to do about Debi's wild ways. Then he goes back to his own reality:

They got out the rest of the frag., and took more x-rays to-day, and also kicked my big butt out of bed. I feel fine, except believe it or not it's not my wounds that hurt, but a bad cold that I've caught. It only hurts when I laugh! They stopped giving me IV's, and that really made me happy; the only bad thing is now I have to get a couple of shots day and night right in the rear end. It's funny because I can hear the nurses and medic arguing about who has to inject CPT LEWIS. I'm not the most loved patient, and I'm sure they will kick me out soon. Hope so!

P.S. This hospital has nurses that look like boys, but they do a great job.

This is Lewis's armor: bragging about what a poor patient he is. It's also his own form of self-care: Who wants to be a good patient, or a patient at all? Not Lewis.

In the next few letters, we get piecemeal information about what happened, his recovery status, and the half-assed jokes that are likely meant to ease his wife's anxiety. They also reconstruct the Jim Lewis he knew himself to be—self-surgery with a ballpoint pen:

The C.G. and my Col. came to see me today and let me know it was the 33rd Regt. that we fought. The next day they went back in and found a cache that you wouldn't believe. It will probably be one of the biggest ones of the war, at least for this area. It made me feel a little bit better about my losses, but—

My face has really started to get its shape back now. They say that they will take the packing out of my chest & arm in a couple of days and sew me back up. That's no bad deal! I'll probably be a little tender for a while, but no sweat; I'll still be able to kiss & hold you, and no problem at all otherwise.

Tell Jack Shannon that he is honor bound to at least get a toenail shot off! If not then I'll claim a foul and demand my tooth back. (1) inch higher & I would have lost my right nipple—now that would make for a good conversation piece!

Nineteen sixty-nine via airmail was flashed through with events bigger than the tin box the letters have been stored in for more than half a century, there in the gargantuan chest of drawers. Lewis's wounds seem larger than my life, and the disappearance a dozen years after is largest, yet smallest of all.

I'm in love with the layers of things, how they stack and peel, diminish and grow. Here's how I peel back the layers of that day:

- The raw events of what took place July 3, 1969: its infinite angles, the innumerable perspectives, sights and sounds and smells: the moment itself, now lost.

- The article in the *Fayetteville Observer*.[1] My mother opened the paper on Independence Day and chanced upon the mention of her husband's unit, the enemy engagement, the numbers of KIA, WIA, and other facts, none answering her most crucial question: Is he alive?

- My memory of our reading the article a second time: first worries, starting with my mother, who must have been holding the newspaper as we all sat together. Retrieving the paper from the yard that morning, unfolding it, placing it on the corner of the kitchen table until early afternoon, when my mother would read it with a second cup of coffee.

- The preservation of the newspaper as an artifact; its yellowing, the folds becoming creases, the advertisements now quaint; the document become relic, the relic easily turned back into news, the news now history, though up close, with the delicate weight of a footnote on one thin page of a massive tome.

- My memory of playing on the kitchen floor, looking at my mother as she sat for hours, staring at the back of a Red Cross envelope. Lewis's anger, months later, that they'd sent their letter before he could send his.

- The receipt, days later, of more envelopes also marked "RED CROSS": Lewis's letters post-battle about the field hospital, recuperation, and return to his unit.

- Months after, the official documentation: citations, of which I have dainty, onion-skinned, green-and-pink carbon copies: straightforward narratives highlighting heroism, in military language; lists appended to those citations: inventories of every object, however small, left behind that day by the enemy regiment.

- Photographs from the August R&R: Lewis's temporary moustache covering the scar above his lip.

- The Silver Star—downgraded from a Distinguished Service Cross—and the Purple Heart.

- Photographs of the Commanding Officer pinning the medals to Lewis's chest; an earlier snapshot of another senior officer visiting Lewis in the field hospital. Lewis's swollen face, barrel chest, and the white hospital pajamas with the medical unit's insignia on his chest.

- Photographs of the man in uniform in later years, with the requisite fruit salad of ribbons and clusters, some for that day.

- The man's own words about these matters—few and rare, and never directly to me.

- Physical and indexical evidence: the scar and the gap in his teeth, the memo book he'd worn in his breast pocket, with a puckered gap where a bullet had punched through.

- Memories of others who were there, found in various places—veterans' internet chat rooms, in recent years.

- Miscellaneous remnants, such as the folded, yellowed clipping I found years ago, long after he'd disappeared: an account of the death of Cpl. Michael F. Folland, who'd thrown himself on a grenade to save Lewis's life.

- Words in books: in particular, Michael Lanning's *The Only War We Had*, excerpted below.

- Other soldier's letters, other citations, newspaper articles, assumed to exist in other cookie tins, shoeboxes, and so forth.

- Everything that the Other Side might provide as further

layering, parallel to and beyond everything listed above: the many soldiers killed, wounded, that day or another day; wives, mothers, children, multiplying our own. Their photographs, their citations, their letters, their versions of the same history.

- The words I'm writing now, refracting the history into my own purposes.

- All else that I've failed to imagine or add to this list.

Michael Lanning's company was in the vicinity that day. He's written many books, mostly about the Vietnam war. *The Only War We Had*[2] is a refinement, I think, of the journals he kept that year. Lanning frames the story this way:

> Another hundred meters along the trail, I came upon McGinnis and CPT Lewis, the Delta commander. Lewis, a tough-looking man about McGinnis' age, was drawing on the ground with the barrel of a .45 pistol. A bloody field dressing was clinched in his teeth. His RTO[3] explained while Lewis drew pictures.
>
> The teenage radio operator calmly told us their point man had been hit in the legs by machine gun fire. The platoon medic and then the platoon leader had been killed trying to get to the screaming soldier. The three were just across a large deadfall of logs and branches a hundred meters to our front. Each time the platoon had reached the deadfall, the enemy had resumed the machine gun fire. A dust-off trying to drop a jungle penetrator for the wounded had been hit and had to withdraw.

Then, Lanning continues, hand grenades and rockets came into their position. The three officers—McGinnis, Lanning, and Lewis—rallied despite heavy losses. Lanning, from twenty meters away, observes Lewis readying for a renewed assault: "Blood ran down his chin, soaking his fatigue shirt," he notes. "His eyes were calm, however." The three companies try to push against the enemy again, taking more losses. Again they pull back and meet to reassess. "Lewis tried to talk. His top teeth and palate had been knocked loose by pieces of frag grenade. He could only grunt."

They try again, all three units, and in half an hour manage to get thirty meters closer to the enemy, who have trained most of the fire on Lewis's company. Grenades, Lanning says, went back and forth. Then Lanning turns his eye back on my stepfather:

> Tears were now in Lewis' eyes. His RTO was no longer with him. A weeping Delta soldier said the RTO had jumped on a grenade to save Lewis.
>
> Lewis motioned he wanted to try again. McGinnis explained the situation to the Battalion and Brigade Commanders who were orbiting the area in their C&C birds.[4] By now, the fight had been going on for nearly six hours. Darkness was closing around us. The Battalion Commander ordered us to withdraw and get the wounded evacuated. Sounds no longer came from the deadfall.
>
> Lewis was growing weak from the loss of blood. Sassner was working a couple of hundred meters to our rear to clear an area for a dust-off. The night was black when we finally were able to get six of the wounded on the bird. I noticed that the lieutenant with the minor wound was the first to be wrenched up on the cable. Lewis, still protesting, was last.

It's a tightly scripted documentary account, like a film made with a camera held by a steady hand. Lanning's account pulls back and zooms in, crafting a vivid series of tableaux in quick succession, all within the broader, mythic tale of heroism, sacrifice, menace. The North Vietnamese soldiers likely died that day in greater numbers. That other officer, quick to save himself: Think of war movies with cowards or psychopaths playing opposite the noble soldier, either fearless or too human to survive. I don't doubt the narrative—how could I? But I want to see through the narrative, the documents, the words and things, to what was felt; feel what was punched into the hearts of men, brought home by the survivors, still in the blood of the few who might survive.

THE EDGE

SOME NEED THE edge, and the edge must burn bright. Most of us, most of the time—I, for one—are content to watch the fire from a distance. "To risk one's life," says Anne Dufourmantelle,[1] "is first, perhaps, not dying"—the philosopher, who died attempting to save two children in the sea, centers life on risk. She bemoans all the attempts to erase risk in modern life. It isn't the cause but the territory one's unknown chances define.

In the late seventies and early eighties, a number of ex-soldiers, and sometimes a few active-duty, found the edge running drugs, guns, or both. Iran-Contra, the scheme to sell arms to Iran in order to fund Nicaraguan right-wing rebels, defined the new normal for making the immoral seem merely amoral: politics and drugs, money and terror—newly idle ex-soldiers might see the world within such cardinal points. Maybe they were sold on the supposed patriotism of their missions—helping Contras, for example—but risk itself was a drug.

The Smith brothers were so-named by law enforcement because they resembled the cough-drop logo. Brother John Boyd was arrested in 1977, charged, and held on a two-million-dollar bond in Miami, while brother Tracy Boyd skipped. Tracy had been a Green Beret. Both had operated a lawn-sprinkler business in Florida, had financial difficulties, and got into the marijuana Colombia-to-Miami smuggling circuit, making lots of quick cash and flaunting it, reports of the time say. John faked his own death in 1980, but authorities found him in 1983. In the last report I've found online, Tracy was picked up weeks later in Buffalo, New York. He'd wanted to escape but still maintain a normal, domestic life. He didn't disappear far enough.[2]

On the Fayetteville/Vero Beach continuum in 1985, we find two active-duty Green Berets, Keith Anderson and Byron Carlisle, arrested for alleged arms dealing, bribery, and conspiracy. Both men claimed to believe they were taking part in a CIA-connected operation to channel arms to rebels in Central America. They were drawn into the plan by a superior officer who, unknown to them, was a confidential informant for the government. The government that gave us Iran-Contra was also prosecuting its minor players.[3]

Luke Thompson, also Special Forces, was recruited for an overseas, high-paying mission by a man who called himself Pat Loomis. In their first telephone call the scheme remained rather vague. Thompson played along and then, unlike Anderson and Carlisle, went to military intelligence for advice. They checked it out and gave a tentative go-ahead, so Thompson proceeded to meet Loomis in person. Loomis now claimed to be working for the CIA. Thompson, with other soldiers, was meant to train terrorists in Libya—a convoluted plan, at best: morally, politically, strategically. When *The New York Times* published its investigative report on the case in 1985, the mission's organizers had been indicted for illegal arms sales. Loomis, it turned out, had already been dismissed from the CIA when he contacted Thompson—still on the payroll due to bureaucratic complexities, but not really sanctioned for a mission as he claimed. But the article points to a notion that some higher-ups in the agency let it go through—hoping that the convolutions would resolve on the other end as intelligence of value on Libyan terrorism. The convicted, such as Edwin P. Wilson, were freed years later when evidence came out of the government's cover-up.

Why would patriots like Anderson take part in such a scheme, sanctioned or not? The pay was good, it was legal according to someone above their heads—and it was the edge; the tripwire and tightrope, converging.

Thompson had gotten very used to assassinations in Central America and Southeast Asia, in the sixties. "It was a mechanical thing," he says in the *Times* article. "It had to be done. It was a chore just like brushing your teeth."

I'm struck, through the scattered, direct quotations attributed to Thompson, at the ways his experiences worked on his soul.

Thompson, the internet tells me, died in 2012, at eighty-two years old. I don't see much from him over the last few decades: years that might resemble who my father or stepfather would have been, had they survived like Thompson. He says, in 1985, about the one killing that bothered him most—from his time as an assassin and a medic in Vietnam, in the mid-sixties:

Suddenly, someone stepped around a bend in the trail with his weapon on his shoulder. I killed him. Immediately after, it was the greatest thrill in the world—I guess because I was alive—but as the day wore on, I was moved to distraction thinking about this guy. He seemed more like a friend. He was doing exactly what he was told to do, and we had come into conflict and I had beat him. I didn't have any sense of victory. Here's this Joe Gook walking along and I'm G.I. Joe. I didn't know his name. He was a soul in the jungle, I was a soul in the jungle.

"As the day wore on . . ."—and Thompson's soul was suspended, is still suspended, maybe, between that thrill and distraction. The bend in the trail is everywhere. You can't simply rise above to see where you are. You're inside another labyrinth, and your double is ahead of you.

Thompson backed out of the Libya operation. Despite all his edgy experiences, this one bothered him. He went back home, contacted someone higher up again, this time sending ripples upward that came back with the sense that the whole thing was off. Thompson cooperated, left the army, stayed free, and moved with his family to Hawaii, where he sailed his boat and stayed to himself. When he sailed, he told the *Times* reporter Philip Taubman, "I'm transported. If you asked me, though, it would be difficult for me to tell you what I think about." It seems to me a perfect spot for someone with such a life: the middle distance, not over the horizon, but vectored toward it: missingness within the circumscribed world, waiting to die. Sometimes the assassin of assassins takes his time.

A parallel to what might be Lewis's end story is that of Andrew Carter Thornton. The parallels I'm looking for? Men whose fates were recorded in some way: confessions, court cases and subsequent records, or actual books—true-crime, journalism, something more than whispers in the wind, which is all we have for Lewis. But he couldn't have been unique. What happened to him must be traceable in the actions and choices, and fates, of others like him: others driven to see the world, see their own choices, as my stepfather saw his.

Thornton gets full-book treatment in Sally Denton's *The Bluegrass Conspiracy*.[4] His story, at least from its brutal conclusion, was also scattered through the newspapers and TV reports circa 1985. Denton's book fills in the details on the man, his milieu, his cohorts, and the craziness I believe James Lewis got caught up in. Thornton, ex-soldier, ex-cop, son of the Kentucky upper class, died in 1985 when he bailed out of a cocaine-laden plane above western North Carolina, believing Customs aircraft were in pursuit.

Thornton liked to test the edge. Particularly, as an avid skydiver, he liked to open his chute at the last possible moment. That night, he had eighty-eight pounds of cocaine, a weapon, and a bulletproof vest on his body, and he seems not to have accounted for the extra weight. From what investigators could reconstruct, Thornton lost his main chute, opened the reserve, opened too late, maybe got caught in the lines, and smashed into somebody's yard. Meanwhile, the plane itself flew on, further into the wilderness, crashed, and was found second by authorities, first by a black bear who dined on some of the cocaine and died.

Thornton's name first came across my screen when I was searching Lewis for the umpteenth time and came across the Web Sleuths forum with a brief mention—a rare find! Lewis doesn't Google much, having vanished long before the digital era. What's there, other than the NamUs page Kevin and I created, are a few spare references to his skydiving and military career. But someone on this forum—as far as I could tell, a dedicated missing-persons hobbyist with no connection to the case—had proposed a connection between Lewis and a cache of FOIA-released FBI notes and various files posted to Archive.org[5] a few years back by Emma Best, a reporter who specializes in national-security issues. Best has been a prolific user of the Freedom of Information Act for several years, making reams of materials on varied issues publicly available.

Thornton is the star of the FBI file. Among the scraps photocopied in the FBI files are the guts of Thornton's wallet, found after he fell out of the sky. The agents copied his charge cards and other items, including these bits of paper with inspirational quotations. The first appears handwritten:

> Believe nothing:
> Because a wise man said it
> Because it is generally held
> Because it is written
> Because it is said to be devine [*sic*]
> Because someone else believes it
>
> But believe only what you
> Yourself judge to be true.

The inspirational proclamation is, according to a website called "Fake Buddha Quotes,"[6] a fake Buddha quote. According to the author Bodhipaksa, it was possibly cribbed and altered by an anonymous libertarian from a passage in the *Kalama Sutra*, wherein the Buddha advises the Kalamas, who are perplexed by the multitude of teachings, to use reason, but not to depend on reason alone; to trust the experience and the opinions of the wise—and who they are will depend on your experience; that is, on how you perceive the wise ones to have fared in the past. In other words, it's complicated—but keep trying; maybe you'll figure it out. That seems a bit different from the misspelled wallet-wisdom the Cocaine Cowboy had on him when he died.

I supposed, earlier, that these men wanted action. But something in me says that explanation simply can't be all. I want to go deeper, nonwarrior that I am, searcher that I am: What psychic links do we find between the veteran and the smuggler—or the mercenary?

I think these people, these men, were searchers, too. They were searching for themselves. They had lost themselves in war. Any war will make persons go missing from themselves. But the distant wars of the imperium are perhaps more likely to tear a warrior into pieces, at least in the spirit. If the lost part seems lost not within but without, lost in the war now lost itself, where might the lost part have gone? Where to seek it?

The 1980s covert/drug-related activities, which I believe took Lewis further away from himself and from us—for he was already leaning toward his missingness—construct an engagement of promise for someone trying to find what was lost in war. Both can be framed from within as amoral engagements. You and I might define them as palpably immoral. But the warrior has, perhaps, already made of strategy and tactics a frame for the broader life—outside of war, and beyond war, which is always, after all, running along beneath us, whatever actual conflicts are taking place in the world.

In Hammett's Flitcraft, we found a touch of Charles Sanders Pierce. We found that disorder or randomness, which I think is really what "amoral" means, was from at least one perspective in time and space a station on the way to order—though that order might not ever resolve itself in one seeker's lifetime, or in the narrative that composes that individual life. But the purpose, the defining focus, is to test one's methods—and methods are outside of morality—by whatever reports of the day one can count as "results."

In Vietnam it was often firmly rooted in the accounting: of bodies, of distances, of awards, of inventoried matériel, and other created measures. The smuggler/warrior, I suppose, reduces it all to distances, processes, challenges, and, ultimately, money. Money is victory—a clear victory, I imagine, and one that seems, in the moment, to compensate for the narrowly defined victories of the war that somehow totaled up as failure.

Thompson, described as disillusioned in the *Times* article from 1985,[7] opened up—constructing, from facts and more and less, his own narrative: true, false, both. How not to take it as symbolic of who we were, who we are, as a people?

I suppose there's an intersection, for certain types of men, between the totalism of war and the totalism of business. Thornton had a few weeks' combat-related experience as part of the intervention force sent into the Dominican Republic in April–May 1965. He was a paratrooper, later a cop, a lawyer, and eventually a smuggler: a businessman. It's suspected he stole from his Colombian business partners. Life, in his view, was a war, and the warrior—who, when he died, wore Gucci footwear—fought every battle to the utmost. But let us pity the black bear.

Lewis's name isn't in the FBI files. Most names are redacted: the informants as well as the agents, except for one, who died several years ago. A second frequent reference is Gene Paul Thacker. Thacker was on the Golden Knights Army Parachute Team with Lewis. They were founding members in the early sixties. Both men served in Vietnam. Both loved planes and jumping out of them. Thacker retired much earlier, skipping the whole officer thing, unlike Lunday and Lewis. Settling in Hoke County, North Carolina, Thacker bought an airfield and established one of the premiere training and competition facilities for sport parachuting.

When Lewis retired in 1981, he spent a lot of time out at the Raeford place, flying jumpers. The pay, if he got any, was erratic, but he just wanted hours in the air.

Two years after Lewis disappeared, my mother spotted an article in the local paper about Thacker's alleged involvement in a smuggling operation. Overall, forty-two suspects were charged down in Jacksonville, Florida. Officials boasted it was the "largest cocaine ring ever organized."[8] The drugs allegedly came from Colombia, passed through Miami, and mostly proceeded to drop-sites in Carolina, Tennessee, and other states. The number on it, dollar-wise, was 2.2 billion, according to the UPI wire article I'm looking at. The time frame is June 1982 to November 1983—a window that includes Lewis's departure. The others charged included former police officers, ex-military, small businessmen, a former journalist, the owner of an aviation business in south Florida, and, among other South and Central Americans, one Jose Antonio Cabrera-Sarmiento, not in custody as of the date of this article, May 1984. They caught, tried, convicted, and locked up Cabrera-Sarmiento a couple years after.

Thacker was the only one of the forty-two not found guilty. He had a number of character witnesses, and his defense produced three witnesses, members of the Army Parachute Team, who claimed to have been present at the airfield on the day a supposed delivery was made and saw no suspicious activity.[9]

The FBI files include chain-of-custody forms, inventories of evidence, field notes, phone logs, notes from interviews, references to informants (names redacted), interoffice memoranda, and information shared among local law enforcement, state-level investigators, and the FBI. The several pages that focus on Thacker tell of an involved, long-term surveillance and investigation of goings-on at the Raeford airfield, of Thacker's alleged involvement in smuggling, and of his association with other suspects. The main link between Thacker and Thornton, at least as documented in these files, is that Thornton had requested permission from local authorities to practice jumps at Raeford—permission needed, I guess, because Thornton was on probation from an earlier arrest and conviction for arms dealing.

Thacker, as these documents compose the story, had been on the radar of the FBI, the North Carolina Bureau of Investigation, and the Hoke County Sheriff's Department for two or three years. The agent takes a moment to observe that Thacker "leads a 'charmed' life"—so it seemed to the agent just after Thacker's acquittal in the Jacksonville trial. Thacker, according to one of the notes, was "widely known in the Raeford area for trafficking by air narcotics [sic] into the Hoke County area."

The agents kept track of several planes they suspected were used for trafficking: types, identification numbers, condition, provenance, where they'd been seen between Florida and Raeford or elsewhere. One plane was tracked from Florida by Customs authorities, including agents in a Cobra gunship, coordinating with Carolina authorities. By the time the agents and officers on the ground got to the landing site, nobody was present. Along with 1,000 pounds of marijuana, they found what they decided was Thacker's palm print on the outside of the aircraft.

Thacker was never charged in North Carolina. After a couple articles in the local paper about his case, back in the eighties, we never saw anything more about that business. He maintained his operations at the airfield. Kevin got to know his sons, but he never talked with Thacker himself about Lewis's fate.

I proposed the trip to Raeford, maybe a few times over the years. "Why bother?" Kevin said on one occasion. "If Gene Paul's guilty, he won't admit to anything."

"It's just a box to check off," I argued, mainly with myself. I didn't actually want to talk to Thacker. Maybe I didn't want closure, anyway, the way my baby brother did. I just wanted to scratch the itch.

"Listen," said Kevin on another occasion. "If he knows anything, Gene Paul's a danger to anyone poking at that shit." It was maybe twenty years after the disappearance; people involved in the smuggling might still be alive, out of prison, just as lethal as ever.

"And if he doesn't know anything," Kevin continued, "then he doesn't know."

". . . and might feel threatened either way," I added, thinking out loud, "because besides the possible smuggling, there's something there; something sealed tight—something we're not supposed to know."

At that point, I didn't even know what I was talking about. What other secrets festered in the lingering lives of men who had tricked death but not corruption? Before we die, we rot. The sweet, rich, pungent, smell—we add curves to the world in twisting away from what revolts us, though it might be ourselves.

"Anyway," Kevin said, wanting to end the discussion, "If Gene Paul had anything to say, he would have said it by now. So why get up in his face? He's an old man. They're all old men."

Yet Kevin tried, a few times, to set up confrontations—attending the Golden Knights reunions while Thacker was alive, and even after, dragging our mother along though she had no desire to go, in hopes that her presence, their presence, would push someone, anyone, to spill his guts; give us one clue, or the whole story, a confession that stabbed into the heart of the mystery—anything, at any scale of knowledge that Lewis was languishing somewhere.

If we had such knowledge, we could imagine salvation: going to that place, that black hole south of here, tending Lewis's body, catching the last glint of life in his eyes before he died.

When I was home that summer and fall, I remember Lewis referring to Thacker as his best friend. All my growing up, I'd thought of those men—comrades in arms, whose names I still remember from beer parties in our house, from dinner-table conversations, from writing on the backs of photographs. I'd thought of those men as my stepfather's committed comrades. I don't know how many were still alive in 1982, 1983; a good number, I think.

None of them ever said much to my mother about the disappearance. One offered a little grudging help when she lost her home and had to move. I wondered then, as I do now, what was so taboo that they'd conspire to silence and inaction. I doubt many of that circle of friends got involved in drugs, arms, or paramilitary shenanigans. But Thacker, who must have had a cloud about him simply from the charges and the trial, stayed in the middle of things. He was honored when he died. Jim Lewis was largely forgotten.

Like the thousands of shipwrecks off every coast, planes must litter the desolate spaces. Thornton wasn't the only adventurer to fly drug-laden small planes into the Tennessee and Carolina wildernesses.

For some missing people, the searchers can pick a direction, a particular field or a corner of the county or the state, a canyon, or a pond to plumb its depths. Or they take their chances and go right into the faces of the supposed bad men, if there are any. In the end, I can't really tell you why we didn't talk to Thacker. I can't really say if he's a good guy, a bad guy, both, or neither. I suppose it was because those men were like gods to me, and still are, though most are dead.

In those FBI files, there's one small passage of interest—though it hardly stands as evidence, much less proof: "Lieutenant _____ CUMBERLAND COUNTY IDENTIFICATION DIVISION, Fayetteville, North Carolina, telephone number _____ advised _____ that_____ who was a certified flight instructor, was doing commercial flying for THACKER for some time, but according to street word is missing due to crashing his airplane in a South American flight for THACKER. THACKER denies any knowledge of _____ and his demise."

We don't know who _____ is, and we don't know who _____ is, either. But "_____ and his demise" points my imagination toward the Amazon. I see Lewis, or his bones, still hung up in the forest canopy, not even dropped down to the forest floor. Or I see forest, bones, plane, and all, bulldozed and burned in the inexorable destruction.

After forty years, this note is the closest I've come to evidence of Jim Lewis's fate: "a certified flight instructor, was doing commercial flying for THACKER for some time . . ." might be Lewis, or it might be someone else. It's rumor reported to a detective reported to the FBI, without names.

And that might be all we'll ever have, besides what shows itself in dreams.

DESERT DREAMS

I LOOK ALONG the streets in cities I visit for the Missing Person's Reading Room. Walking streets in any town, hiking in a wilderness area, flying miles above land or sea, I think of the membrane between me and oblivion. In some places the boundary between here and nowhere is thinner. In those places you can almost forget your own name.

Where each of us stands at any given moment is n degrees of missingness—our shift from some absolute presence, here-ness, at the center of so-called reality.

The Missing One is a busy signal that lasts for years. What emotion do we have when we hear a busy signal? Before texting, before voice mail, before the death of the phone-as-furniture. We felt frustrated, slightly offended. Remember? Maybe you were different, though. One might have felt, in the old days, that a busy signal was a message itself: don't call me, someone else is more important than you, I'm enjoying my solitude, I'm actually—you know—"busy." After hours or even days of a busy signal—would anyone try so long?—we might fear for someone's life. Certainly, before then we would have driven by, peeked in the window, knocked on the front door, gone around to try the back door. If they were states away, we'd eventually call someone near—even the police, maybe.

In the early days after the disappearance, biological traces are possible. Even the head's indentation on the pillow might persist. Fingerprints, small hairs, bits of beard stubble shaved off and not yet cleaned from the sink. The smell of a body, perfume or aftershave, the sweat in unlaundered shirts, lipstick on handkerchiefs—these will have had meaning. Long hairs will cling to carpets or drapes for years, depending on one's housework habits.

Decades turn to cinder blocks, showing up from nowhere on the porch. I can take up Jim Lewis like an elaborate doll and undo him. I could play with the doll—like the sharp-edged gangster in Nicholas Roeg's *Performance*, devolving under Mick Jagger's Svengali gaze, dazed and staggering in a velvet jacket, silken wig, and makeup. So, let's say—toddler train-jumper, Herculean paper-router, teen-soldier Lewis dropped it all and joined a cult: Esalen, Heaven's Gate, Hari Krishna, the Rajneeshis, take your pick. Grew his hair or painted his shaved skull, donned a robe, and danced into a psychedelic sunset.

I imagine him in a no-man's-land, barbed wire and gun towers distant to the north and south. The world we're making could become a no-man's-land everywhere and forever. I think of the missing as nonpersons in a depopulated world. You and I are spectators looking down through a tin tube from some outer world still bustling and prosperous.

I remember him angry, even seething. Lewis is mostly just below boiling in my memory-nightmares. I remember him laughing. I remember him ardent, loving toward our mother: she would feign/feel embarrassment with appreciation. He had no fear of letting the kids see his affection, raunchy or romantic. It was real, and it was our family theater.

If I squeeze down into the pores of memory, I discover other emotions projected by Jim Lewis: mildly admiring of my academic successes; bemused at buxom starlets on TV; exhausted in his La-Z-Boy, iced tea and cig in hand, some cheddar cheese on a plate by the ashtray. To be missing is to sink down into the unconscious below the usual depths. We forget ourselves. I recall his disavowing belief in God on one occasion, when I was a teenager. I don't know why he would have talked about his religious feelings with me. Perhaps he was muttering to himself, and I was simply there.

The things I later learned about him—that in battle he was exceptionally brave—are easy to accept. I don't have a way of fitting that courage into the space of our home life, across many homes. Only if I think, taking from Aristotle, "the coward is a despairing sort of person; whereas confidence is the mark of a hopeful disposition"[1]—then, seeing his lust and laughter as hopefulness, I see in his face in my mind that courageous character. Then, something of him settles a little deeper in memory.

The easiest thing to imagine, about a typical man that age, might be the lure of another woman. That was why, when we reported Lewis missing in 1982, the cops slyly suggested it, not caring what wounds they might open in my mother. It could have been so and might have been a story with no quirk or depth to it, involving a younger woman with little beyond the temporary bloom and charm, and it might have become another long marriage, a partnership in some American space sideways to this one. Or she might have been his sweet anomaly, someone opposite to his outward life, identical to his burgeoning inner being: its emblem, its shine.

To find the missing, we look where they were, where someone last saw them, where their habits might have led them. We look in the beyond, knowing there are things we might not know or want to know. But the broadest sense of searching, of finding (they're existentially the same) is across these three axes: to find someone on the mapped Earth; to find someone in passing; to find someone in one's own world, not from the random passing, but from seeing more clearly where we are.

In recurring dreams of Lewis, his return is the disappearance undone. It never happened and was itself the dream.

What follows began in a real dream, a vivid mind-movie I had, many years ago. In revisiting the dream, I've added to it from many true and waking dreams that have visited me over the years. It's not a real dream if you think that real dreams are only those onetime shows that play inside our sleeping heads.

I had been as myself in dreams always a man in his mid-thirties. That was true before I was that age and remained so until a few years ago, when versions of my older, sleeping self replaced the younger me: usually missing a bit of flesh, some teeth, patches of hair, or whole limbs. At that age, life felt more sordidly actual and less potential. My mind became mired in its unresolved issues, stewed in constant, underlying fear that shaped my choices and deferrals.

I think most dreams are dreams within dreams. The outer or inner dreams burn off and we remember only part of a formula:

therein the strangeness, nonsensicality, frivolity we are often left with on waking.

"In dreams," said Havelock Ellis,[2] "planes of existence that in waking life are fundamentally distinct are brought together, so that events belonging to different planes move on the same plane, and even become combined." Through that assumption—that dread doesn't deny its kinship with hope—I've tried to recover my master vision of Lewis, allowing the dream and my reimagining of it to invade these pages. Let me address the Missing Man himself, reconstructed from pieces of dreams and musings across four decades. He can't not listen, but I already see him seething with anger. How dare I disturb him?

Here in the desert, the sky isn't black but a blue-almost-green. In the air are phosphorescent creatures that blend with the stars. If you were among them, the luminous creatures or the numberless stars, we'd never know.

We can't point to a particular spot on the map except that area, shrinking though it is, still vast and dense: the Amazon. Does it shrink or enlarge you that we can't pinpoint where you are? Better to meet here, in my desert dream!

Sometimes in the dreams I encounter you in one of our many homes through the years. But often, I see you in the desert. It's unlikely that's where you wound up, but my dream world puts you there. It's that space the child you were rode the freight train through—west Texas, a country all its own.

I've imagined my travels as a trail of selves, a near-endless ribbon of ordinary moments: sitting at my desk, driving the same route to work each day, lying in the sarcophagus of my habits. Imagining your trail is different. It might be a dead end within hours of your departure, a violent demise. Or it might continue still. I can place pushpins on a map: North Carolina, Florida, Colombia, Nicaragua, Libya, Iran. But the map doesn't have the true texture of place. The map lacks cul-de-sacs, endless alleys, or the 360,000 degrees of choice that branch from every moment.

What's a dream? One of those elements allowable in dream alone, such as a room without a house. The idea of "room," but framing it, the idea of "desert" or simply "heat, dryness, desolation." And many meta-things, a naked nakedness, a living dead man, a cube of air, or waves of vultures.

Of dreams, according to Macrobius in his *Commentary on the Dream of Scipio*,[3] we can have ordinary dreams, visions, oracular experiences, waking illusions, or visits from apparitions. Only the first three are of divine origin. The *apparition* is a liminal entity, neither sleep nor waking. The first three, though, help us understand the future. A *vision* in Macrobius is like looking through a scope into future time. The *oracular figure* is a noble being, not fantastical like the apparition. Dreams proper, though bewildering, yield to interpretation. They're divided into dreams about oneself, about another person, about a family or a small group, about a community, or about the world entire. "America," wrote Seymour Krim, "was and is the dream of my life."[4] That's what it is, even now, to be American: everywhere you go is you and yours, at least in your foolish dreams.

It's a fermentation, this recurring dream: a cooked version of the experience, in this world and other dimensions on the meta-map of your disappearance. It's something altered, but also something fused with my body; something that has kept with me, changing in its own course, but still a part of me.

The dreams are a replay of your imagined return, as if I have another chance to do my part. Though the circumstances and locations change, the dreams that take place in one of our houses are always this: You stride into the home after an indeterminate absence, as if it were a perfectly ordinary thing to have vanished. But it's less the fact of the return than it is the sense that returning from the afterlife is ordinary, even inevitable.

I wake from these dreams with that inevitability still aching in my head. My fear-self tells me, "No, no—he hasn't come back, he *can't* come back"—and through the logic of the fear-self, I reenter life. But it was my fear that led me back. For most of my adult life, passing through the horns of this recurring dream, I've walked the ground with a muscle tension left behind by that fear, and it is you.

The space mutates. Beyond here, depressing swamps, mangroves standing and overseeing their pitiful domain. A blurring of species—even of kingdoms!—where's the line between one creature and the next, between human and reptilian, between vegetation and miasmic atmosphere? Then the swirling dust shapes faces in the distance. The heat is our common passion. Moving around each other, we've made this ecstasy of desert.

The storms of missing persons around the world converge here: winds, electric odors, flashes, detritus, and, most of all, the many names in dozens of tongues, in their mothers' voices. This is the vortex of the missing. It was a desert, but now it's a swamp. The lights are living things—fireflies, though I imagine them swimming in the saturated air—or they're raw chemical charges, ruptures of dimension, or simply my own eyes writing what I wish were there.

Part of me believes your vitality was the source of your violence. Violence is so sour and so sweet! I can't separate them. Not that I knew consistently, then or now, what might be rational. I suspected some force beyond my understanding was shaping the brutal limits of the world—right against my skin, my skull, my nose. My brain, hot as phosphorus—your violence, still jarring, blocks your welcome, but you keep on. Thus, the dream recurs.

In Tibetan and other schools of Buddhism, one passes through several states of existence—the bardo states. The first is life itself, from birth to death. The second is the experience of dreams; of dream life as if it were an alternative to the places of our waking life. The third is the place we enter when we meditate. The fourth is the moment of death, quick for most of us, unless we've lived by practicing for this moment. Then, the moment of death might offer something richer: perhaps a closer view of reality, or the fifth bardo, and then the sixth, the bardo of transmigration, with the chance of a positive rebirth.

The bardo states are the middle distance. But here, we're caught between the in-between states: either too close or too far from what we want, who we really are, whom we love, who loves us.

Tibetan mysticism also proposes the existence of tulpas: beings constructed in the mind, the fruits of intense concentration. Tulpas were proxies, capable of travel and simultaneous actions at a distance. You are you, maybe, but you're also my mind puppet—how does it feel?

"There is a breed of desert men," writes Steinbeck,[5] "not hiding exactly but gone to sanctuary from the sins of confusion." In Flaubert, in his account of St. Anthony, they leave confusion for confusion, temptation for temptation without buffer. Thomas Merton[6] said they sought to break their connection with the social order by entering "an apparently irrational void," seeking there a God whom they alone could find. Such a God would be oneself.

I saw you again a few nights ago, fingering a scorched spark plug as if it were a jewel stolen from another world; lipping a cigarette, its smoke writing the illegible name of the place you'd gone to. The dream was a flickering, oscillating dream. Mainly, though, I'm driving east along a state road, for endless miles just a few feet from the tracks: desolation, a town, desolation.

My sight in the dream is sometimes onto the distance, the fields and skyline, and sometimes toward the towns. I see each building, each wind-blasted wall. Now I'm standing just outside a ramshackle by the road, nose up to a slit between splintery boards, light filtering through; then just inside, like a prisoner looking out. Railroad ties slow-cook in the sun, pumpjacks move up and down.

Touch me not, you say with your eyes. *Doubt not*; but why should I doubt? Your spirit touches me in these repeated visitations. When I get close enough—fearing your violence, but plasmic enough in my own dream to withstand it, even consume and reconstitute the violence as some strength of my own—then, I see the depth of feeling in your eyes. You, a collection of desert effects, a man undiscoverable.

I sense a red-and-saffron blur behind my back, a humid stillness, then a thin, minor music. Then you're there, but maybe at an age before or after you'd been my father. You're oscillating: sometimes a boy, sometimes the age at your disappearance, just turned gray and retired from it all, a man about to vanish, but thick and coarse as the landscape.

You stand above the farm implements as if one of them had morphed right in front of me. The sun particles make you spirit-like and distant, though you're close enough to smell of aftershave and cigarettes, barbeque and gasoline. Your short-sleeved shirt shows sinuous stains—rust, blood, or both.

The idea, maybe, for whoever directs this nightmare, is for one of us to take the short step over, to dare the river of light and touch. Matter and antimatter, past and present, peace and war. Which am I?

Then I'm looking at a plump, beaming, redhaired little girl, furiously freckled, obnoxiously happy and completely of her own moment. Who is she? An interloper, a random denizen of my dream, which after all is shaped by randomness. She's an excrescence of meaning. But I'm thinking this is not what innocence should look like. The freckles are so angry, like bees. She's squinty-eyed from the pudge in her cheeks, a big smile, calico dress and ribbons.

I see the glazed tan of piecrust. That's where the sunlight went, sucked down into the pie shell. Your plaid, short-sleeved shirt is brand new and you're smoking a Salem. It's just-lit and the smoke is curling heavenward, still no higher than my head. You raise your hand to take another puff, suck in and flare the glowing end, squint, look me over, and exhale.

Relentless horizon lines, and no undulation from the tip of your nose to that seam between sea and sky. You're lost in the speed and slowness of things, in the mineral traces of eons. Those months of your early to middle-age years, so flat they seemed to have no boundary, were the doldrums: You were action-starved.

I hear the wind whistling through your bones, though right now you're all wave and arabesque of neuro-matter. Your eyes are amethystine and cracked, wet from somewhere inside you, and I think to pluck them out and pocket them: proof of life.

At twilight, the boundary between pink air and blue shadows

makes a route toward valleys in the air, rich with insects and first stars. Down in the barranca, long shadows stand up crookedly, detached from their objects.

I climb to the top of a gray dune. Wind streams sharply across the top, taking flecks of me southward. It's like being inside radio hiss: music of the missing. From the cornice of this dune, a steady stream of sand, millions of souls fleeing, removing themselves from this dune world to the next.

The warrior elements are atrophied now—those warlike parts of you are soft, decadent. When you lie down on the sands, you're all contour.

When I search for the cord to pull you back, it becomes a dotted line on paper. We're measuring your height in longitude, your girth in azimuth. I arrive at the next town, train track and silos, hoppers, chutes, idling trucks, and, always, the slowly seesawing pumpjacks.

Beyond the hills are lunar hills, Martian hills, massive peaks of frozen methane on a moon of Jupiter. You've sipped your coffee, smoked your last Salem, stepped out the kitchen door with a knapsack over your shoulder, headed for those hills beyond all earthly hills.

You're how stones disappear over eons. Others squeeze through the soil after changes in temperature, or imperceptible tremors, or changes in humidity, or purely from the will of their mineral consciousness. Other stones appear suddenly as if mocking the squashes or the melons, infiltrating their rows.

Here you can fly without wings, without instruments. Your flying is you.

A calm; torpor of sleep, even the stones sleeping, sleep like an ether. The world nearly still. Sleep like a settling blanket that was always there, the sleep of all things.

So, if you were to be found, if you were alive somewhere, and I could sit down with you again, I might ask: Now, after so many years, after your story has added chapters and footnotes, codas and sequels, after it has been unwritten more than written—can't you tell me the middle part, what you held back that last night, after we watched the baseball game? Were you judging that young officer on the trail, or yourself, or me—or all of us, or none?

In the shack, in a dark corner away from the dust-speckled rays of the setting sun, the cold kiln sits, a skeleton curled inside. It's yours, but still you sit there, tanned arms, eyes squinting, cigarette in your hand. There's no Cinemascope to it. You're just there in the dream shack a few feet away, sitting on a Pepsi crate, tired from a day at work, off to battle but home by dinner every night. You're smoking your last cigarette, and the smoke finds its way through a hole in the ceiling. Fascinated, I follow.

THE RETURN

"I ENTERED AND saw my father dead," writes Musset[1] in his memoirs. "'Sir,' I said to the physician, 'please have everyone retire that I may be alone here; my father had something to say to me, and he will say it.'"

We might hear this as impertinent, medically and spiritually. Or it's gnomic: How else might someone find release from the dead? They have mouths, for a bit longer. Those eyes are closed, but the lids must be ready to open. That hand on the slab: Why should the deceased not lift it, at least once more? Holbein's dead Christ seems both permanently still and ready to rise. It's essential of the supine that it should rise once more.

In early February 1970, Lewis came home from Vietnam. He flew in a troop ship and took a cab from the airport to our home on Village Drive. He'd been gone a year and spent nearly all of it in combat. He'd killed, he'd been wounded, he'd seen his soldiers wounded, and many had died. Some of his friends had died. I couldn't see his eyes then, but in memory, and in versions in my dream, his eyes are small worlds.

Before the door opened, I must have been engrossed in play. I was in the living room just inside that door, with my little green infantrymen spread out on the carpet. I remember the way my mind would be so focused on the small world: holding up one figurine, studying it, constructing a story and background—open-ended, heroic in the abstract, detached from fate—entirely of the moment, and my small hand was all the figure's moment, all its ground. Here's that figure now—his rifle raised, knees bent for a forward thrust. The green plastic man is an inch from my face. The tip of his bayonet is skewed, but he looks straight at me. Except he has no eyes. I put him down on the carpet, could stomp and crush him—

But the ready rifle: He'll never put it down. He's incapable of wavering. Some men are all one gesture, taking on the world: not certainty, not perfection, but sharpness of will. Show me your elegant hypothesis, its intricate clockworks; I'll show you my green plastic man, knees bent, rifle raised, his stare with no eyes.

I was playing war. Maybe it was the last time, since I was eleven already. Not long after, I put away such things. Other uses of my fancying mind took over: a rock collection, then stamps; rock music, reading books, the smell and shape of girls, the changing contours of my own body and how even my mild efforts at athleticism were so transformative—those, and other things, and as my childhood became my adolescence, Lewis was at a slight distance: caught up, it seems to me now, in conflicted feelings for years before he disappeared. He was still a soldier, but something had changed.

Lewis returned that February day in 1970. It was his home though he'd been gone a year. He turned the knob and came in. He wore dress greens and had a duffel bag slung over his shoulder. It was hazy but bright outside, and he was backlit. The figure there, for an instant unfamiliar to me, was at first faceless and dark: a man standing in the door, neither in nor out—waiting, as if still somewhere between here and a world away.

He stepped forward, tentatively. Then I could see his eyes, and they were tired. I remember so well how deeply exhausted the man seemed.

I've dreamed of that doorway many times, seen his hulking shape with the haze behind it, and the eyes that seemed to stare back into themselves, all the way back to where he'd come from.

You can decide to love someone, and it might be because you know they loved you first. At that moment, I understood that I loved Jim Lewis. It was a clear realization, maybe one of the first I ever had. Lacking words, I only stared back at him. Then I got up to help with his bag and he came inside.

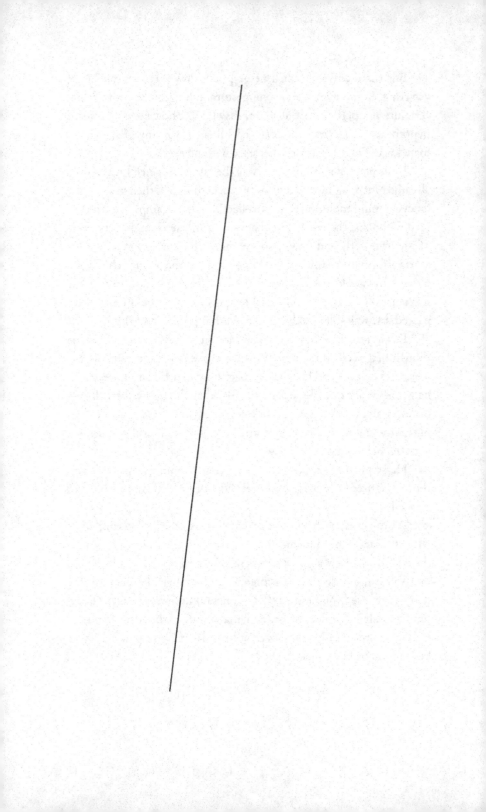

ACKNOWLEDGMENTS

My gratitude goes to Thomas Larson and Randall Watson, who offered valuable advice on the manuscript, along with encouragement and friendship. I am thankful as well to my wife, Yukiko, whose belief has sustained me; to my friend Philip Brady, who has believed in me even longer; to my mother, Patsy Lewis, who has endured so much, like so many other military spouses; and to my siblings Debi Haley and Donald Lewis, but especially my brother Kevin, whose search continues. I hope this book will help unearth what more can be learned of James Lewis's fate.

Some sections of this work, in different form, appeared in the following publications:

- *Coal Hill Review*: "In the Cloud"
- *Drunken Boat*: "Hitchhike"
- *Prick of the Spindle*: excerpts from "Uroboros"

The author gratefully acknowledges permission to reprint the following works:

Excerpt from "Why Brownlee Left" from *POEMS: 1968–1998* by Paul Muldoon. © 2001 by Paul Muldoon. Reprinted by permission of Farrar, Straus and Giroux. All Rights Reserved.

Excerpt from "Disappearing Fathers" from *Telling the Bees* by Faith Shearin. © 2015 by Stephen F. Austin State University Press. Reprinted by permission of Stephen F. Austin State University Press. All rights reserved.

Excerpt from "The Less Deceived" from *The Complete Poems of Philip Larkin* by Philip Larkin, edited by Archie Burnett. © 2013 by Farrar, Straus and Giroux. All rights reserved.

NOTES

Note to Epigraph

Roberto Bolaño, *2666*, trans. Natasha Wimmer (New York: Farrar, Strauss, and Giroux, 2013).

Finding; Understanding

1. Andy Owen, "The Need for an Ending," *Aeon*, April 25, 2019, https://aeon.co/essays/a-missing-person-is-like-a-story-without-an-ending.
2. Idra Novey, *Ways to Disappear* (Boston: Little, Brown and Company, 2016).
3. Tim O'Brien, *The Lake in the Woods* (New York: Penguin Books, 1995).
4. Tim Krabbé, *The Vanishing*, trans. Claire Nicholas White (New York: Random House, 1993).
5. Kazuo Ishiguro, *When We Were Orphans* (New York: Vintage Books, 2001).

Doubles

1. Some of Lewis's letters are edited: lines removed here and there, mainly, to avoid redundancy.
2. Paul Auster, *The Invention of Solitude* (New York: Penguin, 2007).
3. R. D. Laing, *The Politics of Experience* (New York: Pantheon, 1983).
4. Thomas Pynchon, *Gravity's Rainbow* (New York: Vintage, 1995).

Oracles

1. Philip Larkin, *Collected Poems by Philip Larkin* (New York: Farrar, Strauss, and Giroux, 2013).
2. Norman Mailer, *Of a Fire on the Moon* (New York: Signet, 1970).
3. Hester Parr and Nicholas Fyfe, "Missing Geographies," *Progress in Human Geography* 37, no. 5 (December 20, 2012): 615–38. See also Hester Parr and Lucy Holmes, "Returning Missing Adults: The Need for Intervention and Prevention," https://www.missingpeople.org.uk/, accessed 2016.
4. Penny Woolnough et al., "Investigating Missing Persons: Learning from Interviews with Located Missing Adults," *Journal of Homicide and Incident Investigation* 9, no. 2 (November 2014): 14–25.

Relics

1. The FBI's National Crime Information Center database.
2. Lama Anagarika Govinda, *Creative Meditation and Multi-Dimensional Consciousness* (Wheaton, IL: Theosophical Publishing House, 1976).
3. Geoffrey C. Bowker and Susan Leigh Star, *Sorting Things Out: Classification and its Consequences* (Cambridge, MA: MIT Press, 2000).

The Asymptote

1. George J. Veith, *Code Name Bright Light: The Untold Story of U.S. POW Rescue Efforts During the Vietnam War* (New York: The Free Press, 1998).

Nomads and Exiles

1. Pat Conroy, introduction to *Military Brats: Legacies of Childhood Inside the Fortress*, ed. Mary Edwards Wertsch, xvii–xxv (New York: Harmony Books, 1991).
2. Ammianus Marcellinus, *The Later Roman Empire*, trans. Walter Hamilton (New York: Penguin Books, 1986). Thanks to Andrew Hudgins for drawing this passage to my attention.
3. Georg Simmel, *The Sociology of Georg Simmel*, trans. Kurt H. Wolff (New York: The Free Press, 1964).
4. Richard Hofstadter, *The Paranoid Style in American Politics and Other Essays* (New York: Alfred A. Knopf, 1965).
5. Yoshida Kenkō, *The Miscellany of a Japanese Priest: Being a Translation of Tsurezure Gusa*, trans. William N. Porter (London: Humphrey Milford, 1914).
6. Alfred de Musset, *The Confession of a Child of the Century*, trans. Kendall Warren, Project Gutenberg, February 1, 2006, https://www.gutenberg.org/ebooks/9869.

The Middle Distance

1. Havelock Ellis, *The World of Dreams* (New York: Houghton Mifflin Company, 1922).
2. Rebecca Solnit, *A Field Guide to Getting Lost* (New York: Penguin Books, 2006).
3. Kenneth Hill, *Lost Person Behavior* (Ottawa, Canada: National SAR Secretariat, 1998).

Face of Shadows

1. Simone de Beauvoir, *The Second Sex*, trans. Constance Borde (New York: Vintage, 2014).

2. Kevin Lynch, *The Image of the City* (Cambridge, MA: MIT Press, 1960).

3. Iona and Peter Opie, *The Lore and Language of Schoolchildren* (New York: New York Review, 2001).

4. Henri Focillon, *The Life of Forms in Art*, trans. George Kubler (New York: Zone, 1992).

Uroboros

1. Mark Price, "3-year-old boy lost in NC woods tells his family he 'hung out with a bear for two days,'" *The Charlotte Observer*, January 25, 2019, https://www.charlotteobserver.com/ news/local/article225090590.html.

2. Amelia Earhart, *Letters from Amelia: An Intimate Portrait of Amelia Earhart*, ed. Jean L. Backus (Boston: Beacon Press, 1982).

3. John Updike, *The Early Stories: 1953–1975* (New York: Random House, 2004).

4. George Santayana, *Reason and Society*, volume 2 of *The Life of Reason: or the Phases of Human Progress* (New York: Scribner's, 1930).

5. J. Glenn Gray, *The Warriors* (New York: Harper and Row, 1970).

6. Willard Waller, *Veteran Comes Back* (Fort Worth, TX: Dryden, 1944).

The Sun and I

1. Alfred Schuetz, "The Homecomer," *American Journal of Sociology* 50, no. 5 (March 1945): 369—376.

2. Lew Welch, *Ring of Bone: Collected Poems* (San Francisco: City Lights Publishers, 2012).

3. Wright Morris, *The Home Place* (Lincoln: University of Nebraska Press, 1968).

Sayaboury

1. Jacques Nevard, "Laos Army Balks at Attack on Reds; Bars a U.S. Plan Because It 'Would Get People Killed' Heads U.S. Team Fond of Villagers," *New York Times*, May 27, 1962, https://www.nytimes.com/1962/05/27/archives/laos-army-balks-at-attack-on-reds-bars-a-us-plan-because-it-would.html.

2. F. Lionel Pinn Sr., *Hear the Bugles Calling: My Three Wars as a Combat Veteran* (Montgomery, AL: NewSouth Books, 2007).

3. See James Terence Fisher, *Dr. America: The Lives of Thomas A. Dooley, 1927–1961* (Amherst: University of Massachusetts Press, 1997).

4. "Transit Agency Aide Plunges to His Death," *New York Times*, November 6, 1977. https://www.nytimes.com/1977/11/06/archives/transit-agency-aide-plunges-to-his-death-transit-agency-aide-leaps.html.

I am the Grass

1. H. Bruce Franklin, *MIA, or Mythmaking in America* (Rutgers, NJ: Rutgers University Press, 1993).

2. Michael J. Allen, *Until the Last Man Comes Home: POWs, MIAs, and the Unending Vietnam War* (Chapel Hill: University of North Carolina Press, 2012).

3. In Geoff Dyer, *The Missing of the Somme* (New York: Vintage, 1994).

4. Yusef Komunyakaa, *Neon Vernacular: New and Selected Poems* (Middletown, CT: Wesleyan University Press, 1993).

5. Carl Sandburg, *The Complete Poems of Carl Sandburg* (New York: Harcourt, Brace, and Co., 1970).

6. Viet Thanh Nguyen, *Nothing Ever Dies: Vietnam and the Memory of War* (Cambridge, MA: Harvard University Press, 2016).

The Boy Scout Handbook

1. William Hillcourt, *Boy Scout Handbook, 7th ed.* (Irving, TX: Boy Scouts of America, 1969).

2. Paul Fussell *The Boy Scout Handbook and Other Observations* (New York: Oxford University Press, 1985).

Circles

1. In Georges Poulet, *The Metamorphoses of the Circle*, trans. Carley Dawson and Elliott Coleman (Baltimore: Johns Hopkins University Press, 1966).

2. In Gaston Bachelard, *The Poetics of Space*, trans. Richard Kearney (New York: Penguin, 2014).

The Verge

1. Franz Kafka, *Aphorisms*, trans. Daniel Frank (New York: Schocken, 2015).

2. D. H. Lawrence, *Phoenix II: Uncollected, Unpublished, and Other Prose Works* (Portsmouth, NH: Heinemann, 1968).

3. D. H. Lawrence, *Reflections on the Death of a Porcupine and Other Essays* (Cambridge: University of Cambridge Press, 1988).

4. Jay Scott Morgan, "The Mystery of Goya's Saturn," *New England Review* 22, no. 3 (Summer 2001): 39–43.

5. Mary McGarry Morris, *Vanished* (New York: Viking, 1988).

6. Fyodor Dostoevsky, *Notes from Underground & The Dream of a Ridiculous Man*, trans. Constance Garnett (New York: Signet, 1961).

7. Jean Baudrillard, *Why Hasn't Everything Already Disappeared?* trans. Chris Turner (New York: Seagull, 2016).

8. Jean-Paul Sartre, *Baudelaire*, trans. Martin Turnell (New York: New Directions, 1972).

9. Melanie Klein, *Love, Guilt, and Reparation: And Other Works 1921–1945* (New York: The Free Press, 2002).

10. Ilya Prigogine, *Order Out of Chaos* (New York: Bantam, 1984).

Vita Activa

1. Hannah Arendt, *The Human Condition*, 2nd ed. (Chicago: University of Chicago Press, 1958).

2. Louis Ferdinand Céline, *Journey to the End of the Night*, trans. Ralph Manheim (New York: New Directions, 2006).

3. William James, *The Varieties of Religious Experience* (New York: Penguin, 1982).

Disequilibria

1. Havelock Ellis, *The Dance of Life* (Westport, CT: The Greenwood Press, 1923).

2. Mary McCarthy, *Vietnam* (New York: Open Road Media, 2013).

3. Albert Camus, *Lyrical and Critical Essays*, trans. Ellen Conroy Kennedy (New York: Vintage, 1970).

4. Henry Adams, *The Education of Henry Adams* (New York: Modern Library, 1999).

5. Karl Marlantes, *What It Is Like to Go to War* (New York: Grove Press, 2012).

6. Alfred Schuetz, "The Homecomer," *American Journal of Sociology* 50, no. 5 (March 1945): 369–76.

7. Barry Davies, *How to Disappear and Never Be Found: The Ultimate Guide to Privacy, Security, and Freedom* (New York: Skyhorse, 2019).

8. Tobias Wolff, *In Pharaoh's Army: Memories of the Lost War* (New York: Vintage, 2010).

9. Ron Kovic, *Born on the Fourth of July* (New York: McGraw Hill, 1976).

10. Tim O'Brien, *The Things They Carried* (Boston: Mariner Books, 2009).

11. Tim O'Brien, *If I Die in a Combat Zone: Box Me Up and Ship Me Home* (New York: Harper Perennial, 2006.)

12. Sophocles, *Sophocles I: Antigone, Oedipus the King, Oedipus at Colonus*, 3rd ed, The Complete Greek Tragedies, ed. Richmond Lattimore (Chicago: University of Chicago Press, 2013).

13. Stephen Wright, *Meditations in Green* (Boston: Little, Brown, 1983).

14. Erich Maria Remarque, *The Road Back*, trans. Arthur Wesley Wheen (New York: Random House, 2013).

15. Richard O'Connor, *Ambrose Bierce: A Biography* (New York: Little, Brown, 1967).

16. Carlos Fuentes, *The Old Gringo*, trans. Margaret Sayers Peden (New York: Farrar, Strauss & Giroux, 2013).

A Beautiful Death

1. Jean-Pierre Vernant, *Mortals and Immortals: Collected Essays*, trans. Froma I. Zeitlin (Princeton, NJ: Princeton University Press, 1991).

2. Donald E. Wolfe, "A Different Species of Time," in *When War Becomes Personal: Soldiers' Accounts from the Civil War to Iraq*, ed. Donald Anderson, 102–13 (Iowa City: University of Iowa Press, 2008).

3. Pat Conroy, *The Great Santini* (New York: Dial, 2002).

China

1. Andrew Devendorff, "My Brother Went Missing, and the Search for Him Turned My World Upside Down," *Huffpost*, March 5, 2021, https://www.huffpost.com/entry/missing-brother-search_n_5d67e1a5e4b063c341fc2782.

2. Sigmund Freud, *On Murder, Mourning, and Melancholia*, trans. Shaun Whiteside (New York: Penguin, 2005).

3. Pauline Boss, *Ambiguous Loss: Learning to Live with Unresolved Grief* (Cambridge, MA: Harvard University Press, 1999).

The Swerve

1. Maria Flook, *My Sister Life: The Story of My Sister's Disappearance* (New York: Crown Publishers, 1999).

2. Derek Marlowe, *Echoes of Celandine* (New York: Viking, 1970).

3. Seneca, *Letters from a Stoic*, trans. Robin Campbell (New York: Penguin, 1969).

4. Simone de Beauvoir, *The Ethics of Ambiguity*, trans. Bernard Frechtman (Seacacus, NJ: Citadel, 1948).

5. Edward T. Hall, *Beyond Culture* (New York: Anchor, 1977).

6. Arthur Schopenhauer, *The World as Will and Idea*, trans. R. B. Haldane and J. Kemp (London: Routledge and Kegan Paul, 1886).

7. Henri Bergson, *Creative Evolution*, trans. Arthur Mitchell (Garden City, NY: Dover, 1998).

A Feral Presence

1. Luigi Pirandello, *The Late Mattia Pascal*, trans. Arthur Livingston (New York: New York Review Books, 2004).

2. In Jay Robert Nash, *Among the Missing: An Anecdotal History of Missing Persons from 1800 to the Present* (New York: Simon and Schuster, 1978).

3. Lindsay Harrison, *Missing: A Memoir* (New York: Scribner's, 2011).

4. Stephen Wright, *Going Native* (New York: Farrar, Strauss & Giroux, 1994).

5. Beth Gutcheon, *Still Missing* (New York: Putnam, 1981).

6. See Florus, *Epitome of Roman History*, trans. E. S. Forster. Loeb Classical Library (Cambridge, MA: Harvard University Press, 1929).

7. Franz Kafka, "The Metamorphosis," in *Complete Stories*, trans. Willa and Edwin Muir, 89–139 (New York: Schocken Books, 1971).

8. Antonio Porchia, *Voices*, trans. W. S. Merwin (Port Townsend, WA: Copper Canyon, 2003).

9. Margaret Atwood, *Surfacing* (New York: Anchor, 1998).

10. Rubén Darío, *Selected Writings*, trans. Andrew Hurley (New York: Penguin, 2005).

11. Paul Auster, *Oracle Night* (New York: Picador, 2009).

12. Belinda Bauer, *Snap* (Boston: Atlantic Monthly, 2018).

13. Sheena Kamal, *The Lost Ones* (New York: William Morrow, 2018).

14. Kate Crane, "Whatever Happened to Eddy Crane?" *Ozy*, September 12, 2015, https://www.ozy.com/true-and-stories/whatever-happened-to-eddy-crane/61143/.

15. Joan Didion, *The Year of Magical Thinking* (New York: Vintage, 2007).

16. Faith Shearin, *Telling the Bees* (Nacogdoches, TX: Stephen F. Austin State University Press), 2015.

17. J. W. Dunne, *An Experiment with Time* (London: Faber and Faber, 1927).

18. Mona Simpson. *The Lost Father* (New York: Vintage, 1993).

19. Andrew O'Hagan, *The Missing* (London: Faber and Faber, 2004).

Dark Heart

1. Andy Sevilla, "BREAKING: Jawbone Found in Bastrop Belongs to Missing Houston Man, Sheriff Says," *Austin American-Statesman*, August 26, 2019, https://www.statesman.com/news/20190823/breaking-jawbone-found-in-bastrop-belongs-to-missing-houston-man-sheriff-says.

2. Jenny Edkins, *Missing: Persons and Politics* (Ithaca, NY: Cornell University Press, 2016).

3. Eric Carlson, *I Remember Julia: Voices of the Disappeared* (Philadelphia: Temple University Press, 1996).

4. Nathan Englander, *The Ministry of Special Cases* (New York: Vintage, 2007).

5. Jodi Picoult, *Leaving Time* (New York: Ballantine, 2014).

6. Fin Kennedy, *How to Disappear Completely and Never Be Found* (London: Nick Hearn Books, 2008).

7. Aimee Liu, *Flash House* (New York: Grand Central, 2004).

8. Chang-Rae Lee, *Aloft* (New York: Riverhead Books, 2005).

9. John H. Ayers and Carol Bird, *Missing Men* (New York: Putnam and Sons, 1932).

10. James Reidel, *Vanished Act: The Life and Art of Weldon Kees* (Lincoln, NE: Bison Books, 2007).

11. See Nicholas Tomalin and Ron Hall, *The Strange Voyage of Donald Crowhurst* (Middlesex, England: Penguin, 1973).

12. Ben McGrath, "The Wayfarer: A Solitary Canoeist Meets His Fate," *New Yorker*, December 6, 2015, https://www.newyorker.com/magazine/2015/12/14/the-wayfarer.

13. Paul Muldoon, *Why Brownlee Left* (London: Faber and Faber, 1980).

14. See Roger Conover, "Mina Loy's 'Colossus': Arthur Cravan Undressed," in *New York Dada*, ed. Rudolf E. Kuenzli, 102–19 (New York: Willis Locker and Owens, 1986); and Terry J. Hale, ed., *4 Dada Suicides: Selected Texts of Arthur Cravan, Jacques Rigaut, Julien Torma, and Jacques Vaché* (London: Atlas, 1995).

15. Leonardo Sciascia, *The Moro Affair* (New York: New York Review Books, 2004).

16. Giorgio Agamben, *What is Real?* (Stanford, CA: Stanford University Press, 2018).

17. See "We Lived Alone: The Connie Converse Documentary," dir. Andrea McEneaney, 2015, https://vimeo.com/106996853; and Delfin Vigil, "The Musical Mystery of Connie Converse," *SFGate*, March 8, 2009, https://www.sfgate.com/entertainment/article/The-musical-mystery-of-Connie-Converse-3248530.php.

18. Ian McEwan, *The Child in Time* (New York: Anchor, 1999).

19. Hans Koppel, *Never Coming Back* (Berkeley: Pegasus, 2012).

20. Tim Krabbé, *The Vanishing*, trans. Claire Nicholas White (New York: Random House, 1993).

21. Stewart O'Nan, *Songs for the Missing* (New York: Penguin Books, 2009).

22. Maria Flook, *My Sister Life: The Story of My Sister's Disappearance* (New York: Crown Publishers, 1999).

23. Alexis de Tocqueville, *Democracy in America*, trans. Henry Reeve, 7th ed. (New York: Edward Walker, 1847). Archive.org.

24. Kobo Abe, *The Frontier Within: Essays by Abe Kobo* (New York: Columbia University Press, 2013.

25. Emma Healey, *Elizabeth is Missing* (New York: Harper Perennial, 2015).

The Vortex

1. Harmeet Kaur, "Black Kids Go Missing at a Higher Rate Than White Kids. Here's Why We Don't Hear About Them," *CNN*, November 3, 2019, https://cnn.com/2019/11/03 /us/missing-children-of-color-trnd.

2. Rebecca Wanzo, "The Era of Lost (White) Girls: On Body and Event," *A Journal of Feminist Cultural Studies* 19, no. 2 (2008): 99–126.

3. Sierra Crane Murdoch, *Yellow Bird: Oil, Murder, and a Woman's Search for Justice in Indian Country* (New York: Random House, 2020).

4. Danielle Weiss et al., "Lost but Not Forgotten: Finding the Nation's Missing," *NIJ Journal* 279, April 2018, https://nij.gov/journals/279/Pages/lost-but-not-forgotten.aspx.

Flitcraft's Folly

1. Dashiell Hammett, *The Maltese Falcon*. New York: Vintage Books, 1992.

2. C. S. Peirce, "The Doctrine of Necessity Examined," *The Monist* 2, no. 3 (April 1892): 321–37.

3. David Ely, *Seconds* (New York: Harper Voyager, 2013).

Wakefields

1. Nathaniel Hawthorne, *Twice-Told Tales* (New York: Modern Library, 2001).

2. Virginia Woolf, *Essays of Virginia Woolf, Vol. 4, 1925–1928* (Boston: Mariner Books, 2008).

3. W. S. Sebald, *The Rings of Saturn*, trans. Michael Hulse (New York: New Directions, 1998).

4. William King, *Political and Literary Anecdotes of His Own Times* (London: John Murray, 1818). Archive.org.

5. E. L. Doctorow, *All the Time in the World: New and Selected Stories* (New York: Random House, 2012).

6. Eduardo Berti, *La Mujer de Wakefield* (Barcelona: Tusquets, 1999).

7. Antonio Tabucchi, *The Edge of the Horizon*, trans. Tim Parks (New York: New Directions Publishing, 2015).

8. Patrick Modiano, *Missing Person*, trans. Daniel Weissbort (Jaffrey, NH: David R. Godine, 2014).

The Circumambient Self

1. Kobo Abe, *The Box Man*, trans. E. Dale Saunders (New York: Vintage, 1974).
2. Kobo Abe, *The Woman in the Dunes*, trans. E. Dale Saunders (New York: Vintage, 1964).

Subterranean

1. Max Frisch, *I'm Not Stiller*, trans. Michael Bullock (Rochester, NY: Dalkey Archive Press, 2006).

Spirit Radios

1. Henri Lefebvre, *State, Space, World: Selected Essays*, trans. Gerald Moore, Neil Brenner, and Stuart Elden (Minneapolis: University of Minnesota Press, 2009).
2. The reader can learn more about Colonel William Grieves in Douglas Valentine's *The Phoenix Program* (New York: William Morrow, 1990). RMK-BRJ's prodigious construction efforts are recounted in James M. Carter's *Inventing Vietnam: The United States and State Building, 1954–1968* (Cambridge: Cambridge University Press, 2008).
3. Michael Herr, *Dispatches* (New York: Vintage, 1991).
4. Tim O'Brien, "The Vietnam in Me," *New York Times*, October 2, 1994, https://archive.nytimes.com/www.nytimes.com/books/98/09/20/specials/obrien-vietnam.html?_r=2.

Lightness

1. Paul Valéry, *Selected Writings of Paul Valéry*, trans. Malcolm Cowley (New York: New Directions, 1950).
2. J. H. van den Berg, *The Changing Nature of Man: Introduction to a Historical Psychology* (New York: W. W. Norton, 1983).
3. Milan Kundera, *The Unbearable Lightness of Being*, trans. Michael Henry Heim (New York: Harper, 2009).

Foolish Dreams

1. Susan Griffin, *A Chorus of Stones* (New York: Anchor, 1992).
2. Henry Adams, *The Education of Henry Adams* (New York: Modern Library, 1999).

3. "Southern Campaigns American Revolution Pension Statements & Rosters: Pension Application of Edward G. Jacobs S1540," Southern Campaigns Revolutionary War Pension Statements & Rosters, November 2, 2015.

4. Virgil. *The Aeneid*, Book VI, trans. Seamus Heaney (New York: Farrar, Straus & Giroux, 2016).

Old Soldiers Never Die

1. Francis Ponge, "Snails," trans. C. K. Williams, in *Selected Poems*, ed. Margaret Guiton (London: Faber and Faber, 1994).

2. Amélie Rorty, *The Identities of Persons* (Berkeley: University of California Press, 1976).

3. Erich Maria Remarque, *All Quiet on the Western Front*, trans. Arthur Wesley Wheen (New York: Random House, 2013).

4. Guglielmo Ferrero, *Militarism: A Contribution to the Peace Crusade* (Boston: L. C. Page, 1903).

5. Letter from John Adams to Abigail Adams, post May 12, 1780 [electronic edition], *Adams Family Papers: An Electronic Archive*, Massachusetts Historical Society, http://www.masshist.org/digitaladams/.

6. Carl von Clausewitz, *The Essential Clausewitz: Selections from* On War, ed. Joseph I. Greene, trans. James John Graham (New York: Dover, 2003).

Worldness

1. Barbara Newhall Follett, *The House Without Windows* (New York: Alfred A. Knopf, 1927).

2. Laura Smith, *The Art of Vanishing: A Memoir of Wanderlust* (New York: Viking, 2018).

3. Wilson Follett, "To a Daughter, One Year Lost—From Her Father," *The Atlantic*, May 1941.

4. Maria Semple, *Where'd You Go, Bernadette* (New York: Back Bay, 2013).

5. Herman Melville, *Mardi and a Voyage Thither* (Evanston, IL: Northwestern University Press, 1970).

6. David Ely, *Walking Davis* (New York: Charterhouse, 1972).

7. Elias Canetti, *The Human Province*, trans. Joachim Neugroschel (New York: The Seabury Press, 1978).

8. Blaise Pascal, *Pascal's Pensées*, trans. W. F. Trotter (New York: Dutton, 1958).

9. Gerhart B. Ladner, "Homo Viator: Mediaeval Ideas on Alienation and Order," *Speculum* 42, no. 2 (April 1967): 233–59.

10. Georg Simmel, *The Sociology of Georg Simmel*, trans. Kurt H. Wolff (New York: The Free Press, 1964).

11. Cicero, "Tusculan Disputations, Book I," trans. Robert Black, in *Basic Works of Cicero*, ed. Moses Hadas, 61–124 (New York: Modern Library, 1951).

12. Ambrose Bierce, *Ambrose Bierce: The Devil's Dictionary, Tales, & Memoirs*, ed. S. T. Joshi (New York: Library of America, 2011).

13. Peter Fleming, *Brazilian Adventure* (Oxford: Alden, 1933).

14. V. S. Pritchett, *Dead Man Leading* (Oxford: Oxford University Press, 1984).

15. Karl. B. Guthke, *Traven: The Life Behind the Legends* (Chicago: Lawrence Hill, 1991).

16. Nicholas Thompson, "The Unsettling Truth About the 'Mostly Harmless' Hiker," *Wired*, January 1, 2021, https://www.wired.com/story/unsettling-truth-mostly-harmless-hiker/.

17. Kenneth Hill, *Lost Person Behavior* (Ottawa, Canada: National SAR Secretariat, 1998).

18. Roderick Nash, *Wilderness and the American Mind* (New Haven, CT: Yale University Press, 1967).

19. Joan Lindsay, *Picnic at Hanging Rock* (New York: Vintage, 1988).

20. Henry Green, *Concluding* (Rochester, NY: Dalkey Archive Press, 2000).

21. Sheila Nickerson, *Disappearance: A Map: A Meditation on Death and Loss in the High Latitudes* (Boston: Mariner Books, 1997).

22. Rebecca Solnit, *A Field Guide to Getting Lost* (New York: Penguin, 2006).

23. See Aram Saroyan, *Genesis Angels: The Saga of Lew Welch and the Beat Generation* (New York: William Morrow, 1979).

Flying on Fumes

1. In Georges Poulet, *The Metamorphoses of the Circle*, trans. Carley Dawson and Elliott Coleman (Baltimore: Johns Hopkins University Press, 1966).

2. Jane Mendelsohn, *I Was Amelia Earhart* (New York: Vintage, 1996).

3. Katrina Gulliver, "Why We're Still Looking for Amelia," *The Atlantic*, February 27, 2012, https://www.theatlantic.com/national/archive/2012/02/why-were-still-looking-for-amelia/253638/.

4. Helen Macdonald, *Vesper Flights* (New York: Grove Press, 2020).

5. Beryl Markham, *West with the Night* (San Francisco: North Point Press, 1983).

6. "Lake Won't Reveal Location of Plane," *Waco Tribune-Herald*, September 29, 1976.

7. Robert Macfarlane, "Air of Danger," *The Guardian*, April 23, 2005, https://www.theguardian.com/books/2005/apr/23/featuresreviews.guardianreview30.

8. O. G. Sutton, *The Science of Flight* (Harmondsworth, UK: Penguin, 1949).

9. Norman Mailer, *Of a Fire on the Moon* (New York: Signet, 1970).

10. Plato, *The Dialogues of Plato*, two volumes, trans. Benjamin Jowett (New York: Random House, 1937).

11. Michael Makulowich, "Sgt. Lewis Reaches Parachuting Plateau," *Paraglide*, August 12, 1965.

July 3, 1969

1. "North Viets Cut Down U.S. Troops That Stumbled on Red Base Camp," *The Fayetteville Observer*, July 4, 1969.

2. Michael Lee Lanning, *The Only War We Had: A Platoon Leader's Journal of Vietnam* (College Station: Texas A&M University Press, 2007).

3. Radio Telephone Operator.

4. Command and Control helicopters.

The Edge

1. Anne Dufourmantelle, *In Praise of Risk*, trans. Steven Miller (New York: Fordham University Press, 2017).

2. "Tracy Boyd, the Second Man in a Drug-Smuggling Team . . ." June 4, 1983, *UPI Archives*, https://www.upi.com/Archives/1983/06/04/Tracy-Boyd-the-second-man-in-a-drug-smuggling-team/3007342222495/.

3. Jon Peck, "Green Berets Testify They Bribed Comrades," *South Florida Sun-Sentinel*, July 26, 1985, https://webcache.googleusercontent.com/`search?q=cache:3-DCTHy79A8J:https://www.sun-sentinel.com/news/fl-xpm-1985-07-26-8501310051-story.html+&cd=1&hl=en&ct=clnk&gl=us.

4. Sally Denton, *The Bluegrass Conspiracy: An Inside Story of Power, Greed, Drugs & Murder* (New York: Doubleday, 1990).

5. "Andrew Carter Thornton II." Added June 6, 2016. Federal Bureau of Investigation files released through FOIA, Archive.org, https://archive.org/details/AndrewCarterThorntonII.

6. Bodhipaksa, "Believe Nothing, No Matter Where You Read It, or Who Said It, No Matter if I Have Said It, Unless It Agrees with Your Own Reason and Your Own Common Sense," *Fake Buddha Quotes*, June 24, 2012, https://fakebuddhaquotes.com/believe-nothing-no-matter-where-you-read-it/.

7. Philip Taubman, "The Secret World of a Green Beret," *New York Times*, July 4,

1982, https://www.nytimes.com/1982/07/04/magazine/the-secret-world-of-a-green-beret.html?pagewanted=all.

8. "$2.2 billion Cocaine Ring Uncovered," *UPI Archives*, May 3, 1984, https://www.upi.com/Archives/1984/05/03/22-billion-cocaine-ring-uncovered/1899452404800/.

9. Jon Peck, "Jurors Acquit Cocaine Suspect." *South Florida Sun-Sentinel*, May 31, 1985, https://www.sun-sentinel.com/news/fl-xpm-1985-05-31-8501210917-story.html

Desert Dreams

1. Aristotle, *Nichomachean Ethics*, trans. W. D. Ross. (London: Oxford University Press, 1959).

2. Havelock Ellis, *The Dance of Life* (Westport, CT: Greenwood Press, 1923).

3. Macrobius, *Commentary on the Dream of Scipio*, trans. William Harris Stahl (New York: Columba University Press, 1990).

4. Seymour Krim, *What's This Cat's Story? The Best of Seymour Krim* (New York: Paragon House, 1991).

5. John Steinbeck, *Travels with Charley: In Search of America* (New York: Penguin, 1962).

6. Thomas Merton, *The Wisdom of the Desert* (New York: New Directions, 1960).

The Return

1. Alfred de Musset, *The Confession of a Child of the Century*, trans. Kendall Warren, Project Gutenberg, February 1, 2006, https://www.gutenberg.org/ebooks/9869.